Probing
Our Past

Probing
Our Past

MERLE CURTI

FREDERICK JACKSON TURNER PROFESSOR OF HISTORY
UNIVERSITY OF WISCONSIN

HARPER & BROTHERS, PUBLISHERS, NEW YORK

PROBING OUR PAST

Copyright, 1955, by Harper & Brothers

Printed in the United States of America

Library of Congress catalog card number: 54-11009

For My Students

Contents

Introduction

MERLE CURTI has attained an enviable niche in the world of scholarship as a historian of the American mind. In achieving this distinction he has not been content merely to delineate the thoughts of commanding figures; he has also performed the infinitely more difficult task of surveying the attitudes and beliefs of the relatively inarticulate. He has opened up a lode of inquiry in which, if further work needs yet to be done, he has shown himself a master. Certainly no greater responsibility rests upon the historian in a democracy than the one Professor Curti has essayed. The richness of his accomplishment is perhaps best seen in *The Growth of American Thought*, which won the Pulitzer Prize in history for 1943.

In his investigations of the past Professor Curti has not specialized in a few intellectual threads or trends, as so many other scholars have done. On the contrary, he has turned his searchlight on a wide variety of his countrymen's concerns and aspirations, always with particular attention to the humane values that have entered into the national heritage. A native Nebraskan who received his advanced training in the East, he taught as a member of the regular staff of three different colleges as well as of Columbia University before going to the University of Wisconsin in 1942, where he holds the Frederick Jackson Turner Professorship in History. Appropriately enough, one of the essays in the present volume contains his estimate of that great historian of the frontier, whose student he once was at Harvard. Curti has also traveled extensively in Europe and recently served as visiting lecturer to the universities of India. In this varied experience at home and abroad may perhaps be found the key to the breadth of view and the insight with which he invariably approaches his American subject matter.

Professor Curti has written and edited many books and articles. Among the wide-ranging themes which he has illuminated have been the peace movement, the concept of patriotism in United States history, American education at both the lower and higher levels, and divers aspects of America's international role in the world. This collection of essays contains a portion of his fugitive writings in the years from 1926 to 1953. It has the particular merit of being the author's own selection of those studies to which he would like to give more permanent form.

It is fitting that this volume should appear in the year when his professional colleagues throughout the country have accorded him the highest honor in their gift: the presidency of the American Historical Association.

ARTHUR M. SCHLESINGER

Preface

THESE essays, written over the last thirty years, will, I trust, be useful to scholars and students in the field of American social and cultural history. I hope that some of the essays may also interest the general reader who finds pleasure in exploring the less familiar, but not necessarily the less important, chapters of our national history. Some of the essays appeared in periodicals easily accessible, but several were printed in out-of-the-way journals. The one on Frederick Jackson Turner was published in Mexico and has long been out of print.

I am indebted to several periodicals for permission to have reprinted the essays in this volume: to the *Mississippi Valley Historical Review* for "The Democratic Theme in American Historical Literature"; to *Social Education* for "A Great Teacher's Teacher"; to the *Huntington Library Bulletin* and its successor, the *Huntington Library Quarterly* for "The Great Mr. Locke, America's Philosopher, 1783–1861" and "Francis Lieber and Nationalism"; to the *Political Science Quarterly* for "Human Nature in American Thought: The Retreat from Reason in the Age of Science"; to the *Yale Review* for "Dime Novels and the American Tradition"; to the *American Quarterly* for "The Reputation of America Overseas, 1776–1860"; and to *The American Historical Review* for "Young America" and "America at the World Fairs, 1851–1893." I wish also to express my appreciation to the Carnegie Endowment for International Peace for giving permission to reprint my essay in *American Influences Abroad: An Exploration* and to the Comision de Historia of the Instituto Panamericano de Geografia E Historia for permission to include the essay "Frederick Jackson Turner," which originally appeared with its imprint.

I am grateful to Richard Kirkendall for checking the footnotes and to Mrs. Elsie B. Crabb for typing the manuscript.

I am especially grateful for the introduction that my friend, Arthur M. Schlesinger of Harvard University, has written. Some of the essays reflect his influence and leadership. I owe him many debts, as do all those who as graduate students were fortunate enough to have his guidance and, indeed, as do all scholars and teachers concerned with American history.

MERLE CURTI

August, 1954

PART I

Historiography

1

The Democratic Theme in American Historical Literature (1952)

I N RECENT years distinguished scholars have indicted much of the literature of American history in the decades since the First World War.[1] The indictment maintains that, in brief, historical writing has overemphasized or handled with undue sympathy liberal forces and factors in the national experience, and underemphasized those of a conservative nature. One historian has cried out against what he regards as unfair treatment of the so-called "robber barons" whom he sees as constructive architects of our mighty economy. Another has declared that in treating our wars critically, historians failed to prepare youth spiritually for participation in World War II. Still another has deprecated a tendency to expose to the public view what he terms "pathological" aspects of the national past. Not all of these scholars have been explicit, but the indictment has often implied that these shortcomings are somehow closely related to the vogue of relativism and of so-called presentism, or a tendency to see the past through the eyes of the pres-

[1] This paper was presented as the presidential address at the forty-fifth annual meeting of the Mississippi Valley Historical Association in Chicago, Illinois, on April 17, 1952.

ent. The indictment is the more interesting in view of the fact that in 1919 a well-known historian concluded that the profession had been unable to see the American past with any sympathetic understanding of the democratic aspirations and struggles of the people.

The question whether historians have adequately understood the struggles of the plain people is certainly an important one. It is really, in one sense, the question whether they have dealt adequately with democracy in American history, considering the chief factor in democracy to be government of, by, and for the people. Democracy might be treated directly by historians; or it could be given peripheral treatment, that is, the historian might report on events and developments which are aspects of a democratic process, and in so doing would be indirectly dealing with democracy. In considering the democratic theme in American historiography, I shall first ask to what extent certain of our major historians have given central or peripheral treatment to the theme. In considering their contributions I shall keep in mind some questions bearing on ideas of relativism and of what is often called presentism. In what degree did the treatments of democracy by these historians reflect dominant or competing movements of thought in their time? Did those who questioned the view that objectivity, however desirable, is impossible to achieve, overemphasize the democratic theme? Did those who subscribed to the idea that history should be written with an awareness of current problems also overemphasize the democratic theme and also fail to appreciate conservatism? I cannot, of course, provide definitive or even full answers to all these questions. But I shall try to throw some light on them. And I would also like to suggest some of the tasks that remain to be done if we would have a clearer and better understanding of American democracy.

It would be pertinent to consider in some detail a large body of popular historical literature that began to appear in the middle of the last century, but I can only make brief reference to it. All-but-forgotten writers, such as John S. C. Abbott, Benson Lossing, James

Parton, and John Barber, put forth hundreds of histories and biographies for young men, for heads of families and households, for "all people."[2] These writers professed devotion to accuracy and non-partisanship. They also professed a utilitarian purpose—that of inculcating among the masses a veneration for the fathers, and patriotic devotion to national unity. Their folk heroes were not, by and large, champions of democracy, that is, of the rights and interests of the plain people. In treating Shays' Rebellion, these writers failed to display an understanding of democratic grievances and handled the episode in a somewhat perfunctory manner. In discussing the adoption of the Constitution and the Jacksonian contributions to popular rule, these purveyors of history to the people paid their respects not to the plain people but to their betters—to property, order, and authority. In general, the Federalist-Whig view of human nature and of society informed their writing. True, such abstractions as "liberty" and on occasion "democracy" met the eyes of the reader of these flamboyant pages. One of these writers did suggest that democratic theories developed into democratic practices when efforts were made to abridge rights.[3] And another, in the midst of the Civil War, interpreted our history in terms of a long conflict between aristocracy and democracy.[4] But in these popular histories democracy was not a main theme.

The limitations of these early popular histories lie in part in an excess of picturesque and dramatic incident, in an uncritical handling of materials, and in inadequate documentation. Even more,

[2] For example, John W. Barber, *Incidents in American History; Being a Selection of the Most Important and Interesting Events Which Have Transpired Since the Discovery of America, to the Present Time* (3rd ed., New York, 1847), pp. 180–181, 298; Benson J. Lossing, *Our Country. A Household History for All Readers, from the Discovery of America to the One Hundredth Anniversary of the Declaration of Independence* (New York, 1875, 2 vols.), II, 1149.

[3] Benson J. Lossing, *A History of the United States. For Families and Libraries* (New York, 1857), pp. 207–208.

[4] John S. C. Abbott, *The History of the Civil War in America; Comprising a Full and Impartial Account . . . of Touching Scenes in the Field, the Camp, the Hospital, and the Cabin* (Springfield, Mass., 1863–1866, 2 vols.), I, Preface, 17 ff.

they suffer from a pervading presentism, or seeing the past through the eyes of the present. This accounts in part for the undue emotional patriotism of all these histories.

But I must chiefly concern myself now with certain historians whose writings still command the respect of the profession. Francis Parkman wrote of a period in our colonial history before the rise of modern democracy. His theme, of course, was the competition of France and England for the New World. And here and there, notably in *The Old Régime in Canada,* his pronounced antidemocratic bias was reflected.[5] He had no desire to play down his conviction about the dramatic and often decisive role of strong men. Nor could he conceal his patrician view of human nature nor his conviction of the superiority of the Anglo-Saxon "race" with its regard for individual initiative. Parkman realized, as did so many serious scholars in his day, that women are forever inferior to men in reasoning power![6] He could therefore, in explaining why the Anglo-Saxon "race" was peculiarly fitted for self-government, refer to it as "peculiarly masculine" in submitting "its action habitually to the guidance of reason" and in possessing "the judicial faculty of seeing both sides of a question."[7] But insofar as Parkman realized his conviction that the historian as historian should identify himself with the times he was writing about, rather than his own, he succeeded, in his stirring, romantic, and colorful narrative, in holding his markedly antidemocratic bias to a minimum.

Other scholars who took a longer span of history for their bailiwick than Parkman likewise did not discuss democracy as such. Richard Hildreth was chiefly concerned with deflating the overblown filiopietism and patriotism that colored the work of so many of his contemporaries. His aim in *The History of the United States,*

[5] Francis Parkman, *The Old Régime in Canada* (Boston, 1874), pp. 394–396.
[6] For Parkman's views on women, see "The Woman Question," *North American Review* (October, 1879), CXXIX, 303–321. For his antidemocratic position, see "Aristocrats and Democrats," Boston *Daily Advertiser,* July 14, 1863; "The Tale of the 'Ripe Scholar,' " *Nation* (December 23, 1869), IX, 558–560; and "The Failure of Universal Suffrage," *North American Review* (July–August, 1878), CXXVII, 1–20.
[7] Parkman, *Old Régime in Canada,* pp. 397–398.

which he carried to 1821, was to tell the plain unvarnished truth. He did tell the truth as he saw it, but the narrative was varnished by the gloss of his own faiths. Paradoxically, Hildreth championed such democratic values as religious freedom and antislavery on the one hand and several aristocratic doctrines of Federalism on the other.[8] He was both radical and conservative. In reviewing the *History* Theodore Parker regretted that Hildreth's democratic leanings were so feebly reflected. But they were, even so, reflected. Indeed, Parker felt that it was because these values were present in spite of the author that the *History* was so distinguished an achievement.[9] In short, Hildreth determined to write objectively, but the *History* reflected competing movements of thought in his day.[10]

In carrying the story beyond the point at which Hildreth stopped, other historians also gave a peripheral rather than a central place to the democratic theme. Take James Schouler. This New England lawyer and Civil War veteran subscribed, as Hildreth had done, to ardent antislavery views. Unlike Hildreth, he accepted, in a mild form, the natural-rights philosophy. These two tenets often affected his selection of materials, his emphases, and his judgments. He was no lover of the "fierce democracy" of Andrew Jackson, but he nevertheless dealt sympathetically with the movement for universal suffrage.[11] He revered our Anglo-Saxon heritage, but his faith in the natural-rights philosophy led him to write sympatheti-

---

[8] This is explicit in much of Richard Hildreth, *The History of the United States of America* (New York, 1875–1878, 6 vols.). See, for example, II, 424–425.

[9] Donald E. Emerson, *Richard Hildreth* (Baltimore, 1946), pp. 133–134; *Massachusetts Quarterly Review* (1850), III, 386–425.

[10] It is interesting to compare Hildreth's *History* with George Tucker, *The History of the United States, from Their Colonization to the End of the Twenty-Sixth Congress, in 1841* (Philadelphia, 1856–1857, 4 vols.). Although in some respects writing from a Jeffersonian view, Tucker, like Hildreth, expressed much admiration for Alexander Hamilton and George Washington, and declared that some of our "undiscriminatory ancestors, in their love of civil liberty, did not see that, for their sentiment to have any merit, it must be qualified by justice, order, and obedience to the laws. Liberty, in its largest sense, is the desire to do what we please; and it is this desire which animates the tyrant, the criminal, and, in short, every violator of the law." *Ibid.*, IV, 429.

[11] James Schouler, *History of the United States of America under the Constitution* (New York, 1880–1913, 7 vols.), I, 404–405; III, 44–47.

cally about immigrants. For, holding as he did the doctrine that men everywhere are created equal, he had to reject the idea that any one race could alone enjoy the blessings of freedom.[12] Schouler's devotion to popular rule is shown in his presidential address before the American Historical Association in 1897. On that occasion he called for a convention to draw up a new federal constitution designed to make government more responsible to majority will.[13] What president of any historical association in our own day of loyalty purges would dare propose to throw overboard the Constitution? On the other hand, Schouler, like Hildreth, paid proper respects to property rights when these did not operate in an exploitative fashion.

Or take the retired entrepreneur, James Ford Rhodes, who carried the story from 1850 into our own century. Rhodes was a middle-class critic of sudden or drastic social change, an advocate of property and educational qualifications for suffrage, and a warm admirer of John D. Rockefeller.[14] With such a social philosophy he naturally did not emphasize in the *History* the ingredients of democracy, with the exception of antislavery. In virtually ignoring the West and the rising industrial economy, each of which profoundly influenced democracy, Rhodes fell short of giving it adequate treatment. When he did discuss a topic directly related to democracy, such as organized labor or the agrarian revolt, his treatment was highly biased.[15]

Or take Woodrow Wilson, perhaps the first President to make

---

[12] James Schouler, *Ideals of the Republic* (Boston, 1908), pp. 28, 34–38, 173. See also the excellent discussion in Edward N. Saveth, *American Historians and European Immigrants, 1875–1925* (New York, 1948), pp. 158–163.

[13] James Schouler, "A New Federal Convention," American Historical Association, *Annual Report*, 1897 (Washington, 1898), pp. 22–34.

[14] James F. Rhodes, *History of the United States from the Compromise of 1850 to the End of the Roosevelt Administration* (New York, 1928, 9 vols.), III, 634; VIII, 34–35, 232; IX, 165–167. See also Mark A. DeWolfe Howe, *James Ford Rhodes, American Historian* (New York, 1929), pp. 111–112; for views on the direct election of senators and the abilities of women, *ibid.*, pp. 271, 333; and for explicit statements on democracy, *ibid.*, pp. 139, 179, 329.

[15] Rhodes, *History of the United States*, VIII, 46–49, 270–275, 385, 407, 425–427.

sustained and explicit use in state papers and public pronouncements of the term democracy in referring to the United States.
Wilson paid little attention to democracy in his *History*—at least
in the sense in which he used the word in later years. It is true
that he gave ample consideration to constitutionalism, an essential
element of democracy. But he was content merely to suggest that
the frontier and industrialism had bearings on democracy.[16] And
his unsympathetic treatment of labor, immigration, and Populism
caused him no little embarrassment in his later political career.[17]

Again, take Edward Channing. He did, to be sure, deal with
many topics related to democracy—the widening of the suffrage,
the improvement in status of the underprivileged, and public education. But not until the fifth volume, published in 1921, does he
refer explicitly to democracy either in the ideological or substantive
sense. Then he confined the discussion to one note![18] If Channing
had a central theme at all, it was the growth, not of democracy, but
of nationalism. This he deeply appreciated despite the fun he had
in demolishing pet hobbies of filiopietists.

All these historians, Schouler, Rhodes, Wilson in his prepolitical

[16] For Woodrow Wilson's ideas about democracy as expressed in his formal
writings in the fields of history and political science, see *The State. Elements of
Historical and Practical Politics. A Sketch of Institutional History and Administration* (Boston, 1889), pp. 603–609; and the thoughtful commentary on this book in
Arthur S. Link, *Wilson; The Road to the White House* (Princeton, 1947), pp.
21–22. See also Woodrow Wilson, *Division and Reunion, 1829–1889* (New York,
1893), pp. 11–25, 111, 115–129, 161 ff.; *A History of the American People* (New
York, 1903, 5 vols.), V, 82, 99, 127–142, 168, 186, 203, 300. Also illuminating
is Wilson's article "Democracy in the United States, Character of," in *Harper's
Encyclopaedia of United States History From 458 A.D. to 1905* (New York,
1905, 10 vols.), III, 68–78. For Wilson's discussion of aspects of the history of
democracy as developed in his essays and lectures, see Ray S. Baker and William E. Dodd (eds.), *The Public Papers of Woodrow Wilson* (New York, 1925–
1927, 6 vols.), I, 396–415; and "The Course of American History" in *Mere Literature, and Other Essays* (Boston, 1896), pp. 231–245. In addition to the valuable discussion in Link, see Harley Notter, *The Origins of the Foreign Policy of
Woodrow Wilson* (Baltimore, 1937), pp. 23, 40.

[17] *The New York Times*, February 2, 1912, p. 12. See also Link, *Wilson; The
Road to the White House*, pp. 381, 388.

[18] Edward Channing, *A History of the United States* (New York, 1905–1925,
6 vols.), V, 377. For Channing's bias toward "radical elements" in 1798–1800,
see *ibid.*, IV, 220; for his antipathy toward "alien ideologies" of later immigrants,
see *ibid.*, V, 71, 106.

period, and Channing, accepted the doctrine that objectivity is not only desirable but possible. None of these writers subscribed to the view that the past should be interpreted in terms of the present. None of them, however, even in their formal historical writings, succeeded in writing of the past without being influenced by the present. It is not hard to show how various schemes of thought entered into the writings of Schouler, Rhodes, Wilson, and Channing. If one rereads the histories of these men with the controversial issues of their day in mind, he cannot avoid the conclusion that what they wrote could hardly have given much comfort to the liberals and radicals of their time. They took sides, like others of their day.

If one stopped with these historians, one would have to accept the 1919 verdict of William E. Dodd. Writing to his friend Chief Justice Walter Clark, the Chicago historian observed: "You may well say, why can not historians see things from the people's point of view. I agree that most do not, that most historians, like most lawyers, are color blind."[19] In fact, however, Dodd was forgetting an important development in American historiography.

He was, for the moment, overlooking George Bancroft, the first of our major historians to make the democratic theme central in our early history. Bancroft subscribed to the natural-rights philosophy. His view of human nature was a composite of the Enlightenment's faith in the universality of reason in all men and of transcendentalism's faith in the divine intuitive quality of every mind. Bancroft was therefore compelled to make democracy, in the sense of the rightness of majority rule, central in his history.[20] Subscribing further to the Newtonian conception of an ordered universe governed by natural law, Bancroft assumed that the American achievement in self-government represented the implementation in human

[19] William E. Dodd to Chief Justice Walter Clark, June 7, 1919 (Chicago), William E. Dodd Papers (Manuscript Division, Library of Congress), XIV.

[20] This is implicit in George Bancroft, *History of the United States of America, from the Discovery of the Continent* (New York, 1884–1885, 6 vols.), and beautifully explicit on many pages, as, for example, IV, 5–6. It is worth noting that there is little difference between the democratic views Bancroft expressed in the *History* and those appearing in his addresses and private letters.

affairs of the "natural laws" of the universe. The rest of the world would, he was convinced, move toward the American example. Bancroft thus fused American democracy, in the political sense, with American nationalism. He was a presentist in that he wanted to justify American achievement to the American people and to the rest of the world. He also believed that, because he followed in his work the uniquely true dispensation about human nature and society, his *History* was thoroughly objective. Thus he did not take as unqualified praise Leopold von Ranke's remark that it was the best history yet written from the democratic point of view.[21]

We no longer accept the rational and divinely intuitive theory of human nature nor the natural-rights philosophy—at least without qualifications. Nor the teleological conception of American nationalism. Thus we cannot approve the overweening importance Bancroft gave to the early "achievement" of democracy. Modern scholars, reworking the period he surveyed, have corrected his overemphasis. We may here merely mention Charles McLean Andrews. He was an admirable example of a historian who achieved a high degree of the objectivity he believed desirable and who certainly reduced the influence of the present to a minimum. Writing shortly after the First World War, Andrews provided new evidence for the thesis that many historians both oversimplified and carried too far back into the colonial period the beginnings of democracy.[22]

Bancroft was not the only historian to give the democratic theme a central place in his history. Influenced no doubt by the current discussions of democracy and by the profound implications for democracy of the advance of corporate wealth, Henry Adams and Frederick Jackson Turner in quite different ways later gave the topic an important place in their historical writing. Both Adams

[21] Mark A. DeWolfe Howe, *The Life and Letters of George Bancroft* (New York, 1908, 2 vols.), II, 183.

[22] Charles M. Andrews, *The Colonial Background of the American Revolution* (New Haven, 1924), p. 201; "Conservative Factors in Early Colonial History," in *Authority and the Individual* (Cambridge, 1937), pp. 156–169; and *The Colonial Period of American History* (New Haven, 1934–1938, 4 vols.), IV, 423–434 n. This was further developed by one of Andrews' students, Leonard W. Labaree, *Conservatism in Early American History* (New York, 1948).

and Turner were further influenced by certain emergent ideas in
the natural science of their day—ideas which had a great appeal
to thoughtful men of the time. The Darwinian theory of evolution
was especially intriguing. It could be, and was, used in different
ways by Adams and Turner and by other historians. And it provides
an excellent example of the fact that movements of thought in a
time and place, together with problems associated with the economic, political, and social milieu, greatly influenced ways in which
the democratic theme was interpreted.

Henry Adams was convinced that American experience in a
peculiar way exemplified the laws of science. And since he was
concerned with democracy in his own day and regarded it as the
central issue in the first decades of the nineteenth century, it
seemed to him clear that the laws of science could explain democratic development. "The more I write, the more confident I feel
that before long a new school of history will rise which will leave
us antiquated," he wrote to Francis Parkman. "Democracy," Adams
continued, "is the only subject for history. I am satisfied that the
purely mechanical development of the human mind in society must
appear in a great democracy so clearly, for want of disturbing elements, that in another generation psychology, physiology, and history will join in proving man to have as fixed and necessary a development as that of a tree; and also as unconscious."[23]

Adams, in the pages of his great History, assumed that the young
democracy could not survive in a world of force and Realpolitik unless, whatever its reluctance to do so, it took part in the struggle for
existence. So he thought that it was strictly in the order of things
that the United States should have become involved in the Napo-
leonic conflict, in spite of Thomas Jefferson's efforts to stay out.
The war waged by the American democracy brought out the strong-

[23] Harold D. Cater (comp.), Henry Adams and His Friends. A Collection of
His Unpublished Letters (Boston, 1947), pp. 133–134. The letter is dated December 21, 1884. See also Adams to Samuel J. Tilden, January 24, 1883, ibid.,
125–126; and Henry Adams, History of the United States of America (New York,
1889–1891, 9 vols.), I, 1, 5, 59–60.

est qualities in that democracy: such were the terms of survival.[24] In domestic no less than in foreign affairs, Adams made the theory of evolution (adaptation, struggle, and survival) a central key: these doctrines explained the Jeffersonian shift from states' rights to national power, the growing role of the executive, the inadequacy of the old ideas in the postwar world of 1816.[25]

But the mind of Henry Adams was too complex, his range of scientific interests too broad, to make Darwinism explain everything. He had become interested in the teachings of Lord William T. Kelvin regarding physical energy in the universe. In passage after passage in the *History* Adams made energy or force, physiological, psychological, and mechanical, the key to what happened.[26] The historian concluded that the struggle for survival and the laws of thermodynamics in the years he surveyed gave some assurance for democracy in the period after 1818.[27] But only some. For he had discovered the painful shortcomings of the people. Even their most gifted leaders, including Jefferson, seemed helpless to direct the present, let alone the future. Indeed, they appeared "like grasshoppers kicking and gesticulating in the middle of the Mississippi River."[28] Moreover, Adams saw scientific law in recurring catastrophes which were presumably cyclical. From any point of view the *History* was a conscious, sustained, and intellectually sophisticated effort to make democracy the central theme of the period between 1800 and 1818. It testified to Adams' use of our discipline as an instrument for understanding present and future. And within the frame of assumptions suggested by his reactions,

[24] Adams, *History of the United States*, I, 162–163; II, 421–422; IV, 27, 33, 69, 74, 334; V, 234–236, 250; VI, 133–159; IX, 219–220. Mr. James Daffer, who is investigating the relation of Henry Adams to both science and democracy, has independently confirmed and carried further this interpretation.

[25] *Ibid.*, IX, 86, 104, 132, 226–227, 239.

[26] Ernest Samuels, *The Young Henry Adams* (Cambridge, 1948), pp. 134–135; Henry Adams, *Democracy, An American Novel* (New York, 1880), p. 10; Adams, *History of the United States*, I, 116; II, 117; III, 56, 74, 196; VII, 407; VIII, 264; IX, 153, 192–193.

[27] Adams, *History of the United States*, VI, 123; IX, 225–229.

[28] Cater (comp.), *Henry Adams and His Friends*, pp. 125–126.

temperamental and intellectual, to currents of scientific thought, Adams achieved a marked degree of objectivity.

Adams in his earlier essays, and John Fiske[29] and Herbert Baxter Adams[30] later, emphasized the hereditary factor in the evolution of institutions and societies. Frederick Jackson Turner gave a different emphasis. In his view environmental factors were far more important than hereditary ones. The environmentalist view might seem to reduce the scope of individual freedom to create, and subject man to a fate conditioned if not determined by his physical environment. But as Turner saw it, of course, the struggle of men with their environment, the constant beginning over again on new frontiers, developed a self-reliance and individualism, a not necessarily contradictory habit of neighborly coöperation, and an equalitarianism.[31] Turner was aware of the bearings of European democratic ideas and institutions on the course of American democracy; but he emphasized the American frontier environment in giving what he assumed to be a unique quality to democracy in the United States.

It is relevant to add that Turner was sympathetic to the idea that each generation must rewrite the history of the past in terms of its own vantage point and needs.[32] In 1917 he wrote to a former pupil that the historian had too largely held himself aloof from current

[29] John Fiske, *American Political Ideas Viewed from the Standpoint of Universal History* (New York, 1885), pp. 5–6, 49, 94–95, 106–108, 135. For further illustrations of Fiske's views on democracy in American history, see *Essays, Historical and Literary* (New York, 1907, 2 vols. in one), I, 50–51, 115, 134, 146–148, 153–154, 166–167, 173–174, 222–223, 272–273, 301–306; *Old Virginia and Her Neighbors* (Boston, 1897, 2 vols.), II, 315–316, 395–397; *The Dutch and Quaker Colonies in America* (Boston, 1899, 2 vols.), II, 252 ff.; *The Beginnings of New England; or, the Puritan Theocracy in Its Relation to Civil and Religious Liberty* (Boston, 1889), pp. 247–248.

[30] W. Stull Holt (ed.), points out in *Historical Scholarship in the United States, 1876–1901: As Revealed in the Correspondence of Herbert B. Adams* (Baltimore, 1938), pp. 16–17, that Adams, also a champion of the hereditary principle in his historical theory, was aware that the method of the Teutonic school, which influenced him, reinforced conservatism.

[31] Frederick J. Turner, *The Frontier in American History* (New York, 1920), pp. 30–32, 54, 247, 249–251.

[32] Everett E. Edwards (comp.), *The Early Writings of Frederick Jackson Turner* (Madison, 1938), pp. 52, 58; Turner, *Frontier in American History*, pp. 323–324.

struggles. The historian's special knowledge, he felt, might make his contributions to an emergency quite as important as those of the economist and the political scientist.[33] Thus on occasion Turner gave implied support to the contention that government controls must provide the equality of opportunity once provided by free lands.[34]

There is time to speak very briefly of the reactions to the theory of evolution of certain other historians of democracy. The generally neglected book that Bernard Moses wrote in 1898, *Democracy and Social Growth in America,* held that democracy was largely the result of material conditions that were transitory—free land and a simple rural society. Moses concluded that democracy as it developed in response to these conditions could not survive the new era of corporate wealth. If the government failed to control the monopolies, the old democracy was certainly done for; if it succeeded, the swollen government power necessary thereto likewise meant the end of a democracy that had evolved from transitory conditions.[35] The same year, 1898, Frederick A. Cleveland, a lawyer and political scientist who adopted the historical approach, published the first systematic historical account of democracy in which the concept was explicitly made the basis of the treatment. Cleveland viewed democratic, and indeed all institutions, in the light of the cooperative rather than the competitive factors in evolution.[36] Other writers utilized the concept, too.[37] But we must not dismiss this theme without reference to Charles A. Beard's essay, "The Evolution of Democracy." Published in 1919 this piece, one of the many that Beard devoted to the subject, dealt with the evolu-

[33] Frederick J. Turner to Solon J. Buck, May 3, 1917 (Washington), Papers of the National Board of Historical Service, Alphabetical by Authors A-B (Manuscripts Division, Library of Congress).

[34] Turner, *Frontier in American History,* pp. 282–284, 319, 322.

[35] Bernard Moses, *Democracy and Social Growth in America* (New York, 1898), pp. 1–35, 49.

[36] Frederick A. Cleveland, *The Growth of Democracy in the United States; or, The Evolution of Popular Co-operation in Government and Its Results* (Chicago, 1898).

[37] John S. Penman, *The Irresistible Movement of Democracy* (New York, 1923).

tion of society from savagery and the corresponding development of
the state. Beard traced the main aspects of the democratic victory
over governmental institutions of kings and nobles and the adaptation of these to democratic purposes. He pointed to recent democratic forces which were working to subject to popular control all
that the captains of industry had created—especially corporations.[38]

The new science did more than call the attention of historians to
evolutionary theory as a useful tool in their thinking. The implications of the scientific movement also involved a self-conscious effort to achieve objectivity by surmounting the limitations of class,
religion, and politics. Further, natural science suggested to historians that all data, no matter how humble, may be important. Here
was at least one justification for including in historical efforts all
aspects of life, social, economic, and cultural, as well as political
and military.

The broadening conception of the past, to which new social issues contributed, explains John Bach McMaster's determination to
make the people rather than political leaders the chief subject of
his history. It was not clear, however, even at the end of the eighth
volume, just what McMaster meant by democracy, which he talked
about a good deal, or even what he meant by the people. For he
seemed, like Bancroft, to conceive of the people in middle-class
terms and to reject Hildreth's view of social and political groupings
based on property. As Eric Goldman has pointed out, McMaster's
History voted for William McKinley as Bancroft's had voted for
Jackson.[39] Jefferson and Jackson are belittled; Hamilton, the bank,
and the tariff, praised; and the preconstitutional inflationists are
compared with the Greenbackers, those "mischievous schemers,"
whose money policy was labeled vicious and absurd.[40] It would be

---

[38] Charles A. Beard, "The Evolution of Democracy: A Summary," in Frederick A. Cleveland and Joseph Schafer (eds.), *Democracy in Reconstruction*
(Boston, 1919), chap. XXIII, pp. 486–491.

[39] Eric F. Goldman, *John Bach McMaster, American Historian* (Philadelphia,
1943), p. 143.

[40] John Bach McMaster, *A History of the People of the United States, from
the Revolution to the Civil War* (New York, 1914, 8 vols.), I, 201, 282, 476–
477, 490; II, 51, 310; VI, 84.

easy to point to other qualifications of McMaster's democracy. Though he praised many social gains,[41] what had been achieved represented in his eyes finality. There was neither need nor justification for carrying democracy further—especially in the economic sphere. In some degree, then, McMaster too, despite his attention to the people, was writing from the standpoint of his own position in society. His age, as he saw it, seemed to him superior to anything in the past. A certain "presentism" was also evident in his hope that the *History* would be "full of instruction" to the social agitators of the 1880's—that through it they might come to appreciate the great gains made under the peaceful evolution of popular rule.[42]

The decades preceding Dodd's 1919 indictment of historians for failing to see the past from the democratic point of view also witnessed the marked impact on historical scholarship of the interrelated pragmatic philosophy and the progressive movement, broadly defined. Dodd seems to have overlooked—at least for the moment —certain historical writings that appeared in the decade prior to 1919, Albert Bushnell Hart's *National Ideas Historically Traced* (1907), for example. This inadequately appreciated book presented as a key to our democratic development the struggles that resulted in the improved status of disadvantaged persons—slaves, freedmen, women, immigrants, and industrial workers. It emphasized the role of public education in the democratic advance. It traced in a fashion quite acceptable to progressives the new devices to make democracy more efficient and more articulate. And it gave much the same weight to the frontier and the Industrial Revolution in the development of democratic movements as a historian today might give.[43]

The progressivism and pragmatism that illuminated Hart's study

[41] John Bach McMaster, *The Acquisition of Political, Social and Industrial Rights of Man in America* (Cleveland, 1903), pp. 40, 59, 90–100, 110; *With the Fathers; Studies in the History of the United States* (New York, 1896), pp. 239, 251–252.
[42] McMaster, *History of the People of the United States*, II, 616–617; *With the Fathers*, p. 320.
[43] Albert B. Hart, *National Ideals Historically Traced*, 1607–1907 (New York, 1907), in Albert B. Hart (ed.), *The American Nation: A History* (New York, 1904–1918, 28 vols.), XXVI.

also helped historians to rediscover the significance of economic conflicts in the advance of democracy. Here Charles A. Beard was a pioneer. His realistic, pragmatic approach substituted for Bancroft's and McMaster's romantic and amorphous idea of "the people," and for the Marxist doctrine of the class struggle, the notion of a conflict of interest groups. This, Beard held, had marked an American society in which class lines were vague and mobile.[44] The conflict between group interests and its contribution to democratic advance also informed Thomas J. Wertenbaker's description of patrician-plebeian struggles in early Virginia.[45] And Arthur M. Schlesinger's *Colonial Merchants and the American Revolution*[46] was an especially important study, in which the relation of democratic movements to economic interests and group conflicts was well documented. Among these writings, Beard's books on the Constitution and on Jeffersonian Democracy alone seem to have been regarded both by progressives and by conservatives as having an *ad hoc* or presentist bearing.

In indicting the historians for their color blindness to the people's point of view, Dodd must have excluded himself. His work as a historian of democracy has been studied by Wendell H. Stephenson. Like Beard, whose *Economic Interpretation of the Constitution* influenced him markedly, Dodd had shown sensitiveness to the role of group conflicts in American struggles for democracy.[47] Here we shall merely note that, partly in response to the agrarian revolt of the 1890's and its progressive heritage, partly as a result of his experiences in Germany and his studies of Jeffersonianism, Dodd had developed the idea that democracy in American experience

[44] Charles A. Beard, *An Economic Interpretation of the Constitution of the United States* (New York, 1913); *Economic Origins of Jefferson Democracy* (New York, 1915); and *The Economic Basis of Politics* (New York, 1922).

[45] Thomas J. Wertenbaker, *Patrician and Plebeian in Virginia* (Charlottesville, 1910), pp. 214–215. Cf. Richard B. Morris, *Government and Labor in Early America* (New York, 1946), pp. 52–54.

[46] Arthur M. Schlesinger, *The Colonial Merchants and the American Revolution, 1763–1776* (New York, 1918). See also Schlesinger's *New Viewpoints in American History* (New York, 1922), especially chaps. III, V, VIII, IX.

[47] Wendell H. Stephenson, "William E. Dodd: Historian of Democracy," will eventually appear in *Virginia Quarterly Review*.

meant not merely political equality but also economic and social equality.[48] I must at least call attention to a remarkable essay, "The struggle for Democracy in the United States." This appeared in 1918 in the *International Journal of Ethics*.[49] Here Dodd maintained that democracy had been an ideal rather than an actuality in American experience. This he ascribed to the influence of wealth, operating in a frame of ever greater concentration of power in the national government. He also showed how the great leaders of democracy had been forced to compromise with privilege by reason of war as well as by the pressure of property interests. Mrs. Wilson promised to read the essay to the President. Colonel Edward M. House enthusiastically approved it. So did Thomas Reed Powell and many others.[50] The essay was but one of the more or less self-conscious and systematic interpretations of democracy inspired by the crisis of the First World War.[51]

Another interpretation of democracy, likewise related to the challenge of Prussian militarism, came from the skillful pen of Dodd's colleague, Andrew C. McLaughlin. It was expressed, in the first instance, in the presidential address before the American Historical Association in 1914.[52] Analyzing American democracy, McLaughlin saw it in the first place as a composite actuality in which the constitutional convention and the political party were of special importance in realizing self-government. Like Beard and Dodd, McLaughlin called attention to the role of conflict in the advance of

---

[48] These ideas are to be found in many of Dodd's writings, especially *Expansion and Conflict* (Boston, 1915); and *The Old South; Struggles for Democracy* (New York, 1937). The latter is interesting in the parallels it draws between the dangers of centralization and planning in the period after 1660 and similar tendencies in the New Deal.

[49] William E. Dodd, "The Struggle for Democracy in the United States," *International Journal of Ethics* (July, 1918), XXVIII, 465–484.

[50] Mrs. Woodrow Wilson to Dodd, September 18, 1918; E. M. House to Dodd, July 24, 1918; Thomas R. Powell to Dodd, September 3, 1918, February 6, 1919, Dodd Papers (Manuscript Division, Library of Congress), XIV.

[51] Carl R. Fish, "American Democracy," *Minnesota History Bulletin* (February, 1920), III, 251–272, is, for example, a very thoughtful interpretation which weighs the contributions of the several sections to the democratic movement.

[52] Andrew C. McLaughlin, "American History and American Democracy," *American Historical Review* (January, 1915), XX, 255–276.

democratic actuality. He also viewed democracy, in the second place, as a composite ideal. To him this meant simply the belief that men should have a chance to realize their worth without being sifted by artificial theories of value.

In 1920 McLaughlin's *Steps in the Development of American Democracy* amplified the ideas in this address. This brilliant book traced the course of democracy and summed up its implications for the immediate future. It was a pioneer effort in making the democratic theme the focus of our whole history. It was also notable for calling attention to the careless and contradictory ways in which Americans used the term "democracy." McLaughlin held that it was unhistorical to attribute to American democracy of the past anything theoretically involved in democracy in 1920. Eighteenth-century America, he noted, was democratic in comparison with the Europe of that time. It was not democratic in comparison with the Europe or the America of the First World War.[53]

It is worth noting that McLaughlin rejected presentism. And in a spirited correspondence with Dodd, McLaughlin took his colleague gently to task for reading too much of current economic conflict into his critical remarks on the framing and adoption of the Constitution, which McLaughlin regarded as an important step in the development of democracy. Dodd, he felt, was making the same mistake as Beard.[54] But note that Dodd, on his part, felt that McLaughlin was in the same camp with Beard in mistakenly holding that history should be written with an objective—in making it teach "too much."[55] What Dodd said of these historians he might well have said of himself. For he did not hesitate to make history teach lessons, though on this occasion he rejected such a purpose. I do not know whether Dodd ever explicitly accepted any definite doctrine of "relativism." I was, however, surprised to find that in

[53] Andrew C. McLaughlin, *Steps in the Development of American Democracy* (New York, 1920).

[54] McLaughlin to Dodd, February 11, July 19, 1918, Dodd Papers (Manuscript Division, Library of Congress), XIV.

[55] Dodd to Carl Becker, May 21, 1932, Carl Becker Papers (Cornell University Library, Ithaca).

the 1914 address McLaughlin clearly anticipated Beard in expressing the frame-of-reference concept: he frankly said that no historian
could avoid being influenced by his background and experiences.[56]
The point of all this is, of course, that historians tended to see in
the work and position of their colleagues the same limitations that
these in turn saw in them, regardless of whether or not presentism
and relativism were explicitly avowed.

The treatment of the democratic theme in American historical
literature since the First World War was, as in preceding periods,
influenced by changing situations and by new movements of
thought. Among the latter was concern with meanings of terms and
especially with the relativism to which I have just referred. The
precedent of McLaughlin in defining the uses of the word democracy in terms of time, place, situation, and context generally was
continued. It was not until 1939, however, that historians system-
atically probed the meanings attached to the term democracy in the
past. In that year Charles and Mary Beard did so with telling effects.[57] From that time on, few historians discussed democracy without some attention to definition.[58] This emphasis on greater precision has, I believe, increased the degree of objectivity historians
have achieved. Yet some have maintained that the writing of history
since the First World War has become, at least in the hands of
leading historians, less objective than in earlier times. And they
ascribe this to a growing acceptance of the relativist theory and a
"presentism" stimulated by the crisis of depression and the war
against totalitarianism.[59] Let us look, not of course at the whole
body of historical writing in the past three decades, but at that

[56] McLaughlin, "American History and American Democracy," *American Historical Review* (January, 1915), XX, 258–259.

[57] Charles A. Beard and Mary R. Beard, *America in Midpassage* (New York,
1939, 2 vols.), II, chap. XVII, 920–949. See also the admirable discussion of the
meaning attached to the term democracy in Charles A. Beard, *The Republic; Conversations on Fundamentals* (New York, 1943), chap. III, pp. 27–41.

[58] See, for example, Jeannette P. Nichols and James G. Randall (eds.), *Democracy in the Middle West, 1840–1940* (New York, 1941), pp. xiv–xv.

[59] For example, Samuel E. Morison, "Faith of a Historian," *American Historical Review* (January, 1951), LVI, 266–68; and James C. Malin, *Essays on Historiography* (Lawrence, Kan., 1946), chap. IV, pp. 109–168.

considerable segment which has been more or less consciously concerned with the democratic theme, with the question in mind as to whether "presentism" has interfered with objectivity.

It is true that the mood of disillusionment following the First World War influenced interpretations of the past. It is also true that in many quarters there was uncritical complacency regarding our culture, and that this superficial optimism led some historians to search for distinctions between appearances and realities. This search helped give vitality to the Beards' *Rise of American Civilization,* the first really new synthesis of our national history since the prevailing one which had taken shape several decades before.[60] Vernon L. Parrington's *Main Currents of American Thought,* which appeared in the same year, 1927, identified democracy with the agrarian tradition, with American faith in an open universe, and with humane values. It also traced its "decline" before the advancing power of corporate wealth and centralized government.[61] The shortcomings of Parrington are not only obvious but have been so emphasized that we are in danger of forgetting his great contribution to an understanding of the democratic tradition.

The New Deal, evoked by the depression, brought an increased awareness of the problem of democracy in our history, as progressivism earlier had done. Perhaps it inspired well-known historical writings with an undue presentism. Critics have levied such a charge at the author of the *Age of Jackson,* who explored the dynamics of power in the democratic process.[62] Alice Felt Tyler's use-

[60] Charles A. Beard and Mary R. Beard, in *The Rise of American Civilization* (New York, 1927, 2 vols.), deal explicitly with conditions favoring democracy in the colonial period, the advance of democracy during the Revolution, the impact of the agricultural West on its development, Jeffersonian and Jacksonian democracy, the relation of slavery and emancipation to it, the status of women, and the bearings of a machine civilization on it.

[61] Vernon L. Parrington, *Main Currents in American Thought; An Interpretation of American Literature from the Beginnings to 1920* (New York, 1927-1930, 3 vols.). For a penetrating analysis of Parrington's handling of the democratic theme, see Arthur A. Ekirch, Jr., "Parrington and the Decline of American Liberalism," *American Quarterly* (Winter, 1951), III, 295-308.

[62] Arthur M. Schlesinger, Jr., "The Pattern of Democratic Change in the United States," in Carl J. Friedrich, Arthur M. Schlesinger, Jr., and Alpheus T. Mason, *The Democratic Process; Lectures on the American Liberal Tradition* (New London, 1948).

ful synthesis, *Freedom's Ferment*, reflects a sympathy for an earlier phase of the democratic story that became accentuated in the 1930's.[63] Curtis Nettels in *The Roots of American Civilization* viewed colonial history as a struggle between large property owners and lesser folk for the control of political and economic institutions. Ralph Gabriel explored the history of democratic ideology, and argued that there is need in a time of relativist morals for a reassertion of certain values which he speaks of as absolute and as essential elements of the American democratic tradition.[64] Others emphasized the functional role of democratic ideas and forces in the history of American thought and put that history in a social setting which included tussles between competing interests and values.[65] The writings of many of these historians suggested that a new chapter in the history of American democracy had begun in the late nineteenth century. The shift from an agrarian-frontier economy to an industrial one set the stage for a consequent shift from freedom to equality through government planning. No historian developed this theme more cogently than Avery Craven in *Democracy in American Life*.[66]

As if perhaps to put the history of their section into the democratic stream of thought accentuated by the New Deal, southern historians now found much more democracy in the history of their section than had been assumed. The newer school piled up evidence for this thesis.[67] That it was not altogether acceptable was

[63] Alice F. Tyler, *Freedom's Ferment; Phases of American Social History to 1860* (Minneapolis, 1944).

[64] Ralph H. Gabriel, *The Course of American Democratic Thought; An Intellectual History since 1815* (New York, 1940); "Democracy: Retrospect and Prospect," *American Journal of Sociology* (November, 1942), XLVIII, 411–418; and "Thomas Jefferson and Twentieth-Century Rationalism," *Virginia Quarterly Review* (Summer, 1950), XXVI, 321–335.

[65] Merle Curti, *The Social Ideas of American Educators* (New York, 1935); *Peace or War; The American Struggle, 1636–1936* (New York, 1936); and *The Growth of American Thought* (New York, 1943, 1951). Attention should also be called in this connection to the skillful development of this approach in Howard K. Beale, *A History of Freedom of Teaching in American Schools* (New York, 1941); and *Are American Teachers Free? An Analysis of Restraints upon the Freedom of Teaching in American Schools* (New York, 1936).

[66] Avery O. Craven, *Democracy in American Life, A Historical View* (Chicago, 1941).

[67] For example, Bell I. Wiley, *The Plain People of the Confederacy* (Baton

suggested by the work of John Hope Franklin and Kenneth Stampp.[68] In the work of such young scholars was reflected a new concern with democracy in its humanistic and ethnic aspects. Much of what these postwar historians wrote was relative to new currents of thought. But if they were influenced by relativist theories they did not, I believe, champion these in their writings or at professional meetings. The effect of their work, certainly, was to raise further questions and to broaden our knowledge of American democracy. Their "presentism," if present, led them chiefly to call attention to additional data. No one would claim that all these newer contributions forever settled the problem of American democracy in our history. But it is a healthy thing, and conducive to finding out the truth about democracy in American life, that these varied points of view have been represented in research and writing.

The New Deal and its philosophies were, of course, the chief influences in the thirties. But during the late thirties and forties historians like everyone else became increasingly aware of the threat of totalitarianism, and aware too of the rapidly growing importance of the United States as a world power. This new awareness influenced historical writings, especially writings about democracy.

This is not to say that the relations of war and democracy were first explored in these decades. An important discussion of the theme had taken place, in fact, at the meeting of the American Historical Association in 1900. In the view of Professor S. M. Mcvane of Harvard, democracy, through its instruments the telegraph and the popular press, had made several nineteenth-century wars inevitable by interfering with the calm deliberation of statesmen. He was no doubt thinking about the recent Spanish-American

Rouge, 1943), and *The Life of Johnny Reb, the Common Soldier of the Confederacy* (Indianapolis, 1943). See also Clement Eaton, *A History of the Old South* (New York, 1949); Fletcher M. Green, "Democracy in the Old South," *Journal of Southern History* (February, 1946), XII, 3–23; and Frank L. Owsley, *Plain Folk of the Old South* (Baton Rouge, 1949).

[68] John H. Franklin, *From Slavery to Freedom: A History of American Negroes* (New York, 1948); Kenneth Stampp, "The Historian and Southern Negro Slavery," *American Historical Review* (April, 1952), LVII, 123–145.

conflict. John Bassett Moore disagreed, holding that war resulted chiefly from conflicts of national interest.[69] But in 1917 Mcvane's thesis was reinforced by George Blakeslee. The Clark historian held that throughout history the democracies had been quite as warlike as nondemocratic states. Blakeslee suggested that the answer to the quest for peace was not democracy, but federalism.[70] This issue was later exhaustively explored by Quincy Wright, a political scientist who used the historical method, and who concluded, though with many qualifications, that Blakeslee's position was essentially sound.[71] With the exception of Wright, these scholars wrote before "relativism" became an issue.

On the eve of the Second World War, Frederic Logan Paxson brought out his history of our part in the first crusade to make the world safe for democracy. Himself a participant in the effort of historians to publicize democratic war aims but also a representative of the objective school of history, Paxson concluded, in the spirit of Blakeslee and Wright, that the historians had overemphasized the peaceful record of the democracies and the warlike record of the autocracies. At best historians had served democracy by picking out of the American story "validated events with which to construct the sort of picture that Americans wanted to believe; and that, believed, made firmer their willingness to carry out the war." Paxson further maintained that in the crusade the "imagination, manpower, and material strength of American democracy" were mobilized for the first time. To that part of the world which doubted whether democracy, lumbering and inefficient as it undoubtedly was, could be a suitable instrument for implementing national interest, Paxson was on the whole reassuring—more so than Henry Adams had been when in the eighties he discussed a comparable problem in an earlier test. When, continued Paxson, "emotion whittles the minority down to nearly nothing and makes citizens agree among them-

[69] *American Historical Review* (April, 1900), *V*, 434–435.
[70] George H. Blakeslee, "Will Democracy Alone Make the World Safe: A Study of the History of the Foreign Relations of Democratic States," *Proceedings of the American Antiquarian Society*, n.s. (1917), XXVII, 358–374.
[71] Quincy Wright, *A Study of War* (Chicago, 1942, 2 vols.), *II*, 841.

selves, even a democracy may act with speed, directness, efficiency, and weight."[72]

Yet Paxson also saw the weaknesses of democracy in military crises. For he pointed out that democracy, deprived of an effective challenge by a minority, degenerates into the rule of mob psychology against all dissenting elements. He was not surprised at the reactionary aftermath of the war—at the repression of democratic freedoms in a nationalistic hysteria. This he regarded as no less an authentic evidence of American democracy than the high, unified purposes that inspired common action during the struggle itself.

The ideological climate of the Second World War was related both to that of the first crusade and the New Deal. Of note during the years of the contest with the fascist world was the tendency of American historical thought to redefine our democracy and to put it in the broader stream of western civilization. The tendency to relate American democracy to world currents was not entirely new, of course.[73] But it differed markedly from the view of Turner, whose influence on conceptions of American democratic development had been so pronounced.

In 1941, a year of many historical discussions of democracy, Carl Wittke noted that it was hard to define because it was a process never finished. Then he stated, in comprehensive form, the meaning democracy had come to have in many quarters: the conviction that human personality is the first and final reality, never to be used for purposes alien to itself; faith in the essential collective integrity and character of the masses of men and women; government by the consent of the governed, including as an imperative part of the process the functioning of free speech, free assembly, free elections; and a sustaining economic and social order, supplemented by as much government control as necessary to the end that everyone enjoy a fair and a reasonably unfettered chance in life.[74] This opera-

---

[72] Frederic L. Paxson, *American Democracy and the World War* (Boston, Berkeley, Los Angeles, 1936–1948, 3 vols.), II, Preface, 1–3, 48–49, 51, 453.

[73] See, for example, Herbert L. Osgood, *The American Colonies in the Seventeenth Century* (New York, 1904–1907, 3 vols.), II, 254 ff., 433 ff.

[74] Carl F. Wittke, "The Evolution of Democracy," in *Democracy Is Different . . . A Series of Lectures at Oberlin College* (New York, 1941), pp. 1–2.

tional definition reflected the expansion and implementation of the democratic idea in the New Deal era and awareness of the importance in a democracy of protecting minority groups.

Others discussed American democracy within a broad context of values deemed universal at least in western civilization. Carl Becker, who in 1920 had published an interpretation of the American democratic experiment,[75] now in several writings gave the theme the broader treatment.[76] In related disciplines Ralph Barton Perry[77] and Perry Miller[78] accented the democratic aspects of New England Puritanism while locating these in the humanistic currents of the Renaissance. In a striking paper Arthur M. Schlesinger, Sr., pointed out that Americans had long recognized that the democratic movement transcends national boundaries. He further insisted that democracy could be understood only in terms of parallel movements elsewhere, and of world perspective.[79] Of these historians, Carl Becker alone was an outspoken champion of the so-called relativist position in historiography, though others in the group may have subscribed to it in some degree. Yet on the point at issue, the placing of American democracy in a world setting, all were in agreement—all were writing *in relation to* the needs of their times and of their country.

One important contributor to the historiography of American democracy did not entirely share this world orientation. It happened that he, like his friend Becker in the other camp, was a leading spokesman for the relativist position. It was not that Beard ignored the roots of many of our democratic ideas in other places and times.[80] But his emphasis was, like that of Turner, on the uniquely

[75] Carl L. Becker, *The United States; An Experiment in Democracy* (New York, 1920).

[76] Carl L. Becker, *Modern Democracy* (New Haven, 1941); "What Is Still Living in the Political Philosophy of Thomas Jefferson?" *American Historical Review* (July, 1943), XLVIII, 691–796; and the statement in Norman Cousins (ed.), *A Treasury of Democracy* (New York, 1942), pp. 167–168.

[77] Ralph B. Perry, *Puritanism and Democracy* (New York, 1944).

[78] Perry Miller, *The New England Mind: The Seventeenth Century* (New York, 1939).

[79] Arthur M. Schlesinger, Sr., "American and World History," in *Paths to the Present* (New York, 1949), pp. 174–177.

[80] This is clear in a great many of Beard's writings, including *The Rise of*

American aspects of our democracy. In 1932 he had called attention to an important problem in reminding us that the history of democracy had been that of the conquest and adaptation of institutions already established by the privileged classes. In that democratic adaptation America had enjoyed the advantage of having had, at least in the national period, no feudal institutions, no established church, no military caste, no bureaucracy. It had on the other hand inherited and developed constitutional checks on power, many of which were sufficiently local to be close to the people. The country having been for the greater part of its history a nation of freehold farmers, Americans had acquired a daily experience in policy making. Whether the factory could provide comparable experiences and if not, what this fact meant for the general welfare, were questions that Beard raised but that no one could entirely answer.[81]

As the New Deal and the oncoming war concentrated power in the hands of the executive, Beard warned of the importance of preserving constitutional checks and balances. And he saw in the increasing reliance on military power and in overseas activities further danger to American democracy.

Beard's later writings on foreign policy illustrated his own thesis that complete objectivity is impossible. But they raised a basic question. Have we so fully achieved democracy here that the defense of democracy is the same as national defense? This question involves others. Can democracy as Carl Wittke defined it survive in a world placing overwhelming emphasis on military measures? Does democracy need more critical and more informed implementation (both here and abroad) through economic and cultural as well as military means? Should historians, if they can muster the courage, try to help the American people to answer these questions?

This consideration of the democratic theme in American histori-

---

American Civilization, written in collaboration with Mary R. Beard, and in *The Republic*. See also "The Evolution of Democracy: A Summary," in Cleveland and Schafer (eds.), *Democracy in Reconstruction*, chap. XXIII.

[81] Milburn L. Wilson, *Democracy Has Roots* (New York, 1939), Preface. A. Whitney Griswold has challenged this thesis. See his *Farming and Democracy* (New York, 1948).

ography suggests, I think, several things. First, the treatment of democracy in the American story has been for the most part peripheral rather than central—save in times of rapid change, sharp internal tension, or a heightened foreign challenge. Second, it is clear that the treatment of democracy in American experience reflected the reactions of historians to dominant and competing currents of thought about human nature, social relationships, and the place of America in the world at the time of writing. Third, there has been no consensus about either the meaning of American democracy or its origins and conditioning circumstances or the degree of importance it has had in our national experience. It is thus an open question whether or not the current confusion and uncertainty about democracy do not in some measure rest on our shoulders. For we have largely written and taught our history to our people and to the rest of the world.

This study also suggests that recent discussions of "objective versus relativistic" writing have been too heated. As the evidence here presented shows, I have been unable to find any historians whose work has not been influenced by dominant or competing movements of thought in their time or by the position they held in society. The degree of verisimilitude reached appears to have become somewhat greater in the historical writing about democracy since the progressive movement and the First World War—a period in which the democratic theme was given a greater and more realistic emphasis. I submit that scientific method, including the new scientific idea of relativism, has helped to bring this about by lessening the confidence of the historian in assuming he had achieved objectivity.

This survey also bears on the controversy between the advocates of history for its own sake and history for the sake of understanding the present. It has shown, in terms of craftsmanship, justification both for an awareness of the historian's responsibilities to the public and the dangers in mere presentism, whether the emphasis is one primarily critical of the *status quo* or primarily apologetic for it. I have not found evidence that historians who have subscribed to so-called relativism and so-called presentism have been more prone than others to overemphasize and glorify democratic elements in our history, and to undervalue and distort conservative ones. But I have found evidence to suggest that any position which calls for a return to the patriotic affirmations without due regard to our critical functions should give us pause. Any position that calls for suppressing "pathological" episodes in our past, and for using our craft to support a currently held policy,[82] should give us pause.

Finally this report on my study of the writings on democracy may suggest certain questions that invite historical investigation. We need fuller and richer histories of American democracy. These future histories may, and should, approach the subject from various angles of vision and use varying methods. I have been, for example, seeking to test the validity of Turner's contention that the frontier was more democratic than older areas by a more or less microscopic study of a carefully chosen Wisconsin place and period. In this investigation we have supplemented town, county, and state public records, newspapers, and private manuscripts by a quantitative analysis of the data in unpublished censuses. In this study we are asking questions of highly qualified authorities—of authorities so highly qualified as to inspire at least me with awe. We are asking these questions of International Business Machines! We hope their answers may throw some new light on relationships between economic status, political participation and leadership, and social and civic activities. We hope that our study will further clarify the relation between firstcomers or early settlers and later arrivals on the one hand and equality of economic opportunity on the other. And we hope that if our results are promising, similar case studies may be made for many frontier areas at many periods and, for comparative purposes, that similar studies may also be made of the longer-settled areas.

Whether studies in the history of democracy in America be microscopic or broadly gauged, they should take into account the whole of the culture, of which the democratic idea and substance

[82] Conyers Read, "The Social Responsibilities of the Historian," *American Historical Review* (January, 1950), LV, 284.

do not form the entirety. They must consider the problems of definition and meanings. Nor should such histories ignore efforts to state the traditional assumptions of democracy in a form acceptable to modern logic, psychology, cultural anthropology, and theories of knowledge. Such histories should be further informed by the writings about democracy by both American and foreign scholars in the fields of philosophy, education, religion, the other social sciences, and biology. And they should take into full account the relative importance at different times of indigenous and more far-reaching experiences and ideas in shaping democracy.

Such treatments of democracy will serve as warnings against crystallizing the history of American democracy into clichés and dogma for ideological warfare. Our American experience has been related to faith in an open universe, in man's ability to control rather than be controlled by the forces surrounding him; and democracy has been, not a finished accomplishment, but a growing ideal and process. But recent developments suggest that a crystallization of democracy into fixed codes and clichés is not unthinkable.

I am thinking of such aspects of the cold war as loyalty purges and loyalty oaths, of the evidences of reluctance on the campuses to discuss "controversial" questions, and of the growing tendency to associate loyalty with conformity to the particular policies of the most articulate and influential groups. If official crystallization of the democratic faith should take place, perhaps by 1984, it would be impossible to explore any further the history of American democracy. At least we could not explore it freely as our fellow historians, including some of the pioneers of this Association, have explored it—and as I hope our younger colleagues may still want to explore it. But I for one have faith that the democratic theme will continue to be explored and written about, in varied but scholarly ways, by historians who will continue to have not only the humility of scholars but the courage of patriots, and who because of this humility and this courage will keep on trying to rise above the pressures of their time and, just as they find it and see it, present in their writings the truth about the history of democracy.

2

Frederick Jackson Turner, 1861-1932 (1949)

IN CHOOSING Frederick Jackson Turner as one of the two most eminent historians of the United States, the Council of the American Historical Association paid tribute to the scholar who in greater measure than any other in the past half-century has forced the rewriting of the national history. Of the five volumes of Turner's writings, only two deal in anything like a systematic way with specific periods in the development of the United States; and he wrote no comprehensive history of the nation. Thus the mono-graphic and systematic writing of Turner is considerably less in scope and quantity than that of other historians who might have been chosen to stand beside Francis Parkman.[1] But in originality and in influence, Turner has thus far had no superior if he has had any peer. The fact that today one of the major controversies in the scholarship of United States history centers in Turner's frontier

[1] Turner's volumes, not including diplomatic documents that he edited and bibliographies that he prepared or helped prepare, are, in order of the date of publication, *The Rise of the New West 1819-1829* (vol. 14 of The American Nation Series, Albert Bushnell Hart, ed., New York, 1906); *The Frontier in American History* (New York, 1920); *The Significance of Sections in American History* (New York, 1932); *The United States 1830-1850: The Nation and Its Sections* (New York, 1935); and *The Early Writings of Frederick Jackson Turner* (Madison, 1938), with a list of all his works compiled by Everett E. Edwards and an introduction by Fulmer Mood. The bibliography of Turner's writings in this volume includes the large number of essays and reviews that he wrote.

thesis supports rather than detracts from the statement regarding the seminal character of his ideas and the far-reaching influence of his writing and teaching.

Important reasons for the high rank Turner holds in United States historiography are to be found in the problems that he chose for investigation, in the methods by which he broadened and deepened historical research, in the interpretations of his findings, in his inspirational teaching, and in the influence of his work on public thought and even on public action. He who understands the vogue of Turner's ideas understands in large part the chief movements of thought and feeling in the past seventy years.

But even more important than all these is the amazing array of suggestive ideas for investigation that Turner set forth. Virtually no major field of research in the national history, virtually no leading interpretation or approach that others have explored, can be pointed to which Turner did not anticipate. This is true, for example, of such themes, cultivated and reported on by others, as the Industrial Revolution, capitalism, labor, class conflicts, immigration, urbanization, cultural achievements, physiography, and the social uses of historical knowledge in the arena of public action. It is worth emphasizing the point that at the outset of his career Turner urged the study of the United States in terms of world history. He insisted at the start on the necessity of taking account of the contributions of Europe to American development and of the impact in turn of America on the rest of the world.[2] Though he did not develop these themes in his publications, neither did he ignore them in his investigations and teaching; and he encouraged students to explore them. His students who later went into European history, including Carl L. Becker and Guy Stanton Ford, were equally indebted to him.

In view, then, of Turner's pioneer contributions in giving the

---

[2] See in particular his two early essays, "The Significance of History" (1891) and "Problems in American History" (1892), reprinted in *The Early Writings of Frederick Jackson Turner*, and the prescient and stimulating address given on his retirement as president of the American Historical Association, "Social Forces in American History," *American Historical Review* (January, 1911), XVI, 217 ff.

study of American history an economic and social base, of bringing it into a close working alliance with geography, demography, sociology, and other social sciences, and of suggesting a great many fertile approaches and themes, it is unwarrantable to regard him as important merely as the father and sponsor of the frontier interpretation of American history. His name, it is true, has been so intimately associated with that thesis that it must be given due prominence. But the point to emphasize today is that the frontier thesis was but one aspect of Turner's work.

I

By early environment Frederick Jackson Turner came to know at first hand something of the great march of civilization that pushed the wilderness ever westward. He was born in Portage, Wisconsin, on November 14, 1861. His father, Andrew Jackson Turner, and his mother, Mary Hanford Turner, were pioneers who had come to Wisconsin from upstate New York. From them and from neighbors young Turner heard many stories of the Indians, the fur traders, and the loggers that preceded the development of the settled community in which he lived. Portage itself was on the edge of country still largely wilderness. On fishing and hunting excursions young Turner saw Indians pitching their tepees and witnessed other survivals of the frontier. In his day-by-day life he came to know all sorts of people of many national backgrounds, living together with a give and take and with every indication of rapidly becoming Americans. The life of Portage was also thoroughly democratic in its social relations. Turner's father, a local politician, newspaper editor, and historian, was much interested in the transformation of the area from a borderland frontier area to a settled farming community. It is obvious that such an environment, simple, democratic, and on the edge of the wilderness, provided a natural setting for the development in a sensitive youth of an interest in the process by which civilization replaced the forest life of Indians, trappers, and fur traders.[3]

[3] This is based in part on an autobiographical letter of Turner, published in the *Wisconsin Magazine of History* (September, 1935), *XIX*, 96 ff.

But Turner's boyhood comrades, subjected to the same experiences of the departing borderland life, did not become historians of the westward movement. An all-important step in Turner's development was the decision to attend the University of Wisconsin at Madison. Here he received a thorough classical training. The sensitiveness to literary style thus cultivated was another foundation for Turner's later career. His fluid and balanced sentences, his liking for the apt epithet, owed something to his classical studies.

The University of Wisconsin was a small democratic institution, presided over by President John Bascom, a versatile scholar and, for his day, a progressive thinker on social and economic issues. Bascom preached the duty of University students to improve the state which made their higher education possible by using the knowledge thus asquired for the public good. From President Bascom, from other scholars, and from the type of student life that prevailed. Turner was confirmed in the democratic outlook on life that Portage had given him. In two orations, one given in his junior year, and one at his commencement in 1884, Turner expounded his faith in democracy and in a democratic culture.

In one he called for and predicted the appearance of a great epic poet of American democracy. In the other he declared that the world was at last beginning to see that true progress required the enlightenment of all. He had no fear that the utilitarian American democracy would ruin the artistic heritage of the past. It would, on the contrary, Turner insisted, provide for a much greater and richer artistic development: for the squalor of the hovel would no longer mar the beauty of the cathedral. In this emphasis on the functional, democratic interpretation of art and culture, Turner was breaking with the traditional view that associated great achievements in the arts with a privileged order.[4]

At the University of Wisconsin Turner came into close contact not only with cultural democracy but with modern science. In the orations just mentioned the young undergraduate spoke in the most appreciative terms of science. This he associated with both democ-

[4] "The Poet of the Future" and "Architecture through Oppression," *University Press* (May 26, 1883), *XIV*, 4; and (June 21, 1884), *XV*, 12.

racy and progress. From his teachers in biology and geology he learned of the scientific method that was working a revolution in man's knowledge of the external world. It was a natural step to apply the principle of the inductive study of natural phenomena to the inductive study of historical data—a step we shall see him taking under the tutelage of two historians who were pioneers in the United States in the scientific study of history. From Thomas C. Chamberlin, the eminent geologist who presided as president over the University in the years of Turner's graduate studies, he heard of the multiple hypothesis. The development of the earth, Chamberlin held, was too many-sided, too complicated, to be approached by any single hypothesis. It could be understood only through considering multiple hypotheses, each of which was constantly to be tested by the evidence of the data in as detached a way as possible. Turner took to heart this idea and often illustrated it in his later teaching.

As a student at the University of Wisconsin Turner also learned of the doctrine of evolution, at that time still highly controversial. Under the spell of his professor of history, in true evolutionary terms he conceived of society as an ever-growing organism: history was merely the self-consciousness of that organism. The roots of the present, whether the focus of attention were a rock or a flower or an animal or a society, lay deep in the past; and development took place without any break. Thus Turner, thanks to the intellectual currents he met as a student, was prepared to apply to the study of society the concept of development from stage to stage by struggle and adaptation.

One of the most remarkable exemplars in America of the scientific approach to the study of the past was William F. Allen, professor of history at Wisconsin. Trained at Harvard and the German universities of the mid-nineteenth century, Allen taught his students, in the manner of a scientist, the critical evaluation of the evidence in primary sources. This was highly unusual at the time, for most American teachers of history emphasized the mastery of the facts in a historical manual. In addition, Allen set great store on economic and cultural factors in history. Here again he was a pioneer, for in the United States of the time the emphasis was almost exclusively on political and constitutional history. Again, in the spirit of Heeren, under whose spell he had fallen in Germany, Allen emphasized the interrelations of America and Europe. What was more, he acquainted his students with the large problems rather than with the bare isolated facts—the stock in trade of most historians. He likewise made much use of geographical maps. Allen's special interest was Roman history, in the teaching of which he called attention to the expansion of Roman civilization outward and to the movement of peoples. This transplanted Easterner was further a pioneer in emphasizing the importance of the West in American development.[5] There is no doubt that he profoundly influenced Turner. It was the inspiration of Allen that decided the young scholar to give up journalism, in which he spent a profitable year or so, and to become a professional historian. In later years he testified that whatever he had achieved he owed to Professor Allen.

Under Allen's guidance Turner prepared from the rich collection of manuscripts at the State Historical Society of Wisconsin an essay on "The Character and Influence of the Fur Trade in Wisconsin." This fulfilled the requirement for the degree of Master of Arts, which he was awarded in 1888. The study reflected an evolutionary approach to the material, thus exemplifying the impact of natural science on the young historian. In like manner Turner's article on Wisconsin, prepared for the ninth edition of the *Encyclopaedia Britannica*, was outstanding in developing the theme in terms of the evolution of a complex, specialized economy and culture from a simple society.

In the year 1888–1889 Turner went to the Johns Hopkins University, the mecca of young Americans seeking advanced training in their own country. At Baltimore he studied with and became a

[5] Allen's writings are in part available in David B. Frankenburger and others (eds.), *Essays and Monographs by William Francis Allen: Memorial Volume* (Boston, 1890). On Allen see the *Proceedings of the Thirty-Seventh Annual Meeting of the State Historical Society of Wisconsin, 1889* (Madison, 1890), pp. 79–89.

friend of Woodrow Wilson, whose historical work he was to influence; he attended the lectures of the sociologist Albion Small, which may have confirmed him in sociological approaches to history; and he worked under Richard T. Ely, the American exponent of the historical approach in economics. Turner also studied with Herbert Baxter Adams, the best-known university teacher of history at the time. Like Allen, Adams also viewed the development of the present from the past in evolutionary terms. But to him heredity was far more important than environment. In the view of Adams, American institutions could be understood only in terms of their European antecedents or "germs," particularly the political forms that prevailed among the early Teutonic tribes.

To young Turner, all this was unsatisfactory. Admitting that the similarities America shared with Europe were inherited, what of the differences? These could be explained only in terms of environment. The crude unsettled wilderness must have forced the Europeans who came to America to adapt their institutions to new conditions.

Several factors explain Turner's position. He had seen the shaping influence of the borderland in his own Wisconsin community, and in his study of the fur trade of his native state. Sectional pride also led Turner to reject the Adams thesis of the "germ theory" origin of American institutions. Turner's West was at the very moment protesting with much sectional self-consciousness against domination by the East. Turner, taking pride in his section, was thus of no mind to reject its history as negligible. Besides, he was in revolt against the antiquarian nature of historical writing on the West. In reviewing Theodore Roosevelt's *Winning of the West,* he had taken exception to the emphasis on colorful Indian fighting and had insisted that a larger story of westward migration was yet to be told. Likewise the voluminous publications of H. H. Bancroft in California seemed divorced from the central movements of national history, fragmentary and episodical.

In rejecting the prevalent historical interpretations of the history of his country, Turner was expressing a deeply felt nationalism as well as a deeply felt sectionalism. For the Civil War and Reconstruction were now of the past, and the rising generation was fully aware of the great power of the nation, of its potential role on the world stage. Hence, any theory of American history that regarded civilization in America as a mere extension, a bare replica, of that in the Old World hardly answered the emotional needs of young patriots like Turner. In any case, in his expanded and rewritten master's essay which he presented for the doctorate at Johns Hopkins, Turner made only slight concessions to the Adams "germ theory" of American institutions. His study did, to be sure, trace fur-trading institutions back to Phoenicia and Rome; but the text made it plain that the raw environment of the frontier chiefly shaped fur trading in Wisconsin.

The death of Professor Allen in 1889 led to the appointment of Turner as his successor. He was now well-enough prepared to go ahead on his own power, to realize his potentialities. It is noteworthy that in his first research seminar he chose for investigation the movement of immigrant groups into Wisconsin. This choice testified to his conviction that American history could not be separated from that of Europe. The investigations in the seminar called attention anew to the role of cheap lands in attracting immigrants. At the same time Turner announced a course new in the annals of historical teaching—one on the economic and social development of the United States.

II

In 1891 Turner announced his historical credo in a remarkable essay, "The Significance of History."[6] This was prepared to show the usefulness of historical study in the new program of University Extension classes that President Chamberlin was launching. The essay was a historiographical declaration of independence. Turner rejected the dominant emphasis on political and institutional history. He also denied the objective and permanently truthful and

---

[6] This essay is reprinted in *The Early Writings of Frederick Jackson Turner*, pp. 43–68.

adequate character of even the best historical scholarship. In this essay Turner boldly declared "each age writes the history of the past anew with reference to the conditions uppermost in its own time." If this was the case, then historians must learn to discard the idea that there are "standard ultimate histories." Here we find Turner anticipating the recent emphasis that Carl Becker, Charles A. Beard, and others have put on the relativity of historical knowledge —on the frame-of-reference concept. A tribal history, Turner went on, was good enough for a tribal people; but for a modern, complicated society with world orientations, only a comparative and comprehensive approach, indeed a world approach to the nation's past, was adequate if history was to illuminate the present. The study of the history of the United States was still, he argued, in the tribal phase. "Our history is to be understood as a growth from European history under the new conditions of the New World. How shall we understand American history without understanding European history?" From the history of other peoples Americans might surely learn useful lessons.

But Turner was even more the innovator in declaring that the uppermost questions of the day flowed from the new age of machinery, the factory system, and socialism. Thus the historian must understand property relations, the distribution of wealth, the influence of world-wide conditions, "the whole economic base of society." The time had come when the country could no longer be content with ignorance of how the present had come about. In defending historical studies in an institution of higher learning maintained by public funds, Turner held that only through a historical approach to the great current political, social, and economic issues could citizens and statesmen be trained to deal competently with these problems.

Turner was here presenting a view later to be popularized by Professor James Harvey Robinson and others under the term "the new history." This insisted, among other things, on the usefulness of historical knowledge as an instrument for effective living in a modern, complex society. Nor were these mere words, for Turner took the lead in establishing at the University of Wisconsin the new School of Economics, Political Science and History. At Turner's suggestion, Richard T. Ely was brought from the Johns Hopkins University to help in the undertaking. Within no time, the School was a leading center for the training of scholars in public policy and administration.[7]

The rich philosophical content and prophetic eloquence of this manifesto were sustained in a new essay that appeared the following year in a University publication. This was called "Problems in American History." The foremost authority on Turner, Dr. Fulmer Mood, has said that in this essay the historian "for the first time in print put his finger upon the material cause, the fundamental economic factor, that he was to stress in his interpretation of our history." What was that fundamental factor? In Turner's own words, it was this: "In a sense, American history up to our own day has been colonial history, the colonization of the great West. *This ever retreating frontier of free land is the key to American development.*"

The essay was "proof that Turner had evolved from a student of local or regional history into a student of national and continental history."[8] He gathered dry details that would have been dust in other men's hands and molded them into flashing, incisive generalizations that illuminated a subject and a student's mind to their far horizons.

In truth, "Problems in American History" laid down the program of a whole new historiographical school. To quote Fulmer Mood again, "it served notice on those who read it that a revolution had taken place in American historiography." The revolution, briefly, was outlined in certain broad propositions. First, Turner insisted on the necessity of looking behind institutions and constitutional forms to discover "the vital forces that call these organs into life and shape them to meet changing conditions." In terms reminiscent of the

[7] Merle Curti and Vernon Carstensen, *The University of Wisconsin, A History* (Madison, 1949, 2 vols.), I, 630–641.

[8] Fulmer Mood, "Turner's Formative Period," in *The Early Writings of Frederick Jackson Turner*, p. 38.

evolutionist he declared that "the peculiarity of American institutions is the fact that they are compelled to adapt themselves to the changes of a remarkably developing, expanding people. The institutional framework of the nation may be likened to the anatomy of the body politic; its physiology is the social and economic life molding this framework to new uses. Here it is that we find the field for widest study."

The second proposition was that American history in this broader sense could no longer be pursued with conventional tools and materials. In calling for the "thorough study of the physiographic basis of our history," Turner indicated that the geologist, the biologist, the meteorologist, and the historian must join hands and predicted that such a coöperative approach would show "how largely American history has been determined by natural conditions."

The third proposition reminded the reader that natural environment, however important, was not the sole determining factor. For Turner again insisted that European life had entered the American continent and profoundly influenced it; he again declared that America in turn had "modified that life and reacted on Europe."

Fourth, Turner declared that sight must not be lost of the process by which the sectionalization of the Atlantic coast was extended westward with constant modifications of the older culture by new conditions. This process was to be investigated. The historian must discover and explain the distinctive characteristics of the sections, including the moving section that could be described at any moment in time as the West. Nor could he neglect the interplay of these sections on each other and their impact on national development. Such a study, he continued, involved learning more about the Indian, about immigration from Europe, about the distribution of immigrants in the sections, and about the interstate migration of the native-born. Turner ended the essay on a striking note: "What the Mediterranean Sea was to the Greeks, breaking the bond of custom, offering new experiences, calling out new institutions and activities, that the ever retreating Great West has been to the eastern United States directly, and to the nations of Europe more remotely."[9]

III

In some of the most brilliant essays in American historiography Fulmer Mood has shown how Turner arrived at this conception of American history and how it came to be amplified in 1893 in the famous paper Turner read before the American Historical Association.[10] We may merely here remind ourselves that in the later stages of the process Turner owed much to the Bureau of Census and to certain historical atlases. These developed a picture of the westward-moving population, decade by decade; of the resultant conquest of woodland, prairies, deserts, and mountains by the westward advance of population; and of the importance of physiographic areas in this process. Turner, in reading a new bulletin of the Census Bureau, was struck by the statement that "up to and including 1880 the country had a frontier of settlement, but at present the unsettled area has been so broken into by isolated bodies of settlement that there can hardly be said to be a frontier line. In the discussion of its extent, its westward movement, etc., it cannot, therefore, any longer have a place in the census reports." Turner had the remarkable gift of insight and generalization; in terms of his background and studies, this dry official announcement, which most historians would have passed over had it come their way, struck him as highly significant: an era of American history had now ended. He inevi-

[9] *Early Writings*, p. 83.

[10] In addition to the essay already cited, "Turner's Formative Period," see "The Development of Frederick Jackson Turner as an Historical Thinker," Colonial Society of Massachusetts, *Publications* (December, 1939), XXXIV, 283 ff.; "The Historiographic Setting of Turner's Frontier Essay," *Agricultural History* (July, 1943), XVII, 153–155; "The Concept of the Frontier, 1871–1898," *ibid.* (January, 1945), XIX, 24–30; and "Notes on the History of the Word *Frontier*," *ibid.* (April, 1948), XXII, 78–83. Dr. Mood is now engaged in writing a biography of Turner. For another discussion of antecedents of Turner's discovery of the importance of the frontier, see Herman Clarence Nixon, "Precursors of Turner in the Interpretation of the American Frontier," *South Atlantic Quarterly* (January, 1929), XXVIII, 83–89; Nixon shows that Jefferson, Emerson, Tocqueville, E. L. Godkin, and Bryce, among others, anticipated Turner.

tably made this the point of departure in the paper he prepared for
the American Historical Association at its meeting in Chicago in
connection with the World's Columbian Exposition.

In this famous essay, marked by poetic cadences and vivid im-
agery, Turner began with the bold statement that "the existence of
an area of free land, its continuous recession, and the advance of
American settlement westward, explain American development."
Thus American development was chiefly the beginning over again
of civilization in unoccupied areas, the evolution of society from the
simple to the complex. Each new region recapitulated the experiences of former frontiers: the explorer, the hunter and trapper,
the trader, the rancher, and the pioneer farmer followed one another. As the region was transformed from one of pioneer farmers
into one of specialized farmers and manufacturers, into a region
with many towns and cities, it ceased to be frontier country.

In this essay as in later writings, the frontier meant primarily the
region of sparse settlement to the west of settled areas, "the meeting
point between savagery and civilization." At times, to be sure,
Turner used the term in the sense of the line itself, on maps that
separated areas inhabited by less than two persons to the square
mile from those more densely settled; at other times he spoke of the
frontier as the process itself of civilization marching westward into
unoccupied areas; and on occasion he referred to it as a state of
mind. The richness of the land and its relative cheapness and
availability were the magnet; the desire on the part of the potential
frontiersman to better his lot in life was the principal motive for
moving into unoccupied or slightly settled areas.

Turner was more concerned in this essay with the meaning of the
frontier process than with the process itself, though in later researches much attention was paid to the actual occupation. He
maintained that the process of colonization of the new lands chiefly
explained the growth of American democracy and of American
nationalism.

By democracy, Turner meant the democracy of Jefferson, Jackson, and Lincoln; the democracy that meant equality of opportunity

to compete for the natural resources of the unoccupied or sparsely occupied land; the democracy of political participation and decision making by all adult male citizens; the democracy that concerned itself with the well-being of the common man. It was the frontier movement that transformed the democracy of Jefferson into that of Jackson and Lincoln. As long as free land existed, the opportunity for a competency existed: the widely based economic power secured a widely based political power. Turner also saw in the democratizing effects of the westward movement the reinforcing of democracy not only in the older areas of the East but in Europe itself.

In Turner's view the democratizing effects of the colonization of the land between the Atlantic and the Pacific were closely associated with the growth of nationalism, by which he meant the consolidation of sections into the nation, the increasing powers and functions of the central government, and the development of an American self-consciousness. The frontier, he declared, was the line of the most effective and rapid Americanization both of the Old World immigrants and of the native-born peoples of the older sections that settled in it. In the new country the habits, loyalties, and views of Europe, of New England, and of the long-settled Middle and Southern Atlantic regions were gradually replaced by new or modified ones. The frontier, in short, promoted the formation of a composite nationality, for the constant reëxposure to the demands of beginning over again stamped American characteristics on those who colonized the new country. The advancing settlements, moreover, lessened dependence on England; accentuated the powers of the central government, which alone was equal to the task of providing protection against Indians, subsidizing roads, canals, and railroads, and allocating land. Turner also believed that legislation for tariffs as well as for internal improvements and land policy necessitated a broad or loose construction of those clauses in the federal Constitution dealing with the powers of the central government. Finally, the westward movement, he argued, developed the essentially American traits of restless energy, self-reliance, voluntary coöperation on the part of individuals, practical ingenuity and versatility, inventiveness, and a masterful grasp of material things; developed, in short, the individualism, strength, readiness to innovate, and earthy practicality that Europeans described as characteristically American.

Turner was intrigued by the implications of the Census Bureau announcement in 1891 that it was no longer possible to describe on the map a frontier line separating settled from unsettled areas. But he expressed the faith of the late nineteenth-century western mind that the qualities born of the frontier, above all its individualistic democracy, constituted a permanent heritage to the nation. In the survival of frontier ideals in the new America of concentrated economic power, Turner believed his countrymen possessed an instrument well designed to meet the issues of an industrial economy. Under the influence of Populism and Progressivism, in many respects Middle Western movements, he looked to the government to find equivalents for the vanished opportunity implicit in the bygone era of free lands.

In advocating state-supported social services, later liberal leaders, including President Franklin D. Roosevelt, maintained that a democratic politically controlled adjustment must take the place of the earlier equal competition for a share of the nation's natural resources.[11] Yet in combating the social legislation of the New Deal, conservatives argued that such quasi-collectivism ran counter to the characteristically American heritage of individualism and self-reliance.[12] Thus the Turner interpretation of the frontier process was a two-edged instrument used by publicists and politicians in advocating conflicting views on legislation.

In considering the social and political implications of the frontier theory, we may note its bearings on conceptions of foreign policy. Anti-imperialists and isolationists have sometimes argued that over-

[11] Curtis Nettels, "Frederick Jackson Turner and the New Deal," *Wisconsin Magazine of History* (March, 1934), XVII, 257–265. See, for further illustrations of the point, Rexford Tugwell, "No More Frontiers," *Today* (June 22, 1935), IV, 3–4; and Henry A. Wallace, *New Frontiers* (New York, 1934).

[12] James Truslow Adams, "Rugged Individualism Analyzed," *The New York Times Magazine* (March 8, 1934), pp. 1–2, 11.

seas expansion would ruin the democracy born of frontier experience. But a larger number held that the disappearance of free lands at home compelled the United States to seek equivalents in colonialism overseas. Turner himself looked with favor on the movement for oceanic expansion at the time of the Spanish-American War. But it was also possible for the Turner school to contend that the give-and-take of the frontier, the mutual coöperation it had stimulated, its harmonization of different peoples, provided a pattern for a larger coöperation between nations.[13]

The frontier theory not only influenced political leaders and students of United States history. Medievalists compared western movements in America with the expansion of the German people into the forest lands of east-central Europe.[14] Historians of Canada[15] and Latin America[16] examined the relevance of the frontier concept in their own national histories. Students of American law[17] and religion[18] found it a useful key. Literary historians applied it in their field.[19] It became, in brief, a widely used concept in humanistic and social-science scholarship.

Until the 1930's few historians seriously challenged the frontier

[13] Frederic L. Paxson, *When the West Is Gone* (New York, 1930), pp. 134–136. It is noteworthy that Turner prepared for Woodrow Wilson a memorandum on the possible lessons of American frontier and sectional experience for making the League of Nations effective. See *American Historical Review* (April, 1942), XLVII, 545–551.

[14] James Westfall Thompson, "Profitable Fields of Investigation in Medieval History," *American Historical Review* (April, 1913), XVIII, 490 ff.

[15] Walter N. Sage, "Some Aspects of the Frontier in Canadian Thinking," *Annual Report of the Canadian Historical Association* (1928), pp. 62–73; and Morris Zaslow, "The Frontier Hypothesis in Recent Historiography," *Canadian Historical Review* (June, 1948), XXIX, 158–166.

[16] Victor Andrés Belaúnde, "The Frontier in Hispanic America," *Rice Institution Pamphlets* (October, 1923), X, 202–213.

[17] Roscoe Pound, *The Spirit of the Common Law* (Boston, 1921).

[18] Peter George Mode, *The Frontier Spirit in American Christianity* (New York, 1923); Henry K. Rowe, *The History of Religion in the United States* (New York, 1924); and William W. Sweet, *The Story of Religions in America* (New York, 1930).

[19] Among the literary historians influenced by the frontier thesis were Dorothy Dondore, *The Prairie and the Making of Middle America* (Cedar Rapids, 1926); Lucy Lockwood Hazard, *The Frontier in American Literature* (New York, 1927); and Percy H. Boynton, *The Discovery of the Frontier* (Chicago, 1931).

thesis. From that decade to the present, however, it has been subjected to increasing criticism. Some have taken Turner to task for a loose and inconsistent use of such terms as frontier, democracy, and nationalism.[20] Others have regarded the frontier thesis as an oversimplification that violates "the fundamental principles of social causation as the complex product of the unique interaction of multiple causes."[21] Still others insisted that the frontier did little to promote democracy and social innovation; that the East and Europe were in much greater degree responsible for both.[22] Certain historians have held that the frontier thesis was an agrarian interpretation of American history that failed to give sufficient emphasis to the Industrial Revolution, urbanization, and basic class antagonisms and conflicts.[23] Carlton J. H. Hayes has recently gone so far as to attribute to the frontier thesis the intellectual isolationism of the United States—has insisted that the emphasis placed on it by historians has turned the public eye away from Europe, of which our history has been an integral part.[24] We shall not try to evaluate

[20] George Wilson Pierson, "The Frontier and Frontiersmen in Turner's Essays," *Pennsylvania Magazine of History and Biography* (October, 1940), XLIV, 449–478; "The Frontier and American Institutions," *New England Quarterly* (June, 1942), XV, 224–255; and "Recent Studies of Turner and the Frontier Doctrine," *Mississippi Valley Historical Review* (December, 1947), XXXIV, 453–458.

[21] James C. Malin, "Space and History," *Agricultural History* (April, 1944), XVIII, 65–67; and *The Grassland of North America* (Lawrence, Kans., 1947).

[22] Benjamin F. Wright, Jr., "American Democracy and the Frontier," *Yale Review* (December, 1930), XX, 349–365; and "Political Institutions and the Frontier," in Dixon Ryan Fox (ed.), *Sources of Culture in the Middle West* (New York, 1934), pp. 15–38.

[23] Charles A. Beard, "Culture and Agriculture," *Saturday Review of Literature* (October 20, 1928), V, 272–273, and "The Frontier in American History," *New Republic* (February 16, 1921), V; Louis M. Hacker, "Sections or Classes?" *Nation* (July 26, 1933), CXXXVII, 349–350, 108–111, and review of Turner's *The United States 1830–1850* in *The New Republic* (June 5, 1935), LXXXIII, 108. Closely associated with this general criticism is that concerned with the so-called safety valve which Turner suggested and which some of his followers developed. This maintained that the availability of cheap land in the West alleviated economic discontent in Europe. Among the many critics of the theory, the most thoroughgoing has been Fred A. Shannon, "A Post Mortem on the Labor-Safety-Valve Theory," *Agricultural History* (January, 1945), XIX, 27–37.

[24] Carlton J. H. Hayes, "The American Frontier—Frontier of What?" *American Historical Review* (January, 1946), LI, 199–210.

these criticisms or to estimate the degree to which they have been accepted in professional circles. It seems clear that in its extreme form the frontier thesis is no longer tenable,[25] and that more exact analysis and definition are needed. But the last word has not yet been said.

IV

Almost from the first Turner, preoccupied as he was with his studies of geographical atlases, saw the frontier as a sort of moving section. Thus it was a natural step, taken tentatively at the very time he was formulating the frontier concept, for him to emphasize sectionalism as the second and no less important key to American development. As we have seen, he called in his essay of 1892 for a thorough study of the physiographic regions of the United States. "The evolution of sections in our history," he wrote, "is a far deeper fact than the development of state particularism, for whatever force the latter had came in large degree from its association with sectionalism."[26] The Middle Atlantic section, he continued, had been studied much less than either New England or the South Atlantic section; and he urged not only the investigation of these but an exploration of the extension of these, as well as of New England, into the West. "The vast spaces into which the American people moved were themselves a complex of physiographic regions," he wrote later. These physiographic regions, with the type of people moving into them, developed into sections; and these "natural, economic, and social sections" were fundamental in explaining American de-

[25] For the status of the frontier theory in professional circles in 1941, see George Wilson Pierson, "American Historians and the Frontier Hypothesis in 1941," *Wisconsin Magazine of History* (September and December, 1942), XXVI. For a balanced statement by one of Turner's students, see Avery O. Craven, "Frederick Jackson Turner," in William T. Hutchinson (ed.), *Marcus W. Jernegan Essays in American Historiography* (Chicago, 1937). Robert E. Riegel, *America Moves West* (New York, 1947), chap. 40, and Ray A. Billington, *Westward Expansion* (New York, 1949), chap. 11, are thoughtful, balanced statements.

[26] *Early Writings*, p. 27. Frederick Jackson Turner, "The Significance of the Section in American History," *Wisconsin Magazine of History* (March, 1935), VIII.

velopment. In Turner's mind they were in truth comparable to the nations and empires of Europe, each having produced its typical leaders, attitudes, and cultures. "Interacting with each other and in combination they formed the United States." Turner proceeded in his researches to trace the colonization of these areas, their make-up and characteristics, their relations with one another and with the central government and the nation as a whole. In detailed studies he explained how and why the migrations from the older to the newer sections took place, and what followed therefrom. In large degree he came to interpret American political history in terms of "a contest between the economic and social sections." Rival sections made alliances, for no one could by itself determine national policy to suit its needs, whether in regard to tariff, land policy, currency, internal improvements, or foreign relations. Interprovincial relations were complicated by the existence of subsections within the larger sections: this explained political "straddling" and the restraints under which leaders often acted.[27]

In the pursuit of his interest in sections Turner published in 1906 his first major work—*The Rise of the New West 1819–1829.* This analyzed nationalism and sectionalism as major forces in the period, presented characterizations—economic, political, social, and cultural—of the principal sections, New England, the Middle Region, the South, the Middle West, and the Far West. The volume further explained party politics, tariff agitation, presidential elections, economic depression, internal improvements, nullification, and even the Monroe Doctrine largely in terms of sectional drives and ententes. The book, which was a pioneer study, has become a historical classic. Turner published from time to time penetrating essays on various aspects of American sectionalism: these were collected and published as a volume in 1932.

During his later years Turner pushed his researches forward into the period following that covered in *The Rise of the New West.* The same thesis, the significance of the sections in the larger na-

[27] Turner's essays on sectionalism were collected in *The Significance of Sections in American History* (New York, 1932).

tional patterns, provided the key to these investigations. The book on which he labored so long was unfinished when he died, but under the auspices of friendly hands it was prepared for the press and published in 1935. It bore the title *The United States: The Nation and the Sections 1830–1850*. Each section was dealt with separately; the economic, social, political, and cultural developments of each were examined and interpreted, with a wealth of new material, shrewd insights, and brilliant characterizations of sectional leaders. The interrelations of the sections during the period, and their impact on the nation, concluded the volume. While the reception of this book was not entirely favorable, competent historians regarded it as an important contribution to the knowledge and understanding of the period it dealt with.

The sectional interpretation of American history has been no less influential than the frontier thesis. In the work of such students of Turner as Louis Pelzer, Solon J. Buck, L. K. Mathews, U. B. Phillips, C. H. Ambler, Joseph A. Schafer, Herbert E. Bolton, H. C. Hockett, J. A. James, E. M. Coulter, Clarence Carter, Arthur Darling, Avery O. Craven, Frederick Merk, and others, it has borne rich fruits. Leading historians, not pupils or students, have testified with William E. Dodd to their indebtedness to Turner in their own sectional studies. Yet the sectional theme has also met with criticisms. To some it appeared, like the frontier concept, to obscure the importance of class cleavages within physiographical areas. Others have looked on it as no less a temporary phenomenon than the frontier itself. Although Turner recognized that sectional rivalries weakened as intercommunication and standardization increased, and as a national technological culture swept over the land, he did not concede that sectionalism was dying out. "The triumph of Bolshevism or capitalism," he observed in his later years, "would still leave a contest of sections."[28] Sectional rivalries have indeed continued; but the more recent development of the concept of regionalism and regional planning has given the whole matter a new orientation.

[28] *Ibid.*, p. 338.

V

In the years that followed the Chicago address of 1893—the address on the significance of the frontier which quickly gave Turner a national reputation—he continued to investigate the frontier process and the history of sectionalism. To his seminars at the University of Wisconsin came young men and women from all over the country. In a series of notable doctoral dissertations many aspects of the colonization of the West were studied: transportation (L. H. Haney, B. H. Meyer, E. A. Johnson), the influence of the public lands (H. B. Hibbard, G. M. Stephenson, A. C. Ford, R. G. Wellington), immigration (Kate Everest and, later, G. M. Stephenson and Marcus Hansen), the influence of the West on the constitutional development of the federal government (H. C. Hockett, O. G. Libby, and others). Turner himself published investigations of western constitution making and of the influence of the West on foreign policy. A new school of history testified to the appeal of the Turner approach.

The indefatigable research of the master and his devotion to his students did not prevent him from taking a leading part in University affairs. He built up one of the strongest centers for the study of American history, perhaps the strongest American center, a department in which specialists began to explore the history of the different sections. In addition to stimulating graduate studies in the University as a whole, Turner lent a hand in the Extension movement, which disseminated knowledge among the plain people of the state, and in the development of specialized educational services to government agencies, a twofold expression of an ideal of service to the people which came to be known as the Wisconsin Idea. It may be worth noting that he also fought the increasingly professional character of intercollegiate athletics. In 1910, the year he served as president of the American Historical Association, Turner entered a new phase in his career by accepting a professorship at Harvard. At that center of learning he continued to attract able students—Marcus Hansen, who was to become the leading authority on the history of American immigration; A. P. Whitaker, well known to Latin Americanists; and James B. Hedges were only a few. He deepened and extended his own researches. In 1924 Turner retired from Harvard and after a brief residence in Madison, Wisconsin, accepted an invitation to become research associate at the newly established Henry E. Huntington Library at San Marino, California. In 1932 at the age of seventy-one he died, at Pasadena, California.

Turner was one of the great teachers of his time. He was not a polished formal lecturer: his generous use of maps and slides and his spontaneity prevented his lectures from having the finished, systematic character that marked some historical lecturers. Yet his rich, vibrant, melodious voice was always impressive, and his broad humanism, his flair for the picturesque note and phrase, and above all the poetic touch he brought to the lectures distinguished his presentation. Above all he possessed the rare gift of inspiring students, of imbuing them with a deep love of his subject and a belief in its great importance.[29]

In his research seminars Turner achieved his greatest success as a teacher. It was his custom to take a limited period and to suggest closely related subjects to his students. His comments were always illuminating and pertinent and alive. Often they were shrewd and pungent. He could be and was critical of the work of his students; but his way of making them comrades in the quest of truth challenged them to put forth their best efforts. His extraordinary generosity with both his time and his ideas endeared him to those that

[29] Among the students who have written of Turner as a teacher, attention may be called to the essay of Avery O. Craven, already cited; Louise Phelps Kellogg, "The Passing of a Great Teacher," *Historical Outlook* (October, 1932), XXIII, 270–272; Edgar E. Robinson, "Frederick Jackson Turner," *North Dakota Historical Quarterly* (July, 1932), VI, 259–261; Joseph Schafer, "The Author of the Frontier Hypothesis," *Wisconsin Magazine of History* (September, 1931), XV, 86–103; Edward Everett Dale, "Memories of Frederick Jackson Turner," *Mississippi Valley Historical Review* (December, 1943), XXX, 339–358; and Merle Curti, "The Section and Frontier in American History," in Stuart Rice (ed.), *Methods in Social Science* (Chicago, 1931), pp. 353–367. See also Max Farrand, a devoted admirer, "Frederick Jackson Turner at the Huntington Library," *Huntington Library Bulletin* (February, 1933), III, 157–164.

knew him. An out-of-doors man, simple, straightforward, yet perceptive and urbane, he possessed a keen twinkling eye, a youthful vitality, and an enthusiasm that remained with him almost to the end. So did his sense of humor. Few that knew him were ever the same thereafter.

Of the many students that have testified to their indebtedness to Turner, Carl Becker, one of the most distinguished of the men he trained, has admirably summarized Turner's greatness. "Three qualities of the man's mind made a profound and indelible impression," Becker wrote. "These qualities were: a lively and irrepressible intellectual curiosity; a refreshing freedom from personal preoccupations and didactic motives; a quite unusual ability to look out upon the wide world in a humane and friendly way, with a vision unobscured by academic inhibitions."[30]

Before leaving the subject of Turner as a teacher, it may be well to note briefly the original and distinctive methods he brought to historical research. He was among the first, if not the first, historian to study the present in order to find clues to the past. He early saw that if history was really to explain how the present had developed from the past, it was necessary to use the data and methods of economics, sociology, psychology, biology, physiography, and geology, as well as literature and art. Moreover, "the method of the statistician as well as that of the critic of evidence" was "absolutely essential." Turner's intensive use of statistics was basic in his own work. "There has been too little coöperation of these sciences," Turner declared in 1904, "and the result is that great fields have been neglected. There are too many overlapping grounds left uncultivated owing to this independence of the scientists, too many problems that have been studied with inadequate apparatus and without due regard to their complexity."

An example of Turner's use of several disciplines was his development of a method for correlating political and cultural be-

---

[30] Carl L. Becker, "Frederick Jackson Turner," in Howard W. Odum (ed.), *American Masters of Social Science* (New York, 1927), chap. 9. This essay is eloquent and witty, and profoundly sincere.

havior with the physiographic map. This technique, to which one of his early students, O. G. Libby, contributed substantially, enabled Turner to plot the votes of members of Congress on political and economic issues and to correlate these votes with the economic interests and cultural characteristics of the regions they represented. Thus votes for internal improvements were seen to be heaviest in areas producing surpluses; votes for tariffs on raw wool followed the migration of woolgrowing westward; and votes for government control of railroads and monopolies were most numerous in areas suffering from the unfair practice of these business enterprises. By superimposing geological maps on maps indicating the place of origin of the settlers, Turner demonstrated that in general migrants sought a terrain similar to the one with which they were familiar in their old homes. Turner also made some striking correlations between literacy and good soil and between illiteracy and poor soil. This methodology, based on statistics, geological maps, and the plotting on maps of political votes, contributed materially to a realistic understanding of the relationships between physical geography and the colonizations of people, between all these factors and political and cultural phenomena and economic behavior. It is needless to say, perhaps, that Turner's methodology has been widely used in American scholarship.

This, then, was Turner—a pioneer in developing new methods which crossed the barriers of established disciplines and issued in a greater understanding of obscure interrelationships of many kinds; the pioneer who did much to develop the social and economic interpretations of American history; the craftsman who, without ceasing to be an artist, brought historical studies into the sphere of the social sciences; the inspiring and gifted teacher who trained a great number of distinguished students; the originator of seminal interpretations of the national history; the imaginative yet disciplined scholar who, able to glimpse large vistas and yet to work with an almost infinitesimal sense of detail, gave North Americans their first dynamic synthesis of United States history.

3

A Great Teacher's
Teacher (1949)

IT WOULD, no doubt, be proper to begin this essay by defining a great teacher. But I am going to assume that Charles A. Beard was a great teacher as well as a great scholar. Many situations and persons influenced his development as a great teacher. This is the story of his first teacher of social science.

The story begins with the remark Beard once made to me that as an undergraduate at DePauw University he encountered an extraordinary man, a Colonel Weaver. The Colonel, Beard added, had fought in the Civil War, and in the 1880's and 1890's had introduced his students to the writings of Karl Marx. For some strange reason it did not occur to me to ask further about Colonel Weaver. But the remark stuck in my mind. After I began, a few months ago, to satisfy my curiosity about Colonel Weaver, another bit of evidence came to hand confirming my impressions of Beard's regard for Colonel Weaver. "I recall," William W. Sweet wrote me recently, "the day Dr. Charles A. Beard was granted an Honorary Doctorate at DePauw University, and I overheard him say to Colonel Weaver, who came to greet him after the degree had been conferred, 'I am glad to have the privilege of thanking you again as one of my most revered and respected professors.'"

That was all there was to start with—the name Colonel Weaver, and the testimony of his distinguished pupil regarding his instruction.

When the idea struck me that we ought to know something about the teacher of our own great teacher, I turned to the old catalogues of DePauw. These revealed that the full name was James Riley Weaver; that he joined the DePauw faculty in 1885 as professor of modern languages and literature; that from 1886 to 1890 he was listed as professor of political philosophy and modern languages; that from 1890 to 1893 he confined his instruction to history and political science; and that from 1893 to his retirement, the period in which Beard was his pupil, he bore the title professor of political science. But on reading the description of his courses in the catalogues, it was clear enough that whatever he was called he was actually engaged all along in giving instruction in what we would call social science.

This was all highly interesting, of course; but I was still in the dark about what manner of man the Colonel was, what his experience had been before coming to DePauw, even when and where he was born. None of the biographical dictionaries or the early volumes of *Who's Who in America* told me anything about these matters, for he was listed in none.

Remembering that he was a colonel and had fought in the Civil War, it occurred to me, while I was lately in Washington, to see what light might be shed at the National Archives on his career. Surely enough, sheaves of musty, brittle old records in the War Department and in the Bureau of Pensions told me the main facts about his life. The enlistment records and the applications for pensions together made it plain that he was born at Youngstown, Westmoreland County, Pennsylvania, on October 21, 1839; that he was the son of a farmer and one of ten children; that he taught district school and worked his way through Allegheny College, enlisting before graduation on October 21, 1862, as a private in Company B, 163rd Regiment, Pennsylvania Volunteers. We can imagine the sturdy, dark-haired, dark-eyed young man, five feet eight and a half inches tall, pocketing the twenty-five dollars given

him as a bounty and entering on his twenty-third birthday a new
life with a sense of satisfaction and adventure. Promoted to a
sergeancy and a second lieutenancy, Weaver was captured in October, 1863; imprisoned at Libby, at Macon, at Charleston, and at
Columbia; and finally mustered out as a prisoner on parole on
March 13, 1865. He was later breveted first lieutenant, captain,
major, and lieutenant colonel for "meritorious service."

The pension records indicate that in 1865 he was at Concord
(subsequent information reveals he was studying at the General
Biblical Institute), and the next year at the Garrett Biblical Institute at Evanston, Illinois. At this institution he won a S.T.B. degree in 1867. Allegheny gave him the master's degree the following
year. In a curious book entitled *United States Diplomatic and Consular Service: Our Representatives Abroad,* which I stumbled on
accidentally after this sketch was finished, appears the statement—
presumably in the sketch prepared by Weaver himself—that his
teachers testified, concerning his academic record, that during an
experience of eighteen years they had found no student superior to
young Weaver. We have in the pension records the statement that
he taught mathematics and military science in West Virginia College at Morgantown from 1867 to 1868, and that he served as consul at Brindisi, Antwerp, and Vienna from 1869 to 1885.

With no second thought I hurried to the State Department archives, suspecting that the consular reports that Weaver wrote
would tell me more than the bare facts thus far discovered. Miss
Julia Bland, the gracious and capable lady who listened to my
problem, told me about the appointment papers prepared for everyone named to a foreign-service position. These papers revealed the
fact that one of the chief promoters of Weaver for his first consular
appointment was Bishop Matthew Simpson, who emphasized his
unblemished character, his more than ordinary energy, his ambition to acquire foreign experience preparatory to some literary
position, and his disinclination to enter political life. President
Grant referred Bishop Simpson's letter to the Secretary of State
with the notation that he hoped a position could be given the

young Colonel. At this time it had already been decided that Weaver and the Bishop's second daughter, Anna Francis, were to be married. On later occasions Bishop Simpson spared no effort to advance the fortunes of his son-in-law, defending him against criticisms, urging promotion to more important consulates or to a legation, and looking out for him in various other ways. When rumors reached Bishop Simpson that Weaver might lose his job, he intervened not only with the State Department but took the matter to senators, representatives, and the White House itself. Only when Cleveland was elected was it impossible for the Bishop to do anything more for his Republican son-in-law.

Thinking that the Bishop Simpson papers in the Library of Congress might contain letters from Weaver, I plowed through some thirty volumes in this collection. But alas, there were only incidental references to the Colonel in family letters. We catch glimpses of his Sunday School classes in Antwerp, of his wife and children, and his vacations in Tyrol, the Black Forest, and at home. When Bishop Simpson died, the Colonel wrote two beautiful letters of sympathy to his mother-in-law. In view of all the deceased had done for him, well might he say, "O great and good Bishop, model father without peer!"

Weaver's career in the consular service was not without its ups and downs. In his appointment papers is a memorandum dated June 14, 1878, probably written by the official in charge of consular affairs. The document indicates that while Weaver had not been wanting in ability and in the efficient discharge of his duties, he had given offense to shipmasters and to American merchants by "large and doubtful charges for official services. . . . His explanations in this matter were thought to be not wholly satisfactory and the disposition to charge large fees was made out. Some of these the Department compelled him to restore." But no fault had been found in the formal returns to the consulate at Antwerp. Weaver, moreover, had worked hard to harmonize the conflicting interests of owners and crews and to promote direct steam connections between Antwerp and New York. And he was promoted to

Vienna. We know that fifty-seven American residents in that city petitioned President Cleveland to keep him on as consul general. They spoke of his efficient management of his official duties, of his zeal to promote American business, of his liberal hospitality, and of his unsparing pains "in attending to the needs and comforts of his fellow-countrymen." Despite such testimony and notwithstanding the efforts of such prominent Middle Westerners as the DePauws, Studebakers, Tafts, and others to effect a new diplomatic appointment in 1889, Weaver did not return to foreign service after the Democratic victory of 1884.

Weaver's consular reports show that his experience admirably fitted him for a professorship in the social studies. Reports on the economics of swine exports and imports, on currency fluctuations, on population statistics, on railroads, tariffs, ethnic problems in the Dual Monarchy, on steel works and other industrial enterprises, and on panics and depressions indicated scrupulous care in assembling data, analyzing it critically, organizing the generalizations logically, and interpreting them thoughtfully. In other words, Consul Weaver learned a great deal, not only about the languages and culture of the Europeans among whom he lived, but about their political, social, and economic institutions and problems. All of this first-hand learning shaped his conception of teaching. As we shall see, at DePauw he inaugurated what was certainly an unusual departure in college instruction in the 1880's.

We may suspect that even before his death Bishop Simpson, foreseeing the possibility of a Democratic return to power, paved the way for his son-in-law at DePauw University. The institution was dear to the Bishop's heart. He had once been its president and he had kept in close touch with its policies.

Thanks to Mrs. Vera Cooper, the current librarian of DePauw, who put at my disposal typescripts of an obituary of Colonel Weaver and of letters between him and a former student, and to Frederick Ogg, William W. Sweet, and Mary R. Beard, who were students at DePauw during Weaver's teaching, it is possible to reconstruct some part of his role in the institution and the community.

We know that his beloved first wife died at Greencastle and that he married subsequently Emma Mattern, of Sandusky; that he grew in reputation and stature at DePauw until his retirement; and that thereafter he lived on in his Greencastle home, highly revered, until his death in 1920. At the time of his death his former pupil and colleague, Professor F. C. Tilden, spoke of his conscientiousness, his high-mindedness, his gracious, stately bearing. He was a model of gentility, a gentleman of the old school, the soul of dignified geniality. At Beechcroft, as he called his home, he generously dispensed hospitality to students. Year after year the initiation of Phi Beta Kappa took place under his roof. "With what dignity and kindly humor did he, as the many years president of the Society, conduct the initiation," wrote Professor Tilden. Later in the evening, at the banquet table in his long dining room, the Colonel, putting everyone at ease, rose to start the loving cup on its round of the banqueters "with an old-world solemnity loved and appreciated by all." We can picture young, salty, amiable Charles A. Beard at such an occasion. William W. Sweet, Frederick Ogg, and Mary Beard have all written me letters confirming the dignified, courtly, but unpretentious and genteel, demeanor of the Colonel.

All these and others have testified to the unusual character of Weaver's teaching. He was no taskmaster, a role he regarded with contempt. On the contrary, he looked on teaching and learning as a never-ending, mutual process. He fitted precisely the definition of the college professor once given by President Harper of the University of Chicago: "An older fellow student in a great guild of students." In an age of textbooks, he repudiated them, for he was convinced that the laboratory or library method was far superior to lectures and cut-and-dried manuals. In describing his approach Weaver wrote that "students are collaborators with the instructor in the investigation of specific subjects. Too much help stultifies the intellect; it must rather be quickened to self-dependence." The very "germ" of his method consisted in and presupposed "an ability of each member of the class to do individualized work; to carry on such an investigation without the immediate help of a tutor or a textbook." The lists of topics chosen for investigation, which varied from year to year and which may be followed in the printed syllabi —the only books Weaver wrote—cover a wide range and are striking for their importance, whether viewed from the angle of vision of the time or from a longer perspective.

Writing in the Yearbook of DePauw University for 1898, Colonel Weaver explained that his department "embraces the Science and Philosophy of the State or society politically organized." As this depended on organized society in general, the science and philosophy of society naturally fell within its scope. Thus he offered courses, each one based on a syllabus, on the theory of states, United States constitutional history, international law, sociology, sociology and its applications, socialism and reform, economics, money, and banking. While the syllabi indicate a topical or problem arrangement, Colonel Weaver was aware of the "vital importance of history"; for, as he said, "all social theory and philosophy must be tested by historical data properly interpreted. The Historical-Philosophical method is the only safeguard against Ideology on the one hand and Empiricism on the other." This might be Beard himself writing, for he often made similar remarks. Indeed, his last public address before the American Political Science Association was, among other things, a plea for the reunion of history and political science.

Regarding his task as a teacher primarily that of encouraging his students in their desire to learn and to understand, to show them how to learn, and to learn with them, Weaver naturally laid down no dogmas. Rather, he said in effect, let us approach every problem with an open mind. He did not, to be sure, believe that there was an open mind in any absolute sense, for the syllabi show that he paid great attention to the existence and role of bias in social thinking. Bringing up to date the old Baconian idols, Weaver emphasized the bias of religion, the bias of class, the bias of the market place. While he himself was a confirmed protectionist, he taught the tariff issue in such a way that a great many students left his classroom ardent free-traders. Who can doubt that Beard owed some part of his concern with the role of bias and underlying assumptions and presuppositions to his old teacher?

Colonel Weaver spared no pains to bring out the best in his students. He encouraged them to explore in the active voice the great problems of their day that they might be thoughtful and constructive in their approach to public issues. For him, training for citizenship was no abstraction, loftily to be contemplated in remote clouds; it was rather a matter of rolling up the sleeves and getting down to hard sustained labor, of coming to grips with facts and with bias, of cutting through the difficulties to lucid but tentatively held understanding.

Those who knew Charles A. Beard will recall his devotion to the study of the great classics in social science. Colonel Weaver was of like mind. This is clear from the remarkable syllabi. In each course he expected his students to familiarize themselves with the relevant classics. These included Aristotle, Plato, Machiavelli, Locke, Rousseau, Hegel, Bagehot, and *The Federalist* papers in political theory; the Old Testament, Hegel, Greene, Tylor, Darwin, Spencer, Wallace, Buckle, Guizot, Westermarck, and others in social theory; Adam Smith, Jevons, Senior, Mill, Marshall, and, yes, Marx in economics, to cite only a few.

But Colonel Weaver did not think that all knowledge and wisdom was to be found in the old books. He expected his students to read such contemporary writers as the rising sociologists Giddings, Small, Mayo-Smith, Wines, and others; the new economists, such as Ely and other exponents of the Social Gospel, Henry George, Simon Patton, and Edward Bellamy; and, as a member of the new learned societies dealing with the social sciences, he likewise expected his students to follow and make intelligent use of such journals as the *Annals of the Academy of Political and Social Science*, the *Political Science Quarterly*, the *Quarterly Journal of Economics*, and others. But this was not all! Even undergraduates, at least the more advanced among them, were expected in the investigation of special topics to make use of government documents and current materials of all sorts. There is some amusing correspondence at DePauw between Weaver and a former pupil who had come to be a well-established attorney in New York. The former student, Guy Morrison Walker, wrote that he had thought of giving DePauw his fine set of the *Annals of Congress,* the *Congressional Globe,* and the *Congressional Record,* but that he was unsympathetic at the moment with DePauw's policies and was therefore about to give them to another institution. The Colonel persuaded him that DePauw would make the best use of them. Later Mr. Walker started a movement for raising funds for the James Riley Weaver Political Science Library.

From the logical, comprehensive, and intriguing syllabi, which the librarian of DePauw kindly sent me, I have gathered that in all his courses Colonel Weaver emphasized the social content and the social implications of whatever it was he and his students were investigating. That he set considerable store on the importance of the Industrial Revolution is clear from the fact that Toynbee, Marx, and the Social Gospel school are represented in virtually every course. When Beard went to Columbia later on, Marx, apparently, was regarded as out of bounds even in graduate study; but Beard had already become acquainted with the *Communist Manifesto* and *Capital,* thanks to a Civil War veteran of Republican predilections, in a small Middle Western Methodist institution! It is worth recalling here that the first textbooks of James Harvey Robinson did not mention the Industrial Revolution; it was only after Beard entered into a partnership with Robinson that this great movement was recognized. Long before this, in the 1880's, it had been regarded as of basic importance by Colonel Weaver in every course that he gave.

We have spoken of Colonel Weaver's emphasis on the role of bias in social science. We should also call attention to the interest he had in the framing of the Constitution, in *The Federalist,* and in Hildreth's class-economic interpretation of the early national period. But what strikes one most of all in pondering the syllabi is Weaver's conception of the unity of the social sciences and their functional role in understanding and in acting intelligently in current controversial social, political, and economic questions. It is clear that in the Colonel's mind there was no hard and fast division between anthropology, sociology, political science, economics, and constitutional history. Each one, in his view, interpenetrated the other. In due time Beard himself in his own research, writing, and teaching exemplified this conception. Moreover, in using scholarship as an instrument for clarifying thought and guiding action, as Beard did in his early books on the Constitution and as he continued to do throughout his life, he was a good pupil of the Colonel.

To say all this is not, of course, to say that Beard was not influenced by others as well. At DePauw he learned much, according to Mary Beard, from Professor Priest, who instilled in his pupils a high regard for the force and beauty of forensics. At Hull House, at Toynbee Hall, at Cornell, where Beard worked with Moses Coit Tyler and plunged more deeply into the basic writing of the Revolutionary era, at Oxford and at Columbia, he met many scholars who contributed to his techniques and his understanding. But the admiration and affection Beard always felt for his first real teacher of the social sciences should not be forgotten. There is no doubt about his indebtedness to the intellectually modest, open-minded, versatile, enthusiastic searcher for social understanding. As Mary Beard has written to me, "it was unquestionably social education which this teacher fostered."

In the archives of the Department of History at the University of Wisconsin there is a letter which Colonel Weaver wrote in behalf of young Beard when he applied for a teaching position. "Mr. Charles A. Beard has done over two years' work of his undergraduate course in my department, and has proven himself in every way a first class student. He is full of zeal, fond of investigation, and has a keen insight into truth. He has been one of the best men in my work during the last thirteen years, and I regard him as eminently fitted for advanced work and original research. I commend him to your highest consideration." The old Colonel was a good student of the ability of his students. He was, besides, a good prophet!

PART II

The Transmission and Context of Ideas

4

The Great Mr. Locke,
America's Philosopher,
1783-1861 (1937)

ALTHOUGH no one has seriously questioned the great influence of John Locke[1] on American thought during the later part of the eighteenth century, students of American intellectual history have assumed by and large that his ideas were for the most part replaced during the first half of the nineteenth century by those of other philosophers. The purpose of this paper is, first, to test this assumption and, second, to explain the findings.

The importance of the first problem becomes clear when the extent of Locke's influence on Americans of the late eighteenth century is taken into account.[2] Political thought both before and during the American Revolution was profoundly affected by the *Two Treatises on Civil Government*. Otis, John and Samuel Adams, and other leading revolutionists quoted "the great Mr.

---

[1] For an excellent study of Locke's philosophy, see Sterling Power Lamprecht, *The Moral and Political Philosophy of John Locke* (New York, 1918).

[2] Alice M. Baldwin, *The New England Clergy and the American Revolution* (Durham, N.C., 1928), pp. 7, 10: Lewis Rosenthal, "Rousseau at Philadelphia," *Magazine of American History* (July, 1884), XII, 46–47; Howard Mumford Jones, *America and French Culture, 1750–1848* (Chapel Hill, 1927), pp. 361, 366, 368; Carl Becker, *The Declaration of Independence: A Study in the History of Political Ideas* (New York, 1922), pp. 27–28, 53, 56–57, 75; Benjamin F. Wright, *American Interpretations of Natural Law* (Cambridge, 1931).

Locke" reverently; Franklin, Hamilton, and Jefferson read and praised him. His natural-rights philosophy, including the doctrine that all government rests on the consent of the governed and may be overthrown by revolution if it persistently violates individual life, liberty, and property, was incorporated in the Declaration of Independence itself.[3] The similarity between his social and economic doctrines and those of the framers of the Constitution has likewise been pointed out.[4] However, Locke had nearly as great an impact on theology as on political and social thought. Furthermore, the influence of his treatise on education should not be overlooked. His justification of religious toleration, his rationalistic theology, and his conception of the plastic character of human nature were all dear to America's children of the Enlightenment. It is scarcely too much to say, even when the importance of other thinkers is taken into account,[5] that Locke was America's philosopher during the Revolutionary period.

Yet it has been generally assumed that when the nation found itself torn by "the second American Revolution" in 1861, Locke's name was not cherished as it had been three-quarters of a century earlier. Indeed, even a superficial inspection of the conventional literature of the fifties indicates that his authority no longer figured in any lively way in theological discussions and that his "mental philosophy" had long been under attack, and, if we follow leading students of American philosophy, had been largely replaced by the Scotch school of "common sense," French eclecticism, and German idealism. Locke's political ideas, according to authorities on the history of American political thought, no longer enjoyed their pre-eminence.[6]

[3] Herbert Foster, "International Calvinism through Locke and the Revolution of 1688," *American Historical Review* (April, 1927), XXXII, 475.

[4] The Rev. Paschal Larkin, *Property in the Eighteenth Century, with Special Reference to England and Locke* (Dublin and Cork, 1930), pp. 145 ff.

[5] Charles F. Mullett, in his *Fundamental Law and the American Revolution* (New York, 1933), qualifies Locke's influence on political thought by emphasizing that of Burlamqui, Pufendorf, and others.

[6] R. M. Wenley, *The Life and Work of George Sylvester Morris* (New York, 1919), p. 239; I. Woodbridge Riley, *American Thought from Puritanism to*

The belief that Locke's influence during these seventy-five years was a waning one is probably due to a failure to examine sufficient evidence. Historians of ideas in America have too largely based their conclusions on the study of formal treatises. But formal treatises do not tell the whole story. In fact, they sometimes give a quite false impression, for such writings are only a fraction of the records of intellectual history. For every person who laboriously wrote a systematic treatise, dozens touched the subject in a more or less casual fashion. Sometimes the fugitive essays of relatively obscure writers influenced the systematizers and formal authors quite as much as the works of better-known men. The influence of a thinker does not pass from one major writer to another without frequently being transformed, or dissipated, or compressed in the hands of a whole series of people who responded to the thinker and his ideas. It is reasonably certain, moreover, that in the America of the early nineteenth century ephemeral writings, widely scattered as they were in pamphlets, tracts, and essays, reached a much wider audience and are often more reliable evidence of the climate of opinion than the more familiar works to which historians of ideas have naturally turned. The student of the vitality and modification of ideas may well direct his attention, then, toward out-of-the-way sermons, academic addresses, Fourth of July orations, and casual guides and essays.[7] By examining such irregular channels for the expression of ideas, it may be possible to learn to what extent Locke's ideas survived in any vital way during the period between the American Revolution and the Civil War.

Pragmatism and Beyond (New York, 1915), chap. II; Harvey Gates Townsend, *Philosophical Ideas in the United States* (New York, 1934), pp. 101–102; Howard Mumford Jones, "The Influence of European Ideas in Nineteenth Century America," *American Literature* (October, 1935), VII, 251; Raymond G. Gettell, *History of American Political Thought* (New York, 1928), p. 569.

[7] The Huntington Library is particularly rich in this type of fugitive material. I have examined there some five hundred academic addresses, Fourth of July orations, and election sermons.

I wish to express my indebtedness to Professor Marjorie Nicolson and to Dr. Fulmer Mood for their contributions to my thinking on the problem of materials in intellectual history. I am also grateful to members of the staff of the Huntington Library for valuable comments on this paper.

Whether, on the one hand, Locke's ideas largely gave way to those of competing philosophers or, on the other, they survived in some form, there is need for explanation. To a considerable extent students of intellectual history have sought to account for the disappearance of ideas by assuming that they were supplanted by concepts that were either more valid or that in some way better fitted the spirit of newer times. This, however, is too vague an explanation to be very satisfactory.

The doctrine that men seek ideas to justify their activities and to promote their interests, that they think as they live, is hardly startling. If this is true, it should follow that the vitality of ideas depends at least in part upon the effectiveness with which they function, on their usefulness to the interests which they serve. Ideas might be expected, then, to flourish when they answer a need and to wane when that need is no longer urgent. Although it is now almost thirty years since John Dewey asserted that thinking can best be explained in terms of functional relationships to human problems and needs, students of intellectual history have for the most part been little influenced by this concept. Nor have they been much affected by the still older but related contention that ideas are always associated with particular interests, and that the latter, broadly defined, have a way, in the never ending conflict with antagonistic interests, of adopting, modifying, and even inventing ideas serviceable to themselves. Before attempting to appraise this hypothesis, let us test it by finding out what light it throws on the survival or the disappearance of Locke's ideas in the three-quarters of a century following the American Revolution. In short, one should be able to determine what interests or groups challenged Locke's ideas, and for what reasons; what groups defended his teachings, and why; and what happened as a result of this contest.

Locke's ideas are, of course, closely interrelated and not always consistent. They can nevertheless be grouped, for present purposes, into fairly well-defined categories such as education, religion and theology, mental philosophy, and political and economic theory.

I

We may begin by considering the fate of Locke's educational theories which were embodied in *Some Thoughts Concerning Education* (1693). Horace Mann regarded this treatise as superior to all Locke's other works, and it was therefore with the more regret that the father of the common-school revival in Massachusetts, writing in 1840, felt compelled to admit that the great book had been "almost wholly neglected and forgotten."[8] A study of contemporary educational literature confirms Mann's observation. Locke's *Thoughts* had been reprinted in the United States but once in all this period, and an examination of the leading educational periodicals and reports reveals that they mentioned Locke only very occasionally in the period between 1800 and 1860. Even when he was cited, it was chiefly to buttress some particular school program: for instance, the Boston School Committee in 1837 quoted his recommendation that music be taught in the schools, on the ground that he had defined recreation as "easing the weary part by change of business" and that music admirably served such a purpose.[9] Not until 1859 did Henry Barnard's *American Journal of Education* devote an article to Locke's pedagogy, and this, characteristically, was merely a translation of a critique of his educational theories from the pen of Karl von Raumer, a German whose word carried much weight among American schoolmen.[10]

This apparent neglect of Locke's *Thoughts Concerning Education* is all the more interesting in view of the educational awakening that took place between 1825 and 1860. To say that the educational essay was, unlike his other writings, unknown even to eighteenth-century Americans is inaccurate, because there is considerable evidence pointing to the familiarity of not a few colonial

[8] Mary Tyler Mann, *Life and Works of Horace Mann* (Boston, 1891, 5 vols.), II, 255.
[9] *The Common School Journal* (1841), III, 189. *The Academician* (February 7, 1818), I, 6, quoted Locke in support of the idea that a certain amount of one's time should be given to trifles if any of the remainder was to be employed with efficacy and vigor.
[10] *The American Journal of Education* (1859), VI, 200–222.

Americans with the work. To American children of the Enlightenment there was, indeed, a strong appeal in many of the educational doctrines it laid down. Liberal spokesmen of the middle class, which attached great value to enterprise, had welcomed Locke's emphasis on the importance of a sound body and on wisdom in managing affairs. As active, practical people, they had also relished Locke's insistence on the training of the senses rather than the memory; as critics of many sanctions of the past, they had liked his stressing of reason rather than authority. Benjamin Franklin and Joseph Priestley had quoted Locke and were influenced by his educational theories: Franklin's *Sketch of an English School* reflected the utilitarianism of Locke,[11] while Priestley helped to popularize his criticism of indoctrination, a practice which Locke had said was little more than the inculcation of error and prejudice in the name of imposing "right principles" on immature minds.[12]

If Locke's educational theories were favorably known to liberal representatives of America's important middle class in the late eighteenth century, the absence of direct reference to them in the great quantity of educational literature in the first half of the nineteenth century is the more noteworthy. It must be remembered that Locke favored private rather than public education—his treatise, in fact, had been written primarily for tutors in the families of well-to-do gentry and merchants. Hence the groups in nineteenth-century America which stood for mass education at public expense naturally found little in Locke to give them aid or prestige. But those who adhered to the older concept of family or tutorial instruction, who went on thinking of education as a private matter, could continue to derive sustenance from Locke. And they did. An examination, not of the formal treatises and reports of the great

[11] Albert H. Smyth (ed.), *The Writings of Benjamin Franklin* (New York, 1907, 10 vols.), II, 387; III, 28. See also Theodore Hornberger, "A Note on the Probable Source of Provost Smith's Famous Curriculum for the College of Philadelphia," *Pennsylvania Magazine of History and Biography* (1934), LVIII, 377.

[12] Joseph Priestley, *Miscellaneous Observations Relating to Education* (New London, 1796), p. 14; and especially Appendix No. 3 in *Memoirs of Dr. Priestley . . .* (London, 1806), p. 369.

leaders in the public-school revival, but of the casual, fugitive guides for parental and tutorial education for middle-class families, shows that the ideas of Locke remained influential.

Readers of the *Memoirs of the Bloomsgrove Family* (1790), for instance, were treated to a generous feast of Locke. The author of this engaging manual, Enos Hitchcock, a Congregationalist clergyman of Providence, revealed that it was from "the great Mr. Locke" that Mrs. Bloomsgrove, a model educator, drew her ideas on the importance, in education, of a sympathetic understanding of child nature and of fresh air and exercise—in short, of "a sound mind in a sound body."[13] A generation later, to take another example from this informal type of manual, Mrs. Louisa Hoare, in her *Hints for the Improvement of Early Education and Nursery Discipline,* quoted Locke time and again.[14] Like other authors of this genre of pedagogical guides, Mrs. Hoare shared Locke's belief that the road to knowledge may well be made short and easy. But what impressed her most was that he considered proper manners more important than learning, and second only to religion and virtue. How well adapted to the rising, ambitious middle class was this idea! Good manners, which could be acquired by anyone, added luster to virtue and served generally as a passport to preferment. Moreover, Mrs. Hoare was not alone in upholding as a pattern Locke's conception of a gentleman.[15]

Locke's educational precepts, as well as his "mental philosophy," were spread broadcast in the widely read *Improvement of the Mind,* by Isaac Watts, the famous English nonconformist writer of hymns and moral guides. This work, known familiarly as "Watts on the Mind," was almost universally used in the private academies and seminaries that sprang up so rapidly in the early years of the republic. It would, indeed, be hard to overstate the influence of

[13] Enos Hitchcock, D.D., *Memoirs of the Bloomsgrove Family* (Boston, 1790), pp. 86–87, 95, *passim.*
[14] [Mrs. Louisa Hoare] *Hints for the Improvement of Early Education and Nursery Discipline* (Keene, N.H., 1826), pp. 24–25, 31.
[15] For example, see Francis Lieber, *Reminiscences, Addresses, and Essays* (Philadelphia, 1881, 2 vols.), I, 247.

Watt's popularization of Locke among middle-class Americans who patronized these institutions of learning.

However, it was not only through these informal pedagogical guides in the domestic circles of the well-to-do, and popular texts in the private seminaries, that Locke's educational ideas survived. While, as we have seen, the champions of the public schools did not find Locke's emphasis on private education useful, indirectly they were subject to his influence; for in going to school to Rousseau, Fellenberg, and Pestalozzi, they went to school to Locke. In their emphasis on health, learning through doing, and character training, these men were reflecting Locke's teachings. Above all, they shared his faith in the possibility of modifying human nature by changing the environment of youth. It was this faith which inspired American democrats with devotion to education as the best means of insuring the success of their republican experiment and of solving social ills.[16] Rousseau, Pestalozzi, and the French materialists, and back of them Locke, were the intellectual fathers of the American faith in education as the road to Utopia.

If one asks why the fathers of the common-school revival during the 1820's and 1830's turned to continental writers rather than to Locke himself, an explanation has already been suggested in part. For inspiration and guidance, the Horace Manns, the Henry Barnards, and their colleagues quite naturally looked to the Continent, and especially to Germany, where a state system of public schools for all children had been put on a firm footing. They also cast their eyes on Switzerland, where the schools of Fellenberg and Pestalozzi, which combined learning with the doing of practical tasks, seemed particularly congenial to Americans who saw the value of an immediately useful education for a new society engaged in building a physical civilization in the wilderness. Locke, who had favored the private education of children of the middle class and who believed that a minimum of instruction in the principles

[16] See Joshua Bates, *An Inaugural Oration Pronounced March 18, 1818, at Middlebury College* (Middlebury, 1818), for an example of an explicit correlation of Locke's philosophy with the American faith in education.

of religion and trade was sufficient for the rest, seemed to have little to offer to sponsors of a truly democratic and publicly supported school system.[17] So they did not quote him, but contented themselves with borrowing from the continental writers that portion of his educational theory which did fit their needs. In this manner the ideas of Locke, insofar as they served interests or filled needs, continued to live on different levels and in different ways. On the one hand, they persisted directly in the casual manuals for private education; on the other, indirectly through the adoption of Lockean precepts which, combined with precepts of continental educators, met the demands of practical-minded leaders of the public-school revival.

II

Turning from the educational to the theological doctrines of Locke, one recalls, first of all, that he was indirectly among the fathers of both English and American deism.[18] In various writings, notably in *The Reasonableness of Christianity*[19] and in *An Essay for the Understanding of St. Paul's Epistles*[20] as well as in his *Letters on Toleration*, Locke subjected the tenets of Christian theology to reason and maintained that natural knowledge was more certain than miracles and revelation.[21] These writings, like the *Essay Concerning Human Understanding* (1690), tended to

[17] It is clear that while some of the educational writers discussed in Allen Oscar Hansen, *Liberalism and American Education in the Eighteenth Century* (New York, 1926), showed a direct familiarity with Locke, most of the essayists borrowed more heavily from the continental writers.

[18] S. G. Hefelbower, *The Relation of John Locke to English Deism* (Chicago, 1918), pp. 173 ff.; Norman L. Torrey, *Voltaire and the English Deists* (New Haven, 1930), pp. 173 ff.; Herbert M. Morais, *Deism in Eighteenth Century America* (New York, 1934), pp. 16–17, 29, 35, 38.

[19] In addition to the various English editions of Locke's writings which were easily accessible to American readers, this work could be read in separate American editions: Boston, 1811; and New York, 1836.

[20] Republished in Boston in 1820 and in 1823.

[21] Boston, 1743; Windsor, Vt., 1788; Stockbridge, Mass., 1790. For an interesting example of the practical influence of the *Letters on Toleration*, see George Willis Cooke, *Unitarianism in America, A History of Its Origin and Development* (Boston, 1902), p. 43.

break down barriers between the world of matter and the world of spirit, between man and nature—in short, tended to make it less difficult for men to believe that they themselves "correspond with the general harmony of Nature." Although Locke maintained that reason and experience are confirmed by divine revelation, his whole approach paved the way for the later and more thoroughgoing deists. For his God was, after all, a constitutional God, who did not trespass too much on the daily concerns of his creatures. Moreover, the *Essay Concerning Human Understanding* likewise fed the springs of deism, inasmuch as its plea for reliance on sensory experience and reflection, rather than on innate ideas and the "mysterious," tended to undermine the traditional sanctions of orthodoxy. Locke's position was, in many respects, anticipatory of that maintained a hundred years later by the early Unitarians.

Indeed, it is clear that Locke and his disciples, particularly Samuel Clarke, explicitly influenced American Unitarians from Charles Chauncey to Joseph Buckminster, Joseph Priestley, Charles Follen, William Ellery Channing, and Andrews Norton.[22] Locke's religious writings, including his *Letters on Toleration,* were frequently cited in the discussions of liberal Trinitarian as well as Unitarian clergymen, in their efforts to defend their position against both orthodox criticism and "atheistic" attacks.[23] Thus, in the *Christian Examiner* in 1832, and in reviewing Lord King's *Life of Locke,* the Reverend W. B. O. Peabody not only paid high tribute to Locke's *Reasonableness of Christianity* but virtually claimed him as a Unitarian. "We admire Locke as an example of the manly Christian character, and the union of vast intellectual growth with calm

[22] Cooke, *Unitarianism in America,* pp. 12–13, 43; *Memoirs of William Ellery Channing, with Extracts from His Correspondence and Manuscripts* (Boston, 1848, 3 vols.), I, 149; *Memoirs of Rev. Joseph Buckminster, D.D., and of His Son, Rev. Joseph Stevens Buckminster, By Eliza Buckminster Lee* (Boston, 1849), p. 246; John Towill Rutt (ed.), *The Theological and Miscellaneous Works of Joseph Priestley, LL.D., F.R.S.* (London, 1817–1822, 25 vols.), II, 221, 257; VII, 411; XIV, 91 ff.; XVII, 10; XXIII, 339; *The Works of Charles Follen* (Boston, 1841, 5 vols.), III, 99, 101, 168.

[23] For example, Romeo Elton, D.D., *The Literary Remains of the Rev. Jonathan Maxcy, D.D., with a Memoir of His Life* (New York, 1844), pp. 427–428.

and fervent devotion, so beautifully displayed in his life and writings, shows what our religion is when it resides in a powerful mind and an open heart."[24] We shall see that Locke's writings were regarded by conservative Unitarians as a first line of defense when the transcendentalists raised the flag of revolt. On the other hand, the left-wing deists who popularized the cult—men like the militant, fearless Elihu Palmer—drew heavily on Locke, as well as on Holbach, Hume, and Bolingbroke. Palmer wrote in his *Principles of Nature:*

It was not the discovery of physical truths alone that bore relation to the revelation of the human species; it was reserved for Locke, and other powerful minds, to unfold the eternal structure of the intellectual world—explain the operations of the human structure of the human understanding—explore the sources of thought, and unite sensation and intellect in the same subject, and in a manner cognizable by the human faculties. Locke has, perhaps, done more than Newton, to subvert the credit of *divine Revelation.*[25]

In the forties and fifties, however, the religious writings of Locke no longer played a notable role in theological discussions. There was a variety of reasons for their decline in favor. Popular deism, reaching its high-water mark at the turn of the century, had been identified by conservatives with the excesses of the French Revolution. Discredited, it provided the soil for a conventional religious reaction which expressed itself, in part, in the evangelical revivals that swept the country. In such a climate of opinion and feeling, the rationalism of Locke lost its influence, for advocates of evangelical religion found no comfort in its cold, reasoned, apologetic treatises. Circuit riders, camp meetings, and revivals answered the emotional needs of pioneers and ill-adjusted city people far better than any kind of rationalism. The new conservative religious attitude toward Locke was well expressed in an article in the *Encyclopaedia Americana* of 1836. In attempting to analyze the human

---

[24] *The Christian Examiner,* n.s. (January, 1832), VIII, 381 ff., 402.
[25] Elihu Palmer, *Principles of Nature; or, A Development of the Moral Causes of Happiness and Misery among the Human Species* (London, 1819), pp. 94–95.

soul, "as an anatomist proceeds in investigating a body, piece by piece," Locke had, according to this article, unintentionally supported materialism; for he had suggested that God could, by his omnipotence, make matter capable of thinking—a doctrine considered dangerous to orthodox belief by virtue of its identification of God and mind.[26] And when at length Locke's psychology and philosophy came to be rejected by a growing number of intellectuals, it was natural for liberal defenders of the faith to turn to writers like De Wette, Baur, and Schleiermacher, whose basic philosophical assumptions were more congenial.[27] Thus, in 1817 an English visitor found the religious works of Locke practically unknown to New York book dealers.[28] Even the new edition of *The Reasonableness of Christianity*, published in New York in 1836, was but a belated echo of an earlier vogue.

III

Locke's influence on American philosophy and psychology has been profound. His leading theories in these fields—theories which at the beginning of the eighteenth century had been considered so subversive that Calvinistic Yale warned its students against the *Essay Concerning Human Understanding*—gradually made their way in academic circles. Samuel Johnson, a tutor at Yale, broke the ground at least as early as 1719; and Jonathan Edwards, in his fifteenth year, read and was deeply influenced by the *Essay*. Even after Samuel Johnson became a disciple of Berkeley, he recommended Locke to his pupils at King's College. Certainly by 1800 Locke dominated philosophic studies in American colleges.[29]

In 1829, however, President Marsh of the University of Vermont could write to Coleridge that, whereas Locke had formerly been

[26] *Encyclopaedia Americana, A Popular Dictionary of Arts, Sciences, Literature, History, Politics, and Biography* (Philadelphia, 1836, 13 vols.), VIII, 38.
[27] *The Dial* (April, 1842), II, 485–528.
[28] Henry Bradshaw Fearon, *Sketches of America* (London, 1818), p. 35.
[29] P. Emory Aldrich, "John Locke and the Influence of His Works in America," *Proceedings of the American Antiquarian Society at the Semi-Annual Meeting, Held in Boston, Apr. 30, 1879* (Worcester, Mass., 1879), pp. 22–30.

taught in colleges, Stewart, Campbell, and Brown had replaced him.[30] Although Locke was restored at Harvard in 1833 by Joel Giles and used at least until 1841, the statement of President Marsh was substantially true.[31]

Yet this fact need not be interpreted to mean that Locke's influence thereby came to an end. In 1830 a generation of young men trained by his *Essay* was just beginning its active life. Moreover, many of the American texts on mental and moral philosophy which were widely used in colleges embodied ample portions of Locke's philosophical treatise. At Bowdoin, for example, Thomas C. Upham, professor of mental and moral philosophy, substituted his own text in 1827 for Locke, but his book, in fact, both summarized the essential ideas of Locke and paid him high tribute.[32] It will be recalled, also, that the widely read "Watts on the Mind" was a popularization of Locke. In conceiving of mind as possessing functions, powers, or faculties of behaving, such as memory, observation, and reason, it provided the basis of "faculty psychology." Implicit in this system of psychology was the belief in the desirability of formal discipline through concrete experiences and particular mental disciplines. Less used texts in mental philosophy, which were for the most part eclectic, seldom failed to pay high tribute to Locke and to draw heavily from his *Essay*.[33]

Thus it was that an entire generation of Americans knew Locke's mental philosophy better than that of any other writer. The *Essay Concerning Human Understanding* was considered indispensable. Washington Irving, touring Europe in 1804, included it in his

[30] J. L. Torrey (ed.), *The Remains of the Rev. James Marsh, D.D.* (Boston, 1843), p. 136.

[31] Benjamin Rand, "Philosophical Instruction at Harvard University, 1639–1900," *Harvard Graduates Magazine* (September, 1928), XXXVII, 46; I. Woodbridge Riley, *American Philosophy, The Early Schools* (New York, 1907), pp. 316, 476; *The Dial* (July, 1841), II, p. 89.

[32] Thomas C. Upham, *Elements of Mental Philosophy* (New York, 1848), *passim*.

[33] George Payne, *Elements of Mental and Moral Science* (New York, 1829), p. iv; Lyman W. Hall, *Elementary Outline of Mental Philosophy; for Use of Schools* (Cleveland, 1845), III, 115, 117; Margaret Mercer, *Popular Lectures on Ethics, or Moral Obligation* (Petersburg, Va., 1841), pp. 66–68.

"solemn reading list."[34] Daniel Webster at Dartmouth devoured it and actually committed to memory great portions of both the *Essay* and of "Watts on the Mind."[35] Emma Willard struggled with the *Essay* at Middlebury in 1812, on the threshold of her educational career.[36] James Russell Lowell, "rusticated" from Harvard in 1838, agreed to read and report on it to a private tutor,[37] while Thomas Wentworth Higginson, on leaving the same institution in 1841, had acquired "something of Locke's philosophy."[38] Even after it was subjected to frontal attacks, new champions such as Frederick Beasley, Alexander Everett, Andrews Norton, and Francis Bowen rose up to defend it. That the demand for it continued is borne out by the chronological distribution of the twelve American editions between the Revolution and the Civil War. So much, in fact, was the *Essay* a household phrase that James Kirke Paulding could make one of his characters in a novel of 1832 declare that Locke's analysis of the human understanding was the only one which the human understanding could comprehend.[39] If further evidence of the persistence of Locke's philosophy be needed, a goodly number of references to it in academic addresses and similar fugitive literature could be cited. It is, in truth, the frequency of the Lockean assumptions in this sort of material which provides the most convincing proof of the pervasiveness and tenacity of Locke's philosophy.

What was back of this vogue for "the great Mr. Locke" during the first three or four decades of the republic? During a period of

[34] Stanley T. Williams, *The Life of Washington Irving* (New York, 1935, 2 vols.), I, 67.

[35] Rev. Joseph Haven, *An Address Delivered before the Students of Amherst College and the Citizens of the Town, Nov. 17, 1852* (Amherst, 1853), p. 13.

[36] Alma Lutz, *Emma Willard, Daughter of Democracy* (Boston and New York, 1929), p. 45.

[37] Horace Elisha Scudder, *James Russell Lowell, a Biography* (Boston and New York, 1901, 2 vols.), I, 47.

[38] Thomas Wentworth Higginson, *Cheerful Yesterdays* (Boston and New York, 1898), pp. 69–70.

[39] James Kirke Paulding, *Westward Ho! A Tale* (New York, 1832, 2 vols.), I, 56. See also Thomas Wentworth Higginson, *Henry Wadsworth Longfellow* (Boston and New York, 1902), p. 55, for the influence that Locke's *Essay* later had on Longfellow.

democratic faith in the future, in an age in which it was necessary to take an optimistic view of the possibilities of the American experiment, a plastic conception of human nature was highly desirable if not indispensable. So those who were eager to demonstrate the possibility of a successful democracy welcomed Locke's concept that man is largely a creature of his experience, of his environment in the larger sense. If liberal, humane, and democratic influences could be guaranteed through proper training and institutions, the highest potentialities of mankind might be realized; then a democracy might function satisfactorily.

A study of the fugitive literature of the early republic indicates that Locke was frequently appealed to as an authority for belief in the plastic, democratic conception of human nature—a conception which his disciples, the French materialists, had also done much to spread. But Locke was preferred, in general, to the French school. Indeed, he was the choice of even the followers of Jefferson who were in closer sympathy with the France of the Revolution than with the England of the reaction.

Closely paraphrasing the essential ideas in the *Essay Concerning Human Understanding*, Abraham Holmes of New Bedford declared in an oration of 1796 that all social happiness depends on proper early experience, and that for the first time in history America, having thrown off tyranny, had established equal rights and individual freedom—had, in short, provided the proper environment for realizing man's potentialities. Have a care for public worship, universities, libraries, literary societies, and similar conditioning institutions, Holmes admonished, and the injurious and shameful practices which have long been a disgrace to the very name of human nature will disappear.[40] Another champion of democracy, Tunis Wortman, a New York lawyer and publicist, likewise denounced the view that man's vices are stamped on his original constitution. He attributed the evils hitherto so destructive to

[40] Abraham Holmes, *An Oration, Delivered at the First Precinct Meeting-House in Middleborough, before the Philological Society, on the First Wednesday in June, A.D. 1796* (New Bedford, 1797), pp. 8–12, 21 ff.

human happiness to the errors and abuses that had inhered in political arrangements—that is, in monarchical and aristocratic institutions. He cited Locke to prove that man was not born with innate ideas but that nine out of ten parts of a man's traits are what they are, good or evil, useful or not, by virtue of experience and training. Wortman insisted that, once human nature was thought of as malleable, there was no need for despairing of the ability of men to govern themselves intelligently and for the public good.[41] Moreover, these were not lone voices; as any thorough investigation of the out-of-the-way literature of the early republic proves.

Such a picture of human nature was indispensable to certain groups and interests in the first decades of the nineteenth century. The period was one of rapid migration from rural areas to mill towns and cities, with consequent social poverty, vice, and general degradation. In the Old World, republican institutions were generally regarded as utterly incapable of dealing with these new evils or even with the most traditional problems of government. It was a period when the eighteenth-century vision of the heavenly city, temporarily beclouded by the chaos and fear of the French Revolution, was nevertheless seizing the imaginations of tender-minded Americans, who became pioneer exponents of the gospel of social progress. Locke's conception of human nature, differing as it did from the Calvinistic idea of predestination, was good ammunition for the humanitarian and reform groups which began, in the second decade of the last century, to form associations to uproot war, outlaw intemperance, and abolish slavery, poverty, and every social ill. The underlying psychology of Frances Wright, Robert Owen, and the Utopian Socialists is essentially that of "the great Mr. Locke."[42] Although reformers did not find Locke's philosophy and psychology

[41] Tunis Wortman, *An Oration, on the Influence of Social Institutions Upon Human Morals and Happiness, Delivered before the Tammany Society* (New York, 1796), pp. 7–8, 24.

[42] Robert Owen, *Two Discourses on a New System of Society; as delivered in the Hall of Representatives of the United States* (Pittsburgh, 1825), pp. 22–23; Frances Wright, *Courses on Popular Lectures* (New York, 1829). For the attitude of later American social reformers toward Locke, see William D. P. Bliss, *The New Encyclopedia of Social Reform* (New York, 1908), pp. 727–728.

adequate for all their purposes, its importance to crusading humanitarianism can scarcely be overemphasized.

These three or four decades after the American Revolution were also years when the individual was being rapidly released from traditional ties. The Industrial Revolution was disrupting the system of apprenticeship and undermining the family as an economic unit, and both were still further thrown out of joint by the lure of free lands in the West. As a result the individual was more and more coming to think of himself as a free agent. In a relatively limited cultural environment the necessity of self-education was likewise good gospel. Thus Locke's philosophy, emphasizing the doctrine of individualism, the idea that man, within limits, was a free agent, ministered to the needs and desires of a people in such a time and on such a stage.[43] As Professor Becker has observed, men in general are influenced by writings that clarify their own notions, that suggest ideas which they are prepared to accept. In other words, ideas thrive according to the importance of the function that they serve.

American society during the first half of the nineteenth century, however, was by no means homogeneous. The wide variety of interests and needs that were in conflict with each other cannot even be suggested here. But one major contest in our intellectual life demands emphasis. By the early thirties the Northeast was becoming so rapidly industrialized that, to many, America seemed to stand for canals and railways, wharves and factories. From this industrialization sensitive souls drew back in horror and dismay, for it seemed to them that the mechanical trend in American civilization, the preoccupation with "curious mechanical contrivances and adaptations of matter, which it discovered by means of its telescopes, microscopes, dissections and other mechanical aids," was destroying human and spiritual values. And was not all this mechanism in our industrial organization, in morals, and in politics the in-

[43] Nicholas Baylies, *An Essay on the Powers and Faculties of the Human Mind* (Montpelier, Vt., 1828), Preface, *passim*. Baylies was a learned lawyer and judge. For a sketch of him, see *Vermont Historical Gazetteer* (1867), I, No. 4, p. 352.

evitable and direct result of a sensationist philosophy which denied the primary intuitions of the soul? Was not the solution for such misfortunes to be found, in part at least, in a repudiation of Locke and the empiricists and in drinking deeply of the spiritual nourishment of the Cambridge Platonists, Coleridge, and the German idealists?[44]

Some of these protestants against mechanism in American life, moreover, were sensitive to the social injustices seemingly inherent in the new mechanical order—injustices patent enough, they felt, to anyone whose eyes were not blinded. The empirical and sensationist philosophy, by virtue of the plastic character with which it endowed human nature, was sometimes used to support democratic ideals. But by 1840 a fresh generation of New Englanders saw that it could be used against the doctrine that all men are created equal. As Jonathan Saxton, farmer and transcendentalist, put it:

Sensation, then, does not, and by its own terms cannot, see man but in his outward condition, and his personal and social rights are such only, as can be logically inferred from the circumstances in which he is placed. Whatever is, in relation to society, is right, simply because it is. . . . [Sensation] finds man everywhere divided into high and low in social position, and concludes that gradation of ranks is of divine appointment. . . . This philosophy looks calmly on, and bids these ignorant, starving, scourged, and bleeding millions take comfort, for their lot is ordained by destiny that though the earth spreads out provisions liberally for all her children, the arrangements of nature would be defeated, if all should partake of them. . . . As this philosophy begets skepticism and infidelity in religion, so it has no faith, and no promise for man in his social and political relations.[45]

Unwilling to reject faith in equality, which seemed divine and transcendent, some radicals thus felt forced to repudiate the whole philosophy of empiricism and sensationism and to fall back on that

[44] Jonathan A. Saxton, "Prophecy, Transcendentalism, Progress," *The Dial* (July, 1841), II, 88–89, 103 ff. Saxton was graduated from Harvard in 1813, edited journals in Northampton, Troy, and Greenfield, and then settled down as a farmer in Deerfield. He was one of the earliest abolitionists and wrote and lectured on coöperation and social reform. See G. W. Cooke, "*The Dial*," in *The Journal of Speculative Philosophy* (July, 1885), XIX, 259.
[45] *The Dial* (July, 1841), II, 100.

of innate ideas. For if the idea of equality of men did not originate in experience, if indeed it was refuted by the facts of observation and historical investigation, then it must be an innate idea, an in-born truth, having its validity in an appeal to "the universal spir-itual intuitions of Humanity." There can be no doubt, as a study of *The Dial,* and more particularly of a vast quantity of random literature, indicates, that this social dissatisfaction with the new in-dustrial order and all its abuses and inequalities and material em-phasis led many to reject Locke's philosophy, or upheld them in their rejection of it.[46] Frederic H. Hedge, one of the founders of the Transcendental Club, brought this consideration clearly to the fore in a Fourth of July oration at Bangor in 1838. Did Heaven send its divine, transcendent truth of Universal Love, he asked, merely that men might live permanently in a society in which some were high, others low, some rich, others poor, some groveling in misery, others luxuriating in ease?[47] Emerson himself, in his *Lec-ture on the Times,* insisted that the soul of reform could not be sensualism, nor any materialistic force, but rather a transcendent principle—namely, reliance on "the sentiment of men."[48]

Abolitionists likewise found the doctrine of innate ideas more congenial than the teachings of Locke. When confronted by the argument of empiricists that the slaves needed experience for the proper use of liberty, William Hosmer insisted that liberty was both an innate idea and an innate capacity in every human being. "Liberty being the birth-right of man, the natural and normal con-dition of his existence, all the preparation he needs for its enjoy-ment is born with him. He gets his fitness for liberty, as he gets his hands and his feet—not by education, but by inheritance. It is born with him, and constitutes a part of his being."[49] In short, it ap-peared to social reformers that the work of regeneration might best

[46] *Ibid.* (April, 1841), I, 422; (July, 1841), II, 88–117, *passim.*
[47] Frederic H. Hedge, *An Oration, pronounced before the Citizens of Bangor, on the Fourth of July, 1838* (Bangor, 1838), pp. 33–36.
[48] Ralph Waldo Emerson, *Lecture on the Times,* in *The Complete Works of Ralph Waldo Emerson* (Autograph Centenary Edition, Cambridge, 1903–4, 12 vols.), I, 276.
[49] William Hosmer, *The Higher Law in Its Relations to Civil Government* (Auburn, N.Y., 1852), pp. 148–150.

go forward with an anti-Lockean psychology, for Locke's political tenets were still held in high regard.

The revolt—for such it was—did not, of course, begin all at once. Even during his college days (1794–1798) William Ellery Channing had been "saved," as he later put it, from Locke's philosophy by the reading of Dr. Richard Price's *Dissertations:* "He gave me the doctrine of ideas, and during my life I have written the words Love, Right, etc., with a capital."[50] Price also gave Channing a zeal for humanitarianism and social reform. It was in Channing's study, in fact, that the peace movement was launched, and he became an early critic of slavery and of unfettered property rights.

One of the first explicit signs of the revolt against Locke was Sampson Reed's "commencement part" at Harvard in 1821—an address which young Ralph Waldo Emerson, an undergraduate, heard with eagerness. "The science of the human soul," declared Reed, who was already on the way to becoming a Swedenborgian, "must change with its subject. Locke's mind will not always be the standard of metaphysics. Had we a description of it in its present state, it would make a very different book from 'Locke on the Human Understanding.' "[51] The reaction against Locke was indeed in the air. Four years later James Freeman Clarke, entering Harvard, read Coleridge and his American interpreter, President James Marsh of the University of Vermont,[52] and was thereby confirmed in his longing for a "higher philosophy" than that of Locke and Hartley, from whom he had taken his first philosophical lessons in his grandfather's library. To use Clarke's own words, "Something within me revolted at all such attempts to explain soul out of sense, deducing mind from matter, or tracing the origin of ideas to nerves, vibrations, and vibratiuncles." Coleridge at this

[50] *Memoirs of William Ellery Channing,* I, 66.
[51] Elizabeth P. Peabody (ed.), *Aesthetic Papers* (Boston, 1849), pp. 63–64; Clarence Paul Hotson, "Sampson Reed, A Teacher of Emerson," *New England Quarterly* (April, 1929), II, 248–277.
[52] Marjorie H. Nicolson, "James Marsh and the Vermont Transcendentalists," *Philosophical Review* (January, 1925), XXXIV, 28–48.

point rescued him. Accepting the English poet's "distinction between the reason and the understanding judging by sense," he lived again in the realization that knowledge begins *with* experience although it does not come *from* experience.[53] At the Harvard Divinity School, Clarke and other candidates for the Unitarian ministry came in contact, after 1830, with Henry Ware the younger, who led his students to Coleridge, Goethe, the Platonists, and church mystics, thus delivering them from "the wooden philosophy" of John Locke, before which as undergraduates they had been made to bend the knee.

The same revolt may be found in Emerson prior to the writing of his classic essay on Nature and his Divinity School Address (1837). On July 4, 1834, at the age of thirty-one, he wrote in his *Journal* that Locke had given him little—that he was much more indebted to persons of lesser names.[54] Locke is as surely the "influx of decomposition as Bacon and the Platonists [are] of growth," he wrote much later.[55] In his essay *The Transcendentalist* (1842), he went even further in his repudiation of the sensationist philosophy of Locke and in his hearty acceptance of Kant's "imperative forms" —intuitions of the mind itself through which experience is acquired.[56]

What one finds in these leaders of the transcendental movement is encountered again and again in many of the commencement addresses and occasional lectures and essays of less-known figures. For example, in pleading for a union of action and speculation, President John Williamson Nevin, of Marshall College, called for a distinctively American philosophy which would right the sad disproportion in American life between outward activity and inward consciousness, full self-possession, and inner control. To him philosophy without action seemed helpless and liable to disease, and

---

[53] Edward Everett Hale (ed.), *James Freeman Clarke: Autobiography, Diary and Correspondence* (Boston and New York, 1892), p. 39.
[54] *Journals of Ralph Waldo Emerson* (Boston and New York, 1909-1914, 10 vols.), III, 501.
[55] *Ibid., VIII*, 492.
[56] *Complete Works, I*, 340; *IV*, 136; *V*, 238.

action without philosophy appeared equally untrustworthy. Responsive as he was to the German idealism in Mercersburg, he believed that Kant was well designed to bridge the gap. Thus he roundly condemned Locke, Hume, and the French materialists for promoting, as he supposed, only the activist, outer, so-called practical elements in the national life.[57] This revolt against what was interpreted as the materialistic implications of Locke, during a period in which physical expansion seemed to be capturing all American life, is an interesting example of ideas and interests in conflict and at work.

Academic leaders in other sections of the country took like ground.[58] Professor D. D. Whedon of the University of Michigan, speaking before the Phi Beta Kappa Society of Wesleyan University in 1850, denounced the "materialism" of Locke, the low expediency of Paley, the lack of will of Edwards, the atheism of Hume—for the first taught that man had no soul; the second, no conscience; the third, no will; and the fourth, no God. The present period demanded, continued Whedon, a philosophy recognizing the soul, "the power of knowing ideas that transcend matter; and so authenticates the belief in a spiritual and immortal nature."[59] Locke's philosophy was many-sided, and certain Americans were reacting against him because some aspects of his work, and the implications involved, were, in a changing scene, uncongenial to their interests and their values.

It was not only, however, from the neo-Platonists, from Cole-

[57] John Williamson Nevin, D.D., *Human Freedom and a Plea for Philosophy* (Mercersburg, Pa., 1850), pp. 34–36, 41–43. Nevin had taken similar ground as early as 1844. See his *National Taste. An Address* (Chambersburg, Pa., 1844), p. 17. For Nevin's life consult Theodore Appel, *The Life and Work of John Williamson Nevin* (Philadelphia, 1889).

[58] For southern criticisms of the materialistic and utilitarian implications of Locke's philosophy, see James Hammond, *Oration before the two Societies of South-Carolina College, Dec. 4, 1849* (Charleston, 1849), p. 44, and *Southern Quarterly Review* (April, 1850), XVII, 44. Still later, Robert L. Dabney devoted a book to an attack on the sensualistic philosophy, in which Locke was not spared, *The Sensualistic Philosophy of the Nineteenth Century Considered* (New York, 1875), pp. 15–22.

[59] D. D. Whedon, *The Man Republic; A Phi Beta Kappa Oration, delivered at the Wesleyan University, August 1859* (Middletown, Conn., 1850), pp. 15–16.

ridge, and from Kantian idealists that the American critics of Locke derived inspiration and a substitute philosophy. The eclecticism of Victor Cousin and Jouffroy was introduced by H. G. Linberg, Orestes A. Brownson, George Ripley, and the Reverend Caleb Sprague Henry.[60] In this group the most unflagging efforts came from Henry, a man of personal magnetism, vivacity, and literary enthusiasm. After graduating from Dartmouth in 1824, Henry studied theology at Andover, entered the Congregationalist ministry, took part in the peace crusade during his residence at Hartford, and became an Episcopalian minister in 1836. Two years later he accepted a professorship of intellectual and moral philosophy at New York University, a post which he held with great success for many years. In 1834 he translated Cousin's *Elements of Psychology*, a treatise destined to become celebrated in American philosophical circles by reason of its criticism of Locke's *Essay Concerning Human Understanding*. Henry was attracted to Cousin by virtue of what appeared to him to be the most thorough, clear, and convincing criticism of Locke that had ever been made. This refutation, he believed, would establish the very foundations of morality and religion against the subversive principles of Locke and his disciple, Paley.[61] Cousin's doctrine of spontaneous reason (according to which reason, when uncontrolled by the will or when left free to develop undirected by the voluntary faculty, always apprehended things as they are) exerted considerable influence on the transcendentalists.[62]

[60] H. G. Linberg (tr.), *Introductions to the History of Philosophy by Victor Cousin* (Boston, 1832); George Ripley, *Specimens of Foreign Literature* (Boston, 1838, 14 vols.); James Murdock, D.D., *Sketches of Modern Philosophy, especially among the Germans* (Hartford, 1842); Henry F. Brownson (ed.), *The Works of Orestes A. Brownson* (Detroit, 1883, 20 vols.), IV, 359. For the relation of French eclectic philosophy and transcendentalism, see William Girard, *Du Transcendentalisme considéré essentiellement dans sa définition et ses origines françaises*, in University of California Publications in Modern Philology (Berkeley, 1916), IV.

[61] *Elements of Psychology; included in a critical examination of Locke's Essay on the Human Understanding, and in additional Pieces. By Victor Cousin. Translated from the French* (New York, 1861), p. 80 of Introduction and Notes by Caleb Henry.

[62] Murdock, *Sketches of Modern Philosophy*.

The appearance of the first edition of Henry's translation of Cousin's *Elements of Psychology*—there were four editions in all —stirred up much opposition, especially in Princeton circles, where Locke had not yet been replaced by the Scottish school. An article in the *Princeton Review*[63] early in 1839 attacked Henry and Cousin as "infidel expounders" of Locke who "sneered" at the great master for not having discovered a hypocritical way of making Christianity easily palatable to the critically minded. Cousin was represented as a mainstay of fatalism, as hostile to divine revelation in the Scriptures, as a pantheist, and even as an atheist who denied the personality of God and the essential difference between right and wrong.

In his preface to the third edition (1841), Henry replied to his Princeton critics by charging them with having displayed superficial and insufficient knowledge both of Cousin and of the German idealists with whom they confused the French philosopher. In fact Cousin, insisted Henry, made freedom of the will a fundamental part of his system, essential to any conception of moral obligation. He taught the absolute difference between right and wrong, the eternal and immutable nature of moral distinctions, and had explicitly denied the charge of pantheism.[64]

The battle was on. Locke was attacked right and left. Dissatisfied with his compromising position on the problem of thoroughgoing materialism, disciples of that school in America (Dr. Thomas Cooper and Dr. Joseph Buchanan, for example) had long before refused to follow Locke when he implied that the physiological explanation of mentality was inadequate.[65] Moreover, men who formerly entertained the highest regard for him had, for one reason or another, transferred their allegiance to the Scotch common-sense school. Jefferson himself represents this tendency, for he came to

[63] James Waddel Alexander and Albert Baldwin Dod [two Princeton professors], "Transcendentalism," *The Biblical Repertory and Princeton Review* (January, 1839), XI, 37–101.

[64] [Cousin's] *Elements of Psychology* (tr. cited), pp. xiv ff. of Henry's Prefaces to 3rd and 4th eds.

[65] Riley, *American Philosophy*, pp. 416, 426, 373–374, 382.

accept the doctrine of innate ideas and, under the influence of his friend Dugald Stuart, the tenets of "realism."[66] Others rebelled at Locke's indictment of "enthusiasm." George Bancroft, thanking Emerson in 1836 for his kind words regarding the first volume of the *History of the United States,* declared that the early annals of Quaker Pennsylvania completely refuted Locke's outcry against "enthusiasm." His notable discussion in the first volume of the *History,* in which he contrasted Locke somewhat unfavorably with Fox and Penn, was symptomatic of the thought of the times.[67] Still others, hungry for consistency and a philosophy which resolved conflicts in a unified higher synthesis, repudiated Locke as a superficial philosopher who, like the typical Englishman, failed to come to grips with ultimate problems, betrayed a lack of severe mental discipline, and made philosophy a welter of compromises.[68] There were also men who, convinced that the philosophy of Locke "bordered hard upon the inner temple of sensualism," and believing that it was but a gradual descent from sensualism to materialism and thence to deism and rank atheism, found in Cousin an antidote against Locke and the French atheists.[69]

The revolt against Locke aroused defense. Conservatives in religion and social outlook were alarmed at the spread of the intuitional philosophy. Bad enough was its association, in their eyes, with reform agitations of social questions and its menace to religious orthodoxy; but even worse was the possibility that it might beguile those who were guided by "enthusiasm" into endless strange cults unsettling to the authority of God, the past, and the present. As James Murdock suggested, the established philosophy of Locke had at least kept its followers from going off on dangerous tangents, for they could be counted on to examine everything and to hold fast to that which was proved. It also befitted men who by temperament

[66] *Ibid.,* pp. 278, 280.
[67] M. A. DeWolfe Howe, *The Life and Letters of George Bancroft* (New York, 1908, 2 vols.), I, 223; George Bancroft, *History of the United States of America, from the Discovery of the Continent* (New York, 1883, 6 vols.), 561–562.
[68] *The Works of Orestes A. Brownson,* I, 1 ff; II, 226.
[69] *The Methodist Quarterly Review* (April, 1863), XXIII, 336–354.

and interest were distrustful of all that could not be put to the test of accepted conventions and cautious experiment.[70]

Of this group of conservative champions of Locke who still saw in him a bulwark against the new and daring intuitionalism, the best-known was Alexander H. Everett. Trained in law and diplomacy, he had exhibited a certain instability in both politics and thought. He embarrassed his brother Edward Everett by deserting federalism for democracy in 1813. He showed favor at times to the French Revolution. Yet he was an apologist, in a sense, for slavery, adhered to the conservative stake-in-society theory of economics and politics, and denied the perfectibility of human nature. In 1830 this well-read scholar, who was at home in classical and contemporary literature as well as in modern philosophy, became editor of the North American Review, in which he had just published his first notable defense of Locke.[71] Francis Bowen, who for a time edited the same periodical, also taught logic, philosophy, and political economy at Harvard.[72] Even more persistently loyal to Locke was Andrews Norton, who in 1819 became Dexter Professor of Sacred Literature at the Harvard Divinity School and a notable apologist for a conservative, rationalistic type of Unitarian Christianity. This grave, erudite scholar, bold and acute in controversy, was later one of the chief critics of Emerson and the transcendentalists.[73] But the most uncompromising and tireless of all Locke's champions was the Reverend Frederick Beasley. Entering Prince-

---

[70] James Murdock, D.D., Sketches of Modern Philosophy, especially among the Germans (Hartford, 1842), p. 12. See The American Whig Review (May, 1851), VII, 460–463, for a conservative's defense of Locke.

[71] Critical and Miscellaneous Essays of Alexander H. Everett (Boston, 1845–1846), passim; William Charvat, The Origins of American Critical Thought, 1810–1835 (Philadelphia, 1936), pp. 182–185.

[72] Bowen later shifted his position, finally coming to support natural realism modified by Kantian idealism. See his Modern Philosophy from Descartes to Schopenhauer and Hartmann (New York, 1896), chap. 3.

[73] William B. Sprague, Annals of the American Pulpit . . . (New York, 1865, 9 vols.), VIII, 430. The Evidences of the Genuineness of the Gospels (Boston, 1837–1844) is Norton's most important contribution to Biblical scholarship. Norton's son, Charles Eliot Norton, always regarded himself as a disciple of Locke and Hume; see Letters of Charles Eliot Norton (Boston and New York, 1913, 2 vols.), II, 364.

ton from a well-to-do North Carolina family, he became an Episcopalian clergyman shortly after his graduation in 1797. It was as
professor of philosophy and provost of the University of Pennsylvania (1813–1828) that Beasley, a forceful figure and proud of his
old-fashioned thought and dress, exerted his greatest influence in
the intellectual controversies of his time.[74] These men took a conservative or middle-of-the-road position on the great social questions
of the day.

The "back to Locke" movement was really inaugurated in 1829,
when Alexander Everett published in the *North American Review*
a long, closely argued paper, "The History of Intellectual Philosophy." This paradoxical and pragmatic critic undertook to explain
the reaction among leading intellectuals against the *Essay Concerning Human Understanding*. To Everett it seemed clear that
a chief reason for the about-face was that conservative critics of
the French Revolution and its aftermath had mistakenly denounced
the essay as the real foundation of all the mischief which even more
superficial commentators had attributed to Voltaire and Rousseau.
De Maistre, for example, had branded Locke as an apostle of ir-
religion, immorality, impurity, and sedition—a strange indictment,
Everett observed, for one who was a firm believer in revelation and
whose life had been noted for its exemplary beauty. But reaction-
aries like de Maistre were not the only ones who had wrongly
ascribed the French Revolution to Locke's teachings. Liberals,
somewhat illogically anxious to shake off responsibility for most of
the acts and opinions of the fathers of the Revolution, which as a
fait accompli they of course approved, shared in the conservative
reaction against Locke's metaphysics. Cousin, and to a certain extent the Scotch school, represented this reaction of liberals.[75]

After weighing the philosophies of Locke, the Scotch school, and
Kant, Everett decided in favor of the great English empiricist who
in rebelling against obscurantism and mysticism had done so much

---

[74] Sprague, *Annals of the American Pulpit*, V, 477–484.
[75] A. H. Everett, "History of Intellectual Philosophy," *North American Review*
(July, 1829), XXIX, 120.

to inaugurate modern liberal thought. German idealism appeared to this man of the world as an unsubstantial dream, whose appeal arose from its supposed essential connection with the existence of God and the immortality of the soul. The present hysteria, Everett thought, was to be explained by reference to actions and reactions in the history of thought. The protest of the restless, disturbed intuitionalists against the materialism which they wrongly associated with Locke was merely a reversion to "the Platonic visions of the childhood of the race."

In a review of a new edition of Lord King's *Life of Locke*, Everett subsequently pointed out even more explicitly that the materialists or the philosophers of selfishness, in reality, found no foothold in Locke for the degrading theories they cherished. At the same time, he held up for the highest esteem—without entire justification—the great philosopher's precision of ideas and correct use of language, "an indispensable instrument for correct thinking."[76]

It was Francis Bowen, however, who, even more than Alexander Everett, admired Locke and his philosophical style, with its homely simplicity and its freedom from bizarre obscurantism and from dogmatism. What Bowen regarded as loyalty to American values and ideals led him, like Everett, to oppose the new fashion which abandoned plain English speech for "fantastic" German notions. Transcendentalism was, in his eyes, a kind of false, imported mixture of sublimated Fichtean atheism and the downright pantheism of Schelling. Moreover, in the transcendentalist reaction against Locke, the Harvard philosopher and historian detected the unAmerican tendency to divorce speculation from the everyday life of men.[77] Bowen wrote for the *Knickerbocker* a popular paper, in the form of an imaginary discourse between Locke and Newton, which defended the former against the common misunderstanding which attributed to his denial of innate ideas the denial also of the certainty of ideas themselves.[78]

[76] A. H. Everett, *Essays, Second Series* (Boston, 1846), pp. 381–451.
[77] Francis Bowen, "Locke and the Transcendentalists," *The Christian Examiner* (November, 1837), XXIII, 170 ff. See also Bowen's *Lowell Lectures* (Boston, 1849), p. 57.
[78] *The Knickerbocker* (November, 1835), VI, 415–419.

An even more vigorous champion of "the great Mr. Locke" was the Reverend Frederick Beasley, who, like Bowen, resented the new tendency to borrow ideas from Europe and who regarded Locke as America's own philosopher. According to one of Beasley's friends, he could scarcely have shown greater warmth and zeal in Locke's defense had he been among his intimate and living associates. Indeed, Beasley went so far as to declare that Locke "never has been and never can be overthrown." Although he befriended him in his teachings and in his daily discussions, it was in *A Search for Truth in the Science of the Human Mind* (1822) that he mustered all his forces for the cause. Casting strictures on the Scotch school and on the French eclectics, Beasley exonerated his master from "the false and absurd charge of representative perception through mediate images."

Other students of philosophy also came to the defense of Locke, but we need not tarry long with them. Thomas C. Upham, of Bowdoin College, replied to Locke's critics by insisting that he had by no means supposed sensation to be the only source of knowledge. This rejoinder was needed, for transcendentalists had overlooked Locke's emphasis on reflection and his implication that there was also something like intuitive reason. What Upham chiefly valued in Locke, however, was his synthesis: Aristotle had seen the connection of the intellect with the material world, and had postulated the external origin of knowledge; Plato had directed attention chiefly to the internal origin of thought; and Locke combined these two great views.[79]

An examination of a great number of commencement and other academic addresses, and of many popular handbooks, seems to in-

---

[79] Thomas C. Upham, *Elements of Mental Philosophy, embracing the two departments of the Intellect and the Sensibilities* (Portland, 1839, 2 vols.), I, 5. See also the *Works of Charles Follen*, III, 99, 168. From the ranks of the American disciples of Francis Bacon, whose influence on American thought has never been adequately investigated, came still further support for Locke. Samuel Tyler, a member of the Maryland bar, in a learned dissertation on Bacon, regarded Locke as a true Baconian of the mind; and many others in defending Bacon likewise defended Locke, with whom in their minds he was associated. See Samuel Tyler, *A Discourse on the Baconian Philosophy* (Frederick City, Md., 1844), pp. 113 ff.

dicate, however, that the Lockean philosophy was by no means completely undermined by the various attacks, many of which did not penetrate into the everyday channels of intellectual life.[80] It is, of course, impossible to determine finally the depth and persistence of the idealistic and eclectic attacks on Locke. There is evidence that they succeeded only in bringing about an increasing qualification and enrichment of the basic Lockean philosophy. No doubt American dependence on English thought was also lessened. But throughout later American thought, it appears certain that Locke's influence continued to be important and that it did not die with the new emphasis on biology and the theory of organic evolution.

Subsequent developments in American philosophical and psychological thought reveal the tenacity of the ideas of the noted empiricist. In his widely read *Outlines of Cosmic Philosophy* (1874), John Fiske maintained that the doctrine of evolution harmonized Locke's great view, that all knowledge was due to experience, with the Leibnitz-Kantian view that the mind even at birth possesses definite tendencies.[81] In other ways, too, the Lockean empirical tradition was expressed in what have been regarded as characteristically American ideas. William James, according to his most authoritative biographer, belongs unquestionably to the British empirical school founded by Locke. More than once James referred to "the good Locke" and his "dear old book," and rejoiced in his devotion to experimentalism, his common sense, and his hatred of obscure, misty ideas. Furthermore, as Professor Perry points out, the chapter on "conception" in James's *Principles of Psychology* is quite definitely founded on Locke—with his view of the *priority* and *preëminence* of particulars James heartily agreed. Even James's own more original thinking, as distinguished from his inheritance

---

[80] For example, see Hon. Robert Strange, *An Address delivered before two literary societies of the University of North Carolina, June, 1837* (Raleigh, 1837), pp. 8 ff.; Charles McCay, *A Lecture delivered to the Senior Class of the University of Georgia* . . . (Athens, 1842), pp. 3 ff.; Herman J. Groesbeck, *Address delivered at the second anniversary celebration of the Alpha Delta Phi Society of Miami University, Aug. 10, 1837* (Cincinnati, 1837), pp. 8 ff.

[81] John Fiske, *Outlines of Cosmic Philosophy* (London, 1874, 2 vols.), II, 161.

from Locke, was characterized by a functional relationship between ideas and reality—a position not so alien to Locke as to his critics, by reason of the fact that Locke had more or less recognized practical motives in the acquisition of knowledge.[82]

Other American philosophers, too, in spite of non-Lockean influences on their thought, were not unaffected by the great empiricist so long regarded as America's particular master. In discussing the significance of Locke, John Dewey shows his own kinship with him. The philosophic empiricism initiated by Locke, Dewey writes, was designed to remove the burden which "blind custom, imposed authority and accidental association" had loaded on science and social obligation; and the best way to liberate man from this burden was "through a natural history of the origin and growth in the mind of ideas connected with objectionable beliefs and customs."[83] Even the idealist Josiah Royce spoke well of Locke, while a contemporary philosopher, Frederick J. E. Woodbridge, pays great deference to him for having taught us that "we must go to our senses, not to our souls, if we are ever to enter into the realm of the mind."[84] Moreover, the persistence, in contemporary thought, of the impact of Locke was not confined to philosophy. Notwithstanding the biological emphasis in modern psychology, the influence of Locke is still a factor to be reckoned with.[85]

Thus, in spite of the defects in his system of knowledge, in spite of all the attacks levied on him, there was something in the empirical, middle-of-the-road, common-sense position taken by Locke

[82] Ralph Barton Perry, *The Thought and Character of William James* (Boston, 1935, 2 vols.), I, 466, 544–547; II, 56, 74, 75, 449–450. For a discussion of the relation of James and his thinking to the conflicting interests of American life, see Merle Curti, *The Social Ideas of American Educators* (New York, 1935), chap. 13.

[83] John Dewey, *Reconstruction in Philosophy* (New York, 1920), pp. 35, 82.

[84] *Contemporary American Philosophy—Personal Statements* (New York, 1930, 2 vols.), II, 427 ff. Professor R. M. Wenley points out that in the case of another idealist, G. S. Morris, it was the ideas fathered by Locke, Milton, and Hoadley that set his perspective in secular affairs; see his *The Life and Work of George Sylvester Morris* (New York, 1917), p. 105.

[85] Edward Stevens Robinson, *Association Theory Today; An Essay in Systematic Psychology* (New York, 1932), *passim.*

which persisted in the main streams of American philosophy. May it not be that the explanation is partly to be found in the consideration that such a philosophy could best perform the work America needed done? Could it not break down the cleavage between speculation and everyday life and safeguard our inherited, liberal, seventeenth-century English tradition from the "fantastic," imported, French and German notions, supposedly so alien to our Anglo-American civilization?

IV

In the fields of political and economic theory in the first seventy-five years of our national experience, the ideas of Locke were of peculiar importance—an importance not to be obscured by the varying interpretations given them. Locke's *Treatises of Civil Government,* published the same year (1690) as the famous *Essay Concerning Human Understanding,* was, of course, even more influential during the years of revolution than the philosophical and religious treatises. There is abundant evidence that his political theories did not die after the Revolution had become history. There was much work for them to do. True, the *Treatises of Civil Government* was seldom cited in the Constitutional Convention of 1787;[86] but the cardinal doctrine that the people in themselves constitute a power superior to the government, that government may be dissolved without affecting civil society, had great weight in the minds of the men assembled in 1787 at Philadelphia to frame a new Constitution, and was also a powerful factor in the fundamental assumptions of those who made and revised state constitutions.

Statesmen continued, during the early republic, to defer to Locke's *Treatises.* Jefferson, who had declared that "Locke's little book on Government is perfect as far as it goes," insisted that it be required reading for law students at the University of Virginia,

---

[86] Max Farrand (ed.), *The Records of the Federal Convention of 1787* (New Haven, 1911, 3 vols.), I, 437. Luther Martin cited Locke to prove that individuals, under primitive conditions, are equally free and independent, and that the case was the same with states until they surrendered their equal authority.

where in general there were to be no requirements.[87] Madison agreed, thinking that Locke was admirably suited to impress young minds with the right of nations to establish their own governments and to inspire a love of free ones.[88] John Quincy Adams, when the question of the separation of powers was uppermost in the discussions of Congress, went straight to Locke rather than to Montesquieu, for he regarded the English thinker as the true originator of the theory.[89] Charles Sumner and many less-learned statesmen quoted Locke in their public speeches during the slavery controversy; and he was remembered during every contest between human and property rights and interests.[90] Moreover, Locke's doctrine of the right of revolution figured largely in popular thought as reflected in hundreds of election sermons, academic addresses, and Fourth of July orations.

Part of the secret of much of Locke's influence on public thought lies in the very inconsistency of his political theories. In the *Essay Concerning Human Understanding* he had repudiated the theory of innate ideas; yet in his *Treatises of Civil Government* he assumed as innate ideas both the state of nature and the law of reason —conceptions which he could not have arrived at empirically. This incongruity, it will be recalled, was partly responsible for the repudiation of his empiricism by social radicals, who, in a conflict between the "innate truths" of equality and the practical lessons of inequality, had no hesitancy in choosing the former. Forced thus to repudiate Locke's psychology and philosophy and aware that their leading defenders were social conservatives, radicals also discovered that Locke's political doctrines, once regarded as bold and even revolutionary, could be used as a bulwark for the *status quo* as well as for challenging it. Likewise, exponents of laissez faire

[87] *The Writings of Thomas Jefferson* ("Library Edition," Washington, 1903, 20 vols.), VIII, 31.

[88] *Letters and Other Writings of James Madison* (Philadelphia, 1867, 4 vols.), III, 481.

[89] *Memoirs of John Quincy Adams* (Philadelphia, 1876, 12 vols.), IX, 226.

[90] For Locke's early influence on American thought regarding slavery, see Mary Stoughton Locke, *Anti-Slavery in America from the Introduction of African Slaves to the Prohibition of the Slave Trade* (Boston, 1901), p. 19.

and of the sanctity of private property found comfort in Locke's individualism—in his natural rights of life, liberty, and property. Hence it was that divergent interests appealed to contradictory doctrines and implications in Locke's political thought.

It will be remembered that Locke not only refuted the doctrine of absolute monarchy but also justified the right of revolution when a government willfully and over a considerable period of time violated the contract with civil society. He did not, however, indicate precisely how the people were to repossess themselves of the government, or just how it was to be determined that the contract had been broken.[91] These questions, he implied, must be left to common sense, to the practical judgment of the majority. There could be no objective test. But clearly Locke denied the right of minorities to make a revolution, although revolutions (at least in their initial stage) are frequently, if indeed not always, minority movements. He was equally outspoken against "seditious factions." Thus hedged about and restricted, the right of revolution was stated and justified.[92]

Still other aspects of Locke's thought appealed to American liberals and radicals in the first half-century of the republic. He stoutly adhered to the law of nature and reason, by which he meant "the law of good will, mutual assistance, and preservation," or, in other words, the sacred rights of life, liberty, and property. Under primitive conditions this law of nature or reason had, with some exceptions, governed men's relations. To avoid the confusion and awkwardness of exceptions, men had contracted with each other to form civil society and to delegate to government the single natural right of enforcing "the law of good will, mutual assistance, and preservation." Thus Locke's political philosophy was one of individualism. In the early days of the republic the principle of individualism best served the interests of radicals, for their fight was

[91] John Locke, *Of Civil Government, Two Treatises* (London and New York, 1924), chap. 19.
[92] *Ibid.*, p. 223.

against the domination of favored classes and centralized government. Hence Locke's doctrine was in many respects as democratic in its implications as his theory of the plasticity of human nature, which, as we have seen, was beloved by antifederalists and social radicals.

An examination of more than four hundred election sermons, academic addresses, and Fourth of July orations written during the three-quarters of a century after the American Revolution indicates that various interests appealed to these doctrines of Locke to support their causes. Church leaders, concerned over the rapid secularization of life, insisted that religion was an indispensable factor in the proper working of any government founded, as ours was, on the Lockean concept of the law of nature and contract. What could oaths taken by magistrates and people to obey their obligations in the contractual relation mean unless these oaths had the sanction of religion? This question was asked by the Reverend Thomas Reese, a Presbyterian minister of Salem, South Carolina, in an essay written in 1788,[93] and it was a very common argument on the part of religious leaders who were bidding for support for the interest they represented.

Critics of aristocratic tendencies in American life likewise appealed to "the great Mr. Locke." If his heritage of the consent of the governed was to be a thing of substance, then such antidemocratic groups as the Society of the Cincinnati must, it was urged, be restrained from promoting aristocracy and discord—behavior which would fatally wound civil liberty.[94] During the debates in the Virginia Constitutional Convention in 1829, the liberals or reformers, who were contending for an enlarged suffrage and a redistribution of representation to weaken the tidewater aristocracy, cited Locke and the doctrine of natural law in an effort to promote their cause. Locke taught that all government was based on consent,

[93] Rev. Thomas Reese, A.M., *An Essay on the Influence of Religion in Civil Society* (Charleston, 1788), pp. 20, 32.
[94] [Aedanus Burke], *Considerations on the Society or Order of Cincinnati* (Hartford, 1783), p. 10.

and an extension of political democracy in Virginia was necessary, they held, if this principle was to be realized in fact.[95]

In other contests for an extension of suffrage, appeals were made to the doctrine of natural rights, the right of revolution, and similar teachings of Locke. The literature of the Dorr Rebellion, which came to a head in Rhode Island in 1842, is a case in point. As early as 1833 the labor leader, Seth Luther, told a Providence audience that every page in history was stained with blood shed in obtaining acknowledgment of the right of self-government, or in acquiring the exercise of it, or in defending it from encroachment. "In all cases, or nearly all, the rights of men have been wrested from the grasp of power, *vi et armis*, by force and arms. The people have been compelled to take by force that which has been withheld from them by force, to wit: the right to govern themselves, by laws made by themselves."[96] In ringing words which appealed to the class consciousness of Rhode Island's disenfranchised thousands, Luther declared that the existing state government, by depriving men of their natural rights, was violating the great tradition of English liberty and completely repudiating the doctrine of the consent of the governed—a doctrine hallowed by the Declaration of Independence.

In other contests between democracy and privilege the natural-rights philosophy and the revolutionary theories of Locke were mustered for service. The Equal Rights party, or Locofocos, declared in 1836 that the true foundation of republican government is the equal right of every citizen in his person and property, and in their management; and asserted, in the spirit and almost the words of Locke, that the rightful power of all legislation is "to

[95] Benjamin Fletcher Wright, *American Interpretation of Natural Law*, pp. 203 ff.

[96] Seth Luther, *An Address on the Right of Free Suffrage* (Providence, 1833), pp. 6–7. See also Joseph S. Pitman, *Report of the Trial of Thomas Wilson Dorr* (Boston, 1844), pp. 79 ff.; *To the Members of the General Assembly of Rhode Island* (n.p., n.d.), pp. 13–14, for a Lockean but anti-Dorr interpretation of the formation of the Commonwealth of Rhode Island; *Address to the People of Rhode Island, March, 1834* (Providence, 1834), *passim;* Elisha R. Potter, *Considerations on the Questions of the Adoption of a Constitution and Extension of Suffrage in Rhode Island* (Boston, 1842), *passim.*

declare and enforce only our natural rights and duties, and is to take none of them from us." Leader after leader appealed as a precedent to the principles of 1776, to the Declaration of Independence. "We have departed, and are continually departing from the simplicity of those principles, which were the price of our father's blood."[97]

In economics no less than in political matters Locke's ideas continued to live because of their usefulness to developing interests. The Constitution, declared John Hunt, had compromised the principles of natural rights by entrenching wealth in high places. Man in America, as man in the Old World, was still a slave, must continue to be a slave until he had freed himself from the despotism of money, until he could enjoy the fruits of his labor from which he was at present stripped by "swaggering pretensions to exclusive privileges." Wall Street must cease governing our legislative lobbies; monopolies must be exterminated; the speculator and profiteer curbed. Then, and not till then, declared this leader of the proletariat, would the full implications of the rights of man and the principles of the Declaration of Independence be realized.[98]

The same appeals to natural rights, and even to the right of revolution, emerged in the arguments of the more militant abolitionists. No sooner was the Revolution over than many men opposed to slavery held that the existence of that institution was a violation of all the rights for which the war had been fought. Dr. George Buchanan, in a Fourth of July oration in Baltimore in 1791, declared that slavery was a cruel, oppressive, and wanton abuse of the rights of man, that the fires of liberty might well be kindled among the slaves, and that they might rally under the standard of freedom and bring devastation and ruin on the country.[99] "Alas," lamented Samuel Miller in speaking of slavery in a sermon delivered before the Tammany Society on July 4, 1793, "that we should

[97] F. Byrdsall, *The History of the Loco-Foco or Equal Rights Party* (New York, 1842), p. 62.

[98] *Ibid.*, pp. 147 ff.

[99] George Buchanan, M.D., *An Oration Upon the Moral and Political Evil of Slavery* (Baltimore, 1793), pp. 13, 17.

so soon forget the principles, upon which our wonderful revolution was founded!"[100] This note was struck again and again. Slavery, asserted the Reverend P. S. Cleland in a Fourth of July sermon at Greenwood, Indiana, in 1841, was diametrically opposed to the self-evident principles of the Declaration of Independence.

If slavery is right, the axioms set forth in that declaration as our apology to the world, for resisting unto blood, the oppressions of Great Britain, are glaringly false; the American Revolution was but a successful rebellion; and our fathers should be regarded as a band of rebels, engaged in unlawful resistance against the lawful tyranny of George III and his parliament. If the principles of the Declaration were fully adopted, we should no longer be guilty of contradicting our principles by our practice.[101]

Other Fourth of July orators reproduced in detail the contract theory of the origin of government and the natural-rights philosophy, in a more or less orthodox Lockean fashion. Sometimes Locke and other revolutionary leaders or theorists of seventeenth-century England were specifically mentioned, but in any case their ideas were expressed with illuminating reiteration.[102]

In the tension occasioned by slavery, particularly at the time of the Fugitive Slave Law, some of the speakers even went to the length of advocating the right of revolution as perhaps the only means by which the free North could uproot the South's peculiar institution. "If the exigency is imminent, the perversion total, and

[100] Samuel Miller, A.M., A Sermon, Preached in New-York July 4th, 1793 . . . at the Request of the Tammany Society, or Columbian Order (New York, [1793]), pp. 27–28.

[101] Rev. P. S. Cleland, A Sermon, delivered, Sabbath, July 4, 1841, in the Presbyterian Church, Greenwood, Indiana (Greenwood, 1841), pp. 10, 13.

[102] The following are representative speeches: Rev. Samuel C. Bartlett, The Duty and the Limitations of Civil Obedience (Manchester, N.H., 1853), pp. 4, 15–18; C. F. Adams, An Oration . . . July 4, 1860 (Fall River, 1860), p. 20; C. W., My Country; as She was in 1776; as She is in 1846. An Address delivered in Coventry, R.I., July 4, 1846 (Providence, 1846), pp. 5, 8–9; Oliver Dyer, Phonographic Report of the Proceedings of the National Free Soil Convention at Buffalo, New York, August 9th and 10th, 1848 (Buffalo, 1848), pp. 7–9; "The Identity of the Liberal Party of 1846 with the Liberty Party of 1776" (Huntington Library, No. 52377); J. T. Tucker, The Citizen and the Commonwealth. A Discourse delivered in the First Congregational Church in Holliston, Mass. . . . April 10, 1851 (Holliston, 1851), pp. 12–13.

other redress impossible, we must admit the desperate and fearful remedy of Revolution," declared the Reverend Samuel C. Bartlett at Manchester, New Hampshire, in 1853. "I need not argue the case that is so powerfully put in the immortal Declaration of Independence."[103] But this was only one among dozens of such statements. Perhaps the most typical, but by no means the most thoroughgoing, of these expressions of the right of revolution is to be found in a leaflet bearing the title "Revolution the only Remedy for Slavery," issued by the American Anti-Slavery Society.[104] For the most drastic statements one must turn to the literature of the "higher law" doctrine and to radical abolitionists' justification of John Brown's attack on Harper's Ferry. The sermons of Gilbert Haven, a prominent Methodist leader, and the speeches and writings of such people as Wendell Phillips and Mrs. Child, contain unequivocal assertions of the right of revolution.[105] The transcendentalist Theodore Parker found Locke's theory of the right of revolution as useful to his scheme of values as he found his empirical psychology unserviceable. And, after the Civil War, abolitionists, in their advocacy of equal rights for the Negro, appealed to Locke more than once.[106]

If, however, the slavery controversy resulted, on the one hand, in an appeal by the abolitionists to the natural-rights philosophy of Locke, on the other it stimulated exponents of slavery to redefine

[103] Rev. Samuel C. Bartlett, *The Duty and Limitations of Civil Obedience,* (Manchester, N.H., 1853), p. 16.

[104] *Anti-Slavery Tracts,* No. 7, "Revolution the Only Remedy for Slavery" [n.p., n.d.].

[105] Some, admitting the theoretical right of resistance and revolution, nevertheless advised submission to "the ordinance of man for the Lord's sake," as, for example, Nathaniel Bouton, *The Good Land in Which We Live. A Discourse Preached at Concord, N.H., on the Day of Public Thanksgiving, Nov. 28, 1850* (Concord, 1850), pp. 17, 26. Cf. *Writings of Thomas Wentworth Higginson* (Cambridge, 1899), p. 269; Lysander Spooner, *The Unconstitutionality of Slavery* (Boston, 1846), pp. 10–13, 36 ff.; *John Brown's Expedition Reviewed in a Letter from Rev. Theodore Parker, at Rome, to Francis Jackson, Boston* (Boston, 1860), pp. 4 ff.; Gilbert Haven, *National Sermons* (Boston, 1869), pp. 13 ff.; L. Maria Child, *The Duty of Disobedience to the Fugitive Slave Act* (Boston, 1860), pp. 3 ff.

[106] *Charles Sumner: His Complete Works* ("Statesman Edition," Boston, 1900, 20 vols.), III, 58; VI, 164; XII, 159; XIII, 156, 300.

natural rights in such a way as to make slavery justifiable, or it led to a complete repudiation of the natural-rights philosophy itself. J. K. Paulding, novelist, satirist, and naval official, endeavored to reconcile slavery with natural-rights theories.[107] President Dew, of William and Mary College, and Albert Bledsoe, a mathematical philosopher at the University of Virginia, undertook the same task. Discarding the traditional theory of individual natural rights, Bledsoe elaborated an idea of natural law which was based on public good and which definitely restricted individual liberty. The greatest number of proslavery apologists, however, rejected the theory of natural rights. They insisted that any observation of the facts of nature was an obvious refutation of the doctrine, for which they substituted the historical or organic conceptions of social development.[108] Thus, interest led southern intellectuals to try their hand at refuting the natural-rights philosophy of Locke which, when put to work by radical abolitionists, threatened the institution of slavery.

In their onslaught the apologists for slavery were aided by conservative Northerners who for one reason or another had no liking for the natural-rights philosophy. No doubt many responded to new currents of thought, particularly the theories of Burke, the utilitarianism of Bentham, and the ideas of the German historical school, whose leader, Savigny, exerted considerable influence on American intellectuals. But at the same time, it is also true that these men were usually conservative by temperament and fearful lest extreme democratic tendencies should jeopardize the established rule of the wise, the good, and the well-to-do. Without completely renouncing all of Locke's political philosophy, John Quincy Adams in 1842 subjected the doctrine of the social compact to severe criticism. Appealing to historical facts, Adams demonstrated that the constitution of Massachusetts had been framed and adopted, not by all the citizens, but by only a certain portion, and that therefore the com-

---

[107] J. K. Paulding, *Slavery in the United States* (New York, 1863), pp. 42 ff.
[108] Albert Taylor Bledsoe, *Is Davis a Traitor?* (Baltimore, 1866), pp. 3–43, 142–143. For an excellent discussion of the proslavery criticism of the natural-rights philosophy, see Wright, *American Interpretations of Natural Law*, pp. 216 ff.

monwealth could in no sense be thought of as democratic.[109] Another New Englander, Dr. Alexander H. Vinton, rector of St. Paul's Church, Boston, in his election sermon of 1848 criticized Locke's theory and concluded that the checks which we had established in our constitutional framework might not be adequate to protect order, duty, proprieties, and established values generally against radical interpretations of the doctrine of natural rights.[110]

In conservative hands Locke's doctrine of the right of revolution was also qualified, and even denied, when established interests seemed to be threatened. A study of more than a hundred Fourth of July orations and sermons emanating from groups specifically devoted to the existing economic order enables us for the first time to understand the reasons advanced for whittling away the doctrine of the right of revolution.[111] It is important, in analyzing this fugitive literature, to show the connection between the arguments on the one hand, and, on the other, the class background, training, and position in society of the authors, as well as the specific occasions of the addresses. When this is done, it very frequently becomes clear that idea and interest were fairly obviously and directly related.

In the years following the conclusion of peace with England in 1783, the Revolution was interpreted in the majority of Fourth of July orations in such a way as to temper the abstract right of revolution itself. Economic depression reminded everyone of the sacrifices which the Revolution had cost, and, at least until 1786, times remained hard. It was therefore natural for ministers and orators to insist that the men of '76 had appealed to the sword only after every other recourse had been tried, and that the right of revolution has been resorted to most reluctantly.[112] Since society was torn by fac-

[109] John Quincy Adams, *The Social Compact, Exemplified in the Constitution of the Commonwealth of Massachusetts* (Providence, 1842), pp. 8 ff.

[110] Dr. Alexander H. Vinton, *The Religious Theory of Civil Government* . . . (Boston, 1848), pp. 15 ff.

[111] In a subsequent study a detailed consideration of this literature will substantiate the analysis that follows.

[112] David Osgood, A.M., *Reflections on the goodness of God in supporting the People of the United States through the late war* (Boston, 1784), pp. 27–31.

tions, it was also desirable for orators and ministers to insist that the Revolution had been carried out by an overwhelming majority[113] —Locke had made that a condition of a justifiable revolution. Little or nothing is to be found in the Fourth of July orations regarding the Tory opposition. And, save for avowed radicals (who were much less frequently called on to make addresses that found their way into print), little is said of the social changes and democratic upheaval which were unmistakably a part of the Revolution. Following Locke, the typical Fourth of July orator insisted that civil society had been in no way affected by the long years of the struggle. Such an attitude would obviously tend to counteract antifederalist restlessness and the rumblings of agrarian revolts in Massachusetts and Pennsylvania.

It was this belief that the American Revolution had been political and not social that caused preachers and orators to contrast at great length the American revolt against England and the French Revolution. With unceasing reiteration conservatives, taking their cue no doubt from Burke, denounced the anarchy, atheism, and violence of the events taking place in France, in comparison with what they insisted was the orderly, calm, and virtually bloodless procedure of the men of '76. Fear of enthusiasm for the social principles of the French Revolution led a great number of orators and preachers to paint the French Revolution and its aftermath in the blackest possible terms. Long after France had achieved relative stability, Americans made her revolution a warning against a similar occurrence here.[114] And, although they had greeted with enthusiasm the

---

[113] Idem, A Discourse delivered February 19, 1795 (Boston, 1795), p. 20; James P. Puglia, The Federal Politician (Philadelphia, 1795), pp. 159–162.

[114] Examples are John Wells, Esq., An Oration delivered on the Fourth of July, 1798, at St. Paul's Church (New York, 1798), p. 7; and John Lowell, An Oration, pronounced July 4, 1799, at the Request of the Inhabitants of the Town of Boston (Boston, 1799), pp. 6 ff. The Origin and Principles of the American Revolution, compared with the Origin and Principles of the French Revolution; Translated from the German of Gentz by an American Gentleman [J. Q. Adams] no doubt supplied much of the material for these arguments. The contrast continued, as, for instance, in Rev. John Gunnison, The Nation's Progress, or Licentiousness and Ruin . . . (Amesbury, 1836), p. 5; and Henry B. Stanton, Ultraists, Conservatives, Reformers (Utica, 1850), pp. 15 ff.

Spanish American revolutions, it became the thing to contrast the anarchy and chaos in the lands to the south of us with our own orderly way of winning independence.[115]

Close scrutiny of the Fourth of July orations and election sermons indicates that it was when the established order at home was overtly threatened by such insurrections as that led by Daniel Shays in 1785, and by the Whisky Boys a few years later, that clergymen, lawyers, and public men most carefully defined the right of revolution and hedged it about with heavy qualifications. In identifying the Shays affair and the Whisky revolt with insurrection, they were following Locke in his condemnation of minority factions and seditious riotings. Certainly the general tendency of the orations and sermons during these crises—the conservatives were far more articulate than the radicals—was to make inroads on the theory of the right of revolution.[116] This was notably true during the Dorr War in Rhode Island in 1842, and after the suppression of slave insurrections.[117]

In the forgotten literature emanating from conservative and even liberal sources, other factors and interests entered into the qualifica-

[115] For example, Henry W. Hilliard, *The Spirit of Liberty, An Oration* (Montgomery, Ala., 1860), p. 19.

[116] Rev. Joseph Lyman, *A Sermon preached before His Excellency James Bowdoin, Esq.* . . . *May 30, 1787* (Boston, 1787), *passim;* Jonathan Jackson, *Thoughts upon the Political Situation* (Worcester, 1788), pp. 50 ff.; David Daggett, *An Oration, New Haven, July 4, 1787* (New Haven, 1787), p. 14; Elizur Goodrich, *The Principles of Civil Union and Happiness Considered and Recommended, A Sermon* (Hartford, 1787), pp. 22 ff.; William White, D.D., *A Sermon on the Reciprocal Influence of Civil Policy and Religious Duty* (Philadelphia, 1795), p. 30; John McKnight, D.D., *The Divine Goodness to the United States of America* (New York, 1795), pp. 14–15; Samuel Kendall, *A Sermon on the day of National Thanksgiving, Feb. 19, 1795* (Boston, 1795), p. 23; John Murray, *The Substance of a Thanksgiving Sermon* (Boston, 1795), pp. 19 ff.

[117] Elisha Potter, *Considerations on the Questions of the Adoption of a Constitution and Extension of Suffrage in Rhode Island* (Boston, 1842), pp. 6 ff.; Rev. Mark Tucker, D.D., *The Deliverance of Rhode Island* . . . (Providence, 1842), pp. 7 ff.; John Robert Godley, *Letters from America* (London, 1844, 2 vols.), II, 208; Joseph S. Pitman, *Report of the Trial of Thomas Wilson Dorr* . . . (Boston, 1844), pp. 79 ff.; William G. Goddard, *An Address to the People of Rhode Island* . . . (Providence, 1843), pp. 27 ff.; *An Address to the People of Rhode Island, from the Convention Assembled at Providence* . . . (Providence, 1834).

tion of the right of revolution. Pious ministers declared that happiness depends, not on the form of government, but on individual righteousness.[118] Expounders of the Constitution insisted that our form of government made further appeal to revolution entirely unnecessary, or even absolutely criminal. Some observed that the American government was a contract, not between governors and governed, but between the governed themselves.[119] In such a government of laws, in such a popular and democratic type of polity, revolution had no place. Others observed that the federal system, by allocating considerable power to the states, prevented encroachments on the part of central authority: nullification was always a remedy when things went too far in the direction of consolidation. Still others maintained that the frequency of elections, the independence of our judiciary, and the possibility of easily amending the Constitution rendered revolution needless.[120] In the first decades of the nation's history it seems clear that all these arguments were prominent because of the general fear that the federal experiment might not prove successful, and that chaos and economic backsliding might replace the newly established central authority and the prosperity associated with it.

As time went on, other arguments, taken from dominant currents of thought, were mustered for service against the particular theory of Locke which was now increasingly uncongenial to controlling interests that favored the existing order. No idea appealed to Americans in the first half of the nineteenth century more than the doc-

118 Miller, A Sermon . . . July 4, 1793, p. 14.

119 Joseph Lathrop, A.M., A Sermon, Preached in the First Parish Church in West Springfield, Dec. 14, 1787 (Springfield, 1787), p. 8.

120 Abiel Holmes, A.M., A Sermon on the Freedom and Happiness of America . . . (Boston, 1795), pp. 10–11; Thomas Brockway, A.M., America Saved, A Thanksgiving Sermon, Preached in Lebanon (Hartford, 1784?), pp. 21 ff.; Andrew Lee's Election Sermon (Hartford, 1795), p. 20; Mathew Carey, Information to Europeans who are disposed to migrate to the United States (Philadelphia, 1790), p. 11; John A. M'Clung, Oration, delivered at Lexington, Kentucky, on the 22d of February, 1844 (Maysville, Ky., 1844), p. 19; Nathaniel Chipman, Sketches of the Principles of Government (Rutland, Vt., 1793), p. 291; Samuel Kendall, A Sermon, delivered on the day of National Thanksgiving (Boston, 1795), p. 19; Speeches of Mr. Silas Wood of New York, on the Proposition to amend the Constitution of the United States (Washington, 1826), pp. 6 ff.

trine of progress; what had been a pleasant theory in Europe seemed to be a patent fact in the rapidly expanding and developing civilization of the New World. Samuel Tyler, a member of the Maryland bar, declared in an essay (1844) that divine wisdom had decreed that restraints on man were to be thrown off, not all at once, but separately as he advanced in mental and moral improvement.[121] Disciples of science quoted both Bacon and Newton to the same effect. The marvelous order governing the universe seemed to deny the idea of revolution.

In the constitution of the material universe we have not failed to discover proofs of the most perfect order. From the beauties of proportion, and the harmonies of arrangement, and the mutual adaptations existing between its diversified parts, and between each part and the whole, arises the inference, that to warrant the introduction of a new principle into its operations would require a new modeling of the entire whole.[122]

It was this faith in order, plan, development within an existing framework, that led sensitive men and women to look to reform, rather than to revolution, as a remedy for existing abuses. "Let us remember," Noah Webster had admonished in 1798, "that force never makes a convert; that no amelioration of society can be wrought by violence; and that an attempt to reform men by compulsion must produce more calamities than benefits."[123] As reform got under way in the first decades of the nineteenth century, revolution was pushed more and more into the background. "A prudent man," the Reverend Joseph McKean pointed out in his election sermon before the governor of Massachusetts in 1800, "will not set fire to his house, and thereby endanger the lives of his family, because some parts are not so perfectly convenient, or some of its proportions not so agreeable to the eye, as they might be made in a

---

[121] Tyler, *A Discourse*, pp. 2 ff.

[122] Amos Dean, A.M., *Address delivered before the Albany Institute, April 3, 1833* (Albany, 1833), p. 1.

[123] Noah Webster, Jr., *An Oration Pronounced before the Citizens of New-Haven on the Anniversary of the Independence of the United States, July 4th, 1798* (New Haven, 1798), p. 13.

new edifice."[124] This refrain became a familiar one, and no doubt tended to help substitute the doctrine of gradualism for that of revolution.[125] Although we meet with this argument in the literature of all reform movements, it was, as might be expected, especially evident in that of the peace movement.[126]

Two circumstances help to explain the growing reliance on reform as a substitute for revolution. In the first place, as a result of faith in reason and enlightenment, sponsors of public schools spread the word that mass education, by raising the general level of intelligence, would remedy social abuses which might otherwise result in revolution.[127] In the second place, it was generally believed that the existence of free lands provided a safety valve for discontent. Even though this belief may not have been well grounded, it must nevertheless have tended to make people think less in terms of revolution and more in terms of education and gradual reform as possible means of social amelioration.[128] Occasionally, fear was expressed that, once free lands were exhausted, proletarian discontent might lead to a reign of terror.[129] This fear was particularly strong in the minds of Southerners who were horrified at Fourierism and other radical social and economic doctrines, and who looked with dismay on the establishment in Paris of national workshops during the revolutionary days of 1848.[130]

[124] Joseph McKean, A.M., *A Sermon, May 28, 1800, being the day of General Election* (Boston, 1800), p. 24.

[125] *The Works of Orestes A. Brownson, XIV,* 33–34; Byrdsall, *Loco-Foco or Equal Rights Party,* p. 74, *passim.*

[126] George E. Ellis, *An Oration delivered at Charlestown, Massachusetts, on the 17th of June, 1841* (Boston, 1841), p. 69; Merle Curti, *The American Peace Crusade, 1815–1861* (Durham, N.C., 1929), pp. 52–53.

[127] Curti, *The Social Ideas of American Educators,* pp. 79–81, 191.

[128] Henry Duhring, *Remarks on the United States of America, with regard to the Actual State of Europe* (London, 1833), p. 23; Edward D. Barber, *An Oration, delivered before the Democrats of Washington County, at Montpelier, on the Fourth of July 1839* (Montpelier, 1839), pp. 15–18.

[129] George Fitzhugh, *Cannibals All or, Slaves without Masters* (Richmond, 1857), p. 61.

[130] *Ibid.,* pp. xiv, 54–55; *Addresses, delivered on Thursday, Dec. 18, 1851, on the occasion of the inauguration of the Rev. Robert L. Staunton, as President of Oakland College, Mississippi* (New Orleans, 1852), p. 17; B. J. Barbour, of Orange County, Virginia, *An Address delivered before the Literary Societies of*

At the same time that these forces were diminishing the once generally cherished idea of the right of revolution, a still more powerful force was at work with similar effect; for, as an examination of Fourth of July orations clearly indicates, the tradition of the Revolution gave way before the spirit of nationalism and patriotism.[131] Our revolution was regarded solely as the instrument by which our nationalism had come into existence. Once the historic mission of revolution had been fulfilled, once we were a nation, there could no longer be any use for revolution. It might even jeopardize the dearly bought nationalism which had not yet been consolidated.

In 1861, when the southern states determined to embark on their separate path as a new nation, they chiefly justified their action by the doctrine of the right of secession, rather than by that of revolution. The idea of revolution was now in such bad odor that relatively few appealed to "the great Mr. Locke," whose theory of revolution had once done such good service.[132] Some Northerners sought, on the one hand, to identify secession with revolution and to condemn it as such, but, on the other, denied that it was at all analogous to what happened in 1776.

the *Virginia Military Institute, at Lexington, on the 4th of July, 1854* (Richmond, 1854), p. 8.

[131] Good examples are P. I. Vanpelt, A.M., *The Goodness of God, to be Praised by Men. A Discourse delivered on the Fourth of July* (New York, 1812); and T. S. Grimke, *Oration on . . . the 4th of July*, [1833] (Charleston, 1833), pp. 19 ff.

[132] For a treatment making a clear distinction between the right of revolution and the right of secession, see John Randolph Tucker, *An Address delivered before the Society of Alumni of the University of Virginia* (Richmond, 1851), p. 60. For advocates of the appeal to the right of revolution, both North and South, see Dwight Lowell Dumond, *Southern Editorials on Secession* (New York, 1931), pp. 167–168; T. L. Nichols, *Forty Years of American Life* (2nd ed., London, 1874), pp. 327–338; *Union, Slavery, Secession; Letter from Governor R. K. Call, of Florida to John S. Littell, of Germantown, Pennsylvania* (Philadelphia, 1861), pp. 25–27; Jesse T. Carpenter, *The South as a Conscious Minority* (New York, 1930), pp. 194–200; *State Sovereignty and the Doctrine of Coercion, by the Hon. William D. Porter, together with a Letter from Hon. J. K. Paulding, former Secretary of the Navy. The Right to Secede by States* (1860 Tract Association, Tract No. 2 [n.p., n.d.]), pp. 26–27. An interesting discussion of the Civil War as a "civil revolution of states" is that of Henry A. Wise in his *Seven Decades of the Union* (Philadelphia, 1881), pp. 252 ff.

Thus it was that, after the Revolution, various growing interests, particularly when challenged by competing ones, led to the qualification of Locke's idea of the right of revolution. In spite of the radicalism of much of Locke's political thought in the seventeenth and eighteenth centuries, it is plain that he himself would in general have approved of the qualifications of the natural-rights philosophy and of the doctrine of the right of revolution, which had been made in order functionally to serve dominant interests in the existing pattern of political and social arrangements. For in considerable part the sanctity of property rights was to Locke the chief reason and justification for the substitution of civil society and government for the original state of nature.[133] It was likewise the sanctity of property rights which in his mind largely warranted men in making a revolution against a government jeopardizing them.[134] Therefore he would have discountenanced attempts to apply his theory of the right of revolution to lend validity to movements to abridge or annihilate property rights.

Locke's belief that the preservation of property was the chief end of government had even more important social implications.[135] In declaring that whatsoever a person "hath mixed his labor with and joined it to something that is his own" was a sacred right, to be protected by government, Locke laid the foundations of the concept of economic laissez faire as well as of the theory that property, being a crystallization of personal achievement, is never to be lightly dissociated from private ownership. Although Locke himself defined property broadly and probably did not intend to give it the general and sweeping sanctity with which it was subsequently endowed,[136] his doctrine became the gospel of liberty and property, in close as-

[133] *Of Civil Government. Two Treatises,* pp. 129 ff., 228 ff.

[134] *Ibid.,* pp. 224 ff.

[135] For an excellent discussion of the conservative social implications of Locke's political theory for the nineteenth century, see C. E. Vaughan, *Studies in the History of Political Philosophy before and after Rousseau* (Manchester, England, 1925), pp. 168 ff.

[136] Larkin, *Property in the Eighteenth Century,* pp. 145 ff.

sociation. For this development the march of events, which he could not have foreseen, must be chiefly blamed.[137]

It is hardly defensible to attach too much weight to Locke's justification of property rights as he understood them, nor to assume that without his ideas on this subject events in nineteenth-century America would have shaped themselves in any fundamentally different way. Yet it is pertinent to note that Locke's theories of property influenced the thoughts and actions of the framers of the Constitution and the advocates of the stake-in-society theory of economics during the Jacksonian period. In other words, advocates of property rights found work for Locke's ideas. When Chancellor Kent was particularly concerned over the dangers to property which he feared the movement for an extension of suffrage involved, he declared, "Give me the writings of Addison and Locke."[138] It is only necessary to examine the writings of such Federalists as Fisher Ames and such Whigs as Daniel Webster to note the similarity between their conceptions of property rights, individualism, and laissez faire and the teachings of Locke. In the debates of the state constitutional conventions which convened to discuss the enlargement of the suffrage, one finds clearly stated the Lockean-Federalist principle that "the great and chief end therefore of men's uniting into commonwealths, and putting themselves under governments, is the preservation of their property."[139] Locke was quoted in those conventions, to the effect that men possessed of property must have power over those who were not.

In a pioneer society, with an abundance of free lands, the individualistic interpretations of the functions of government were not without their progressive, liberal connotations; but in an industrial, stratified society, the case was quite different, for there

[137] This idea is elaborated by Walton H. Hamilton, in an article (*Yale Law Journal* [April, 1932], XLI, 864 ff.) in which he defends Locke against some of the criticisms made by Larkin, *Property in the Eighteenth Century.*

[138] William Kent, *Memoirs and Letters of James Kent, LL.D.* (Boston, 1898), p. 219.

[139] Dixon Ryan Fox, *The Decline of Aristocracy in the Politics of New York* (New York, 1919), pp. 249–250.

Locke's highly individualistic, laissez-faire conception of government and his regard for property rights could only check the development of social legislation and sanctify the accumulation of corporate wealth. Walton H. Hamilton has pointed out that Mr. Justice Sutherland, in condemning as unconstitutional an act of Congress regulating the conditions of labor of women in the District of Columbia, revealed a train of thought similar to that of Locke; even an occasional turn of expression was reminiscent of the seventeenth-century thinker.[140] Without laboring the point, or attempting to establish any personal influence of Locke, it is clear, as Professor Hamilton has suggested, that here we have a continuing stream of thought. This is only one of the indications that Locke's influence remained vital long after the period with which this paper has been chiefly concerned.

"The great Mr. Locke" in a real sense remained America's philosopher, in spite of all the competition of new ideas. And he remained America's philosopher because many of his concepts were useful to interests in the tasks at hand. Above all, it is plain that many of his ideas admirably suited the needs of the more dominant American interests. His philosophy was practical and yet general; it appeared to be liberal, without endangering the individualistic conception of social relations and property rights. Moreover, his essential philosophy had the merit of emphasizing specific facts rather than general presuppositions. In varying degrees this emphasis served both conservatives and reformers. Clearly, Locke's thought—religious, educational, metaphysical, and political—survived to the degree that there was work for it to do; and those aspects of his philosophy which were functional to the needs of ascendant interests were destined to have the longest history.

[140] *Yale Law Journal* (April, 1932), *XLI*, 864 ff.

5

Francis Lieber
and Nationalism (1941)

MY PAMPHLET *Nationalism*,"[1] wrote Francis Lieber two years before his death in 1872, "will be found sticking in my bones, instead of marrow, when I am dead and people should take the trouble of applying the cleaver to my shins."[2] It is quite true that the thought compressed in this little pamphlet was indeed the very marrow of Lieber's bones. Nor is it any less true that his contribution to the philosophy of American nationalism in particular, and of nationalism in general, was of far greater importance than either students of Lieber or of nationalism have generally been aware.

When, in 1827, Francis Lieber began the task of Americanizing himself, of analyzing the problem of nationalism in the United States, and of contributing to its furtherance, he was not, of course, breaking virgin soil. Other immigrants before him—Alexander

---

[1] The full title is *Fragments of Political Science on Nationalism and Internationalism* (New York, 1868). The pamphlet, portions of which had appeared elsewhere (*American Presbyterian and Theological Review*, n.s., April, 1868, VI, 304–305), was dedicated to General Grant. K. S. Pinson, in his *Bibliographical Introduction to Nationalism* (New York, 1935), refers to it as the first American publication on the theory of nationalism. An edition in Spanish, translated by the Mexican Minister to the United States, was published in New York in 1870.

[2] Francis Lieber to Charles Sumner, New York, January 25, 1870, in Lieber Collection (Huntington Library). This collection (which will hereinafter be cited as the Huntington Collection) has been described by C. R. Robson in *The Huntington Library Bulletin* (February, 1933), No. 3, pp. 135–155.

Hamilton, Mathew Carey, and Albert Gallatin come at once to mind—had become stanch nationalists and had contributed to the growth of American nationalism, or to its theoretical exposition. Native-born Americans, including Tench Coxe, Noah Webster, Jeremy Belknap, Jedidiah Morse, and Henry C. Carey, together with such poets and critics as Joel Barlow, Philip Freneau, William Ellery Channing, and C. J. Ingersoll, had formulated concepts of American nationalism.[3] A unique past and a unique future, a distinctive people, a God-given and a God-blessed topography designed for the glorious experiment to which Americans were dedicating themselves—all these ideas had figured in the discussion.[4] Innumerable parsons and Fourth of July orators had popularized the idea that America differed from Europe not only in possessing republican institutions but in being designed by Providence to achieve the glorious mission of realizing the natural rights of man to life, liberty, property, and happiness.[5] Countless writers and

[3] For discussions of the nationalism of these and other figures, see A. O. Hansen, *Liberalism and American Education in the Eighteenth Century* (New York, 1926); Harry Warfel, *Noah Webster, Schoolmaster to America* (New York, 1936); C. W. Cole, "Jeremy Belknap: Pioneer Nationalist," *New England Quarterly* (December, 1937), X, 743–751; H. H. Clark, "Nationalism and American Literature," *The University of Toronto Quarterly* (July, 1933), II, 492–519; J. C. McCloskey, "The Campaign of Periodicals after the War of 1812 for a National American Literature," *PMLA* (March, 1935), L, 262–273; R. W. Bolwell, "Concerning the Study of Nationalism in American Literature," *American Literature* (January, 1939), X, 406–416; H. Hutcheson, *Tench Coxe: A Study in American Economic Development* (Baltimore, 1938); K. A. Rowe, *Mathew Carey: A Study in American Economic Development* (Baltimore, 1933).

[4] For typical examples, see Ezra Stiles, *The United States Elevated to Glory and Honor* (New Haven, 1783); S. S. Smith, *An Essay on the Causes of the Variety of Complexion and Figure in the Human Species* (Philadelphia, 1787); J. P. Johnson, *An Oration on Union . . .* (New York, 1794); Samuel Dickinson, *An Oration, in Celebration of American Independence . . .* (Northampton, Mass., 1797); Abiel Abbot, *Traits of Resemblance in the People of the United States of America to Ancient Israel* (Haverhill, Mass., 1799).

[5] See, e.g.: Elnathan Winchester, *A Plain Political Catechism* (Greenfield, Mass., 1796); F. W. Hotchkiss, *On National Greatness: A Thanksgiving Sermon . . .* (New Haven, 1793); Enoch Huntington, *Political Wisdom, or Honesty the Best Policy* (Middletown, Conn., 1786), p. 16; Samuel Austin, *An Oration, Pronounced at Worcester on the Fourth of July, 1798* (Worcester, Mass., 1798); De Witt Clinton, *An Oration, on Benevolence, Delivered before the Society of Black Friars, in the City of New York* (New York, 1795); Mrs. Mercy Warren, *Poems, Dramatic and Miscellaneous* (Boston, 1790), p. 101; Tunis Wortman,

speakers in addresses before the literary societies of colleges had reëchoed these sentiments and proclaimed the doctrine, so dear to magazine editors, that America must also achieve a distinctive literature and culture.[6] Foreign visitors had written at length about American nationalism and patriotism.[7]

To these materials for a synthesis of American nationalistic philosophy must be added *The Federalist,* Hamilton's basic writings on economic nationalism, and Kent's *Commentaries on American Law* (1826–1830), as well as Marshall's great decisions. No systematic treatise had appeared, however, when Francis Lieber established himself in America in 1827. Indeed, apart from Tocqueville's *Democracy in America,* which met many but by no means all the specifications of an analysis of American nationality and nationalism, no elaborate or formal treatise on the subject was written until after the fate of American nationalism was settled by Lee's surrender at Appomattox.

It was not Lieber who wrote this formal treatise;[8] nor, indeed, did he write anything comparable in scope to at least two other volumes which appeared between the collapse of the Confederacy and his death in 1872.[9] Yet in spite of these considerations it was Francis

---

An Oration on the Influence of Social Institutions on Human Morals . . . (New York, 1796).

[6] For interesting examples, see Erastus Root, *An Introduction to Arithmetic* (Norwich, Conn., 1796); Simeon Baldwin, *An Oration, Pronounced before the Citizens of New Haven, July 4th, 1788* (New Haven, 1788); James Marsh, *An Address* . . . (Burlington, Vt., 1826).

[7] Examples are Filippo Mazzei, *Recherches historiques et politiques sur les États-Unis de l'Amérique Septentrionale* (Paris, 1788, 4 vols.), II, 32; IV, 1–10; Ferdinand Bayard, *Voyage dans l'intérieur des États-Unis* . . . (Paris [1798]), p. 191; W. Winterbotham, *An Historical, Geographical, Commercial and Philosophical View of the United States of America* . . . (New York, 1796, 4 vols.), I, 585–586; Charles William Janson, *The Stranger in America* . . . (London, 1807), pp. 284–285.

[8] Orestes A. Brownson, *The American Republic; Its Constitution, Tendencies and Destiny* (New York, 1866).

[9] J. W. Draper, *Thoughts on the Future Civil Policy of America* (New York, 1865); and Elisha Mulford, *The Nation: The Foundations of Civil Order and Political Life in the United States* (New York, 1870). J. C. Hurd did not publish his masterly study, *The Theory of our National Existence as Shown by the Action of the Growth of the United States since 1861,* until the year 1881. Had Lieber lived to read it, he would have been impressed by the way in which Hurd's com-

Lieber, not Orestes A. Brownson, not John Draper, not Elisha Mulford, who may be regarded as the most significant figure during the period in articulating and promoting among intellectuals and public men a theory of nationalism in general and of American nationalism in particular.

One explanation, no doubt, of the failure of students of American nationalism and of Lieber[10] to assess his contributions in this field lies in the fact that his writing on nationality and nationalism was scattered through three formal treatises which in the main were devoted to other themes in political science. Much also appeared in occasional essays, addresses, and reviews, and an even larger proportion of what Lieber said on nationalism must be gleaned from his extensive and largely unpublished correspondence in the Huntington Library.[11] The purpose of this essay is to suggest an explanation of Lieber's intense and lifelong interest in nationalism, to assemble and to interpret his ideas on that subject, and, finally, to assess, so far as possible, the importance of his contribution to the philosophy of nationalism.

I

Francis Lieber's interest in nationalism was born of his experiences as a child and a youth. When Napoleon's troops entered Berlin on

prehensive conception of nationalism resembled his own. Of the writings on American nationalism which appeared between the victory of the North in 1865 and his death, Lieber expressed special interest in the work of Mulford, an Episcopalian clergyman who applied Hegel's political philosophy to the development of American civilization. (Lieber to Sumner, September 11, 1870; April 14, 1871 (New York), in Huntington Collection.)

[10] T. S. Perry, *The Life and Letters of Francis Lieber* (Boston, 1882), should be supplemented by L. R. Harley, *Francis Lieber: His Life and Political Philosophy* (New York, 1899). See also C. S. Phinney, *Francis Lieber's Influence on American Thought and Some of His Unpublished Letters* (Philadelphia, 1918); and L. M. Sears, "The Human Side of Francis Lieber," *South Atlantic Quarterly* (January, 1928), XXVII, 42–61. The best account to date (1941) is that of Joseph Dorfman and Rexford Tugwell, "Francis Lieber: German Scholar in America," *Columbia University Quarterly* (September, December, 1938), XXX, 161–293. See also Vernon L. Parrington, *The Romantic Revolution in America, 1800–1860* (New York, 1927), pp. 93–98.

[11] The larger part of the research for this paper was done at the Huntington Library. I wish to express my indebtedness to the Library for its generosity in making possible this and other researches which I engaged in there, and to thank its staff for innumerable kindnesses.

October 26, 1806, some of them, hearing vehement sobs, looked up at the window from which they came. So poignant was the grief of the six-year-old lad at the defeat of his country at Jena, and at the humiliation which the military occupation symbolized, that his father had to remove him from the window by force.[12]

Within a few years the youth's patriotism and zeal for German freedom and unification were being strengthened by his gymnastic master, Friedrich Ludwig Jahn, the great promoter of national regeneration. Like other German boys, Lieber was fired with enthusiasm for the liberation of his country from the French and for the unification of its distracted fragments. Though a mere stripling, he took part in the Battle of Waterloo, and was severely wounded. But the Congress of Vienna neither united Germany nor insured it freedom, and Lieber, with other liberal students, continued the struggle against the reactionary Metternich regime. Hounded out of the land by the Prussian police, Lieber was forced to abandon his efforts to help achieve the unification of Germany along liberal lines.[13] When, after a long residence in America, he returned to his native land in 1849 to be of what aid he could in the liberal movement for national unity, he once more met with defeat.

Lieber's love for his homeland—his regret that Germany did not throughout the middle of the nineteenth century achieve national unification—was a basic factor in his life. "In early manhood," he remarked in 1854, "I once wrote to a friend that I considered it the highest blessing if a man could study the history of his country with pleasure and with pride, and live among institutions which lead him back to the earliest history of his country, as is the case with an Englishman. It is a fountain of manliness. And it is a crushing burden if the earnest study of the history of one's own people can only fill the heart with grief."[14] And, in the same year, he wrote to George Hillard, a Boston lawyer to whom he was much attached:

[12] Francis Lieber to Hamilton Fish, October 26, 1870, in Hamilton Fish Papers (Library of Congress).

[13] To the frustration imposed on his spirit by the failure of the liberal movement to unify Germany after Napoleon's downfall was the added disappointment of his experience in Greece, to which he went in 1821 as a crusader for that country's struggle for national freedom.

[14] Perry, Lieber, p. 274.

"Can you not imagine how deeply a native German must feel again that bitter truth which envenoms his whole life, the sad historic fact that Germany had been cheated out of her noble birthright of being a great and manly nation . . . ?"[15]

Again and again Lieber returned to this theme. And, moreover, ambitious as he was both academically and politically, he felt that his talents would have been more fully realized and honored had he been able to live in a nationally united and parliamentary Germany. As a disciple of the liberal nationalism of the early nineteenth century, Lieber hated to see unification effected by autocratic methods. Yet he was so thoroughly convinced that national unity was the inevitable and desirable goal that he persuaded himself, when Bismarck at last achieved unification through "blood and iron," that the end justified the means. But his joy was quickly diminished: he had to justify the course of events to his American friends, who disapproved of "blood and iron" and who looked with concern on the annexation of the Rhineland provinces.[16] Thus it is plain that Lieber's personal career, from cradle to grave, was constantly affected by the problems involved in struggles for national unity in his homeland.

When Lieber migrated to the United States in 1827, he was disappointed to find that national unity had been achieved there only in name. Having been deeply stirred by the nationalistic movement in Germany and having been defeated in his efforts to help realize national unity, he was more sensitive than many immigrants, and than many native-born Americans, to the fact that the United States was torn by sectional strife. Although Lieber rejoiced in much that America offered and, as we shall see, helped to make articulate in the minds of native-born Americans a definite concep-

[15] *Ibid.*, p. 272. Lieber wrote similarly to friends in Germany, e.g., he thus expressed himself to Karl Joseph Anton Mittermaier: "What a glorious country it [Germany] might be, if the true standard were not wanting—if we had a *national life*" (Lieber to Mittermaier, February 14, 1841, in Huntington Collection).

[16] "What Peace Germany Ought to Make," in New York *Evening Post*, September 14, 1870; Lieber to James Garfield, January 30, 1871, in Garfield Papers (Library of Congress); Perry, *Lieber*, p. 140.

tion of American nationalism, even the American experience was only a partial compensation for his disappointment in the failure of German nationalists. In the first place, Lieber never forgot and never was allowed to forget that he was not a native-born American. Marooned at South Carolina College, he made relentless and even desperate efforts to obtain an appointment at Harvard or Columbia.[17] To the objection of certain trustees at the latter institution that a foreigner should not be given a professorship, Lieber, writing to Samuel Ruggles, himself a trustee, remarked: "If a man throws himself at the foot of an altar of a foreign country; if he does not merely settle in foreign parts for gain, but makes that country his, he weds her, and as a man clings faster to his wife than even to father and mother, so he who does by choice what chance does for the native citizen. Having left his country, he is conscious that if he does not cleave to his wedded country, he floats in unsettled loneliness, and every generous heart requires a *country*, a soil to grow firm in."[18]

Notwithstanding Lieber's staunch Americanism, Know-Nothingism plagued him. And even in the last years of his life, the old bugbear would not down. When he hankered for an ambassadorship, his foreign birth was held against him. "I have a better right," he wrote protestingly to Sumner in 1869, "to say *Civis Americanus sum* than great Paul had to say to the Centurion *Civis Romanus sum*. Let me see—I am an older full citizen than the President, and perhaps came to this country a longer time ago than Grant came into it. If I am not an American, Hamilton, after whom Fish is called, never was one. Tell this to the President."[19]

But it was not alone Lieber's continued sensitiveness about his foreign birth that made him regard his adopted country as an only partially satisfying compensation for his failure and that of his

[17] Dorfman and Tugwell, "Francis Lieber: German Scholar in America," *loc. cit.*, pp. 267 ff.

[18] Lieber to Ruggles, September 14, 1842, in Lieber Papers (Library of Congress).

[19] Lieber to Sumner, December 11, 1869, in Huntington Collection. Lieber wrote in much the same way to Hamilton Fish, Secretary of State (Lieber to Fish, March 18, 1869, in Fish Papers, Library of Congress).

associates to unite Germany after Waterloo. The fact that from many points of view the United States had not achieved a genuine nationalism was not only emotionally depressing but personally uncomfortable. During his residence in South Carolina, from 1835 to 1856, he had too little sympathy with slavery and states' rights to feel at home, to feel that *this* was *his* country. And the fact that he did not dare to jeopardize his academic position at South Carolina College by making his sentiments altogether clear resulted in the alienation of certain of his northern friends, especially Sumner.

Even when he had identified himself thoroughly with the cause of the North, after he became a professor at Columbia in 1857, Lieber was not entirely free from a sense of insecurity which he associated with the absence of a fully matured nationalism. When, at the end of the Civil War, a committee of the trustees of Columbia tried to oust him, Lieber was convinced that it was because he had been "a plain uncompromising Union man who does not believe in *double allegiance* but who most studiously avoids all existing things within the walls. Am I forsooth to be sent away from Columbia Col. because so *'confoundedly national'?*"[20] Though other factors no doubt weighed more heavily in the minds of the trustees than Lieber's accentuated nationalism, in his judgment it was that, and that alone, which lay at the root of the trouble. In short, the fact that the America with which he had identified himself lacked national unity, and that this in truth was not only a cause of emotional frustration but a source of personal insecurity, explains much in Lieber. "Why was I saved at Waterloo?" he asked a friend, in 1856, when he despaired of the possibility of maintaining the national union.[21]

In analyzing Lieber's thought on nationalism it is worth noting, to begin with, that he subscribed in a general way to the so-called historical school. He repudiated, with other exponents of that position, the contract origin of society and the state, and explained

[20] Copy of a letter from Lieber to President King, June 9, 1865, in Lieber Papers (Library of Congress).
[21] Perry, *Lieber*, p. 290. See also a letter written to Allibone in 1860, cited in Harley, *Lieber*, p. 161.

institutions, including the national state, in terms of a long, gradual historical process. But, if he repudiated Rousseau, Jefferson, and other liberal exponents of the contract theory and of much else in the thought of the Enlightenment, he did not, on the other hand, see eye to eye with the more conservative exponents of the historical school. He rejected, for example, Hegel's social philosophy and theory of nationalism. Julia Ward Howe heard Lieber, early in his American period, report unfavorably on the lectures he had attended in Hegel's classroom at the University of Berlin.[22] In addition to referring, on another occasion, to Hegel's arrogance and presumption, to his disregard for facts, Lieber also explicitly rejected his belief in a " 'spirit of the people,' *per se,* existing as a thing in itself. . . ." He likewise thought Hegel's "spirit of history," as an independent, separate entity, was nonsense.[23] Nor did he approve of the Hegel-like way in which George Bancroft glorified the American Revolution as the greatest culminating event in the historical struggle for freedom: the preceding English struggle in the seventeenth century appeared, in fact, the high point in that monumental contest.[24]

In Lieber's own mind he was the first to advance certain ideas in regard to nationalism.[25] He had suggested in his *Manual of Political Ethics,*[26] and more thoroughly developed in his treatise *On Civil Liberty and Self-Government,*[27] the doctrine that in modern times there are several leading nations, in contrast with the ancient world, in which one leading state dominated all the others. By its very nature, then, he reasoned, modern civilization demands both nations and long-living nations; and, in consequence of this, modern nations possess a recuperative power entirely unknown to states in

[22] *The Critic* (December 30, 1882), II, 251.

[23] Lieber to Mittermaier, September 13, 1834, in Huntington Collection; Lieber to Sumner, December (after the 25th), 1864, *ibid.*; Perry, *Lieber,* p. 412.

[24] Lieber to Hillard, January 21, 1842, in Huntington Collection.

[25] Memorandum for Sumner, Sept. 1, 1867, in Huntington Collection.

[26] *Manual of Political Ethics* (Boston, 1838–1839, 2 vols.), II, 500–501, 656. This work was used as a textbook at Harvard College.

[27] *On Civil Liberty and Self-Government* (Philadelphia, 1853). This was used as a textbook at Yale College.

the ancient world. Lieber also thought that he was the first to formulate the theory that "the national polity is the normal type of government of the present time."[28]

Sensitive as he was to the liberal German thought on nationalism, Lieber early distinguished between the nationalization of populations and the centralization of governments. "Centralization," he wrote in 1839, "is the convergence of all the rays of power into one central point; nationalization is the diffusion of the same life-blood through a system of arteries, throughout a body politic, indeed, it is the growing of the body politic as such, morally, and thoroughly cemented, out of a mass, otherwise uncemented."[29] This process, Lieber thought, resulted from an "instinctive social cohesion" which lay beneath and at the same time gave impulse to "the unconscious longing and revealing tendency of the people to form a nation, and to make the minor organization subservient to the great end of modern polity."[30] In ancient civilization the city-state and the universal monarchy sufficed as instruments for the necessary social cohesion. But universal monarchy, realized by Rome and later by Charlemagne, led to the reactionary and pulverizing process known as feudalism, which in turn had been largely replaced by the modern national state—the normal, characteristic expression, and the necessary one, of modern civilization.[31]

Although Lieber, in an interesting essay written in 1849,[32] indicated a general awareness of the existence of the cultural as well as political element in nationalism, he did not fully develop this concept until the Civil War period. In doing so he brought a fresh note into the American discussion of nationalism, which had

[28] Lieber to Sumner, August 28, 1867 (Washington), in Huntington Collection.

[29] *Manual of Political Ethics*, II, 497.

[30] *Two Lectures on the Constitution of the United States, Concluding a Course on the Modern State Delivered in the Law School of Columbia College, during the Winter of 1860 and 1861* (New York, 1861), p. 14.

[31] Lieber to Sumner, August 24, 1867, in Huntington Collection.

[32] "Anglican and Gallican Liberty," first published in a newspaper at Columbia, S. C., on June 7, 1849, appeared in translation in *Zeitschrift für ausländische Gesetzgebung* (1849), XXI Bd., 2 Hft. and was also included in *The Miscellaneous Writings of Francis Lieber* (Philadelphia, 1881, 2 vols.), II, 371–388.

largely but by no means exclusively been concerned with legal and constitutional problems.[33] A nation, he wrote to Sumner in 1867, when that statesman was engaged in preparing an address on the subject[34] (an address in which he borrowed heavily from Lieber), means "a large number of homogeneous people (. . . generally from 20 to 30 or 40 millions) with one prevailing language and literature, or permeating political organism and common law, inhabiting a continuous territory, and distinctly marked out by these from all other similar groups and fellow members of the same Civilisation."[35] In that complete sense the term possessed, clearly, anthropological as well as political meaning. He went on to insist that it always conveyed a meaning of consciousness of union. This consciousness of union—as was true of Germany and Italy before their unification—might be ethnological and cultural, rather than political. It might, on the other hand, be political rather than ethnological: such was the case in the United States, as it would be in Canada and Australia, neither of which possessed distinct languages and cultures.

Lieber's treatment of race as one of the ethnological-cultural elements in nationality was not without a certain haziness. If in contrasting the Celt and Teuton he did not explicitly declare that the differences between them were innate, he was led to reject the doctrine of the original unity of races when he observed the striking

[33] See, e.g.: George Perkins Marsh, The Goths in New England (Middlebury, Vt., 1843); O. J. Falnes, "New England and the Norsemen," New England Quarterly (June, 1938) X, 211–242; Rufus Choate, "American Nationality," in The Works of Rufus Choate (Boston, 1862, 2 vols.), II, 415 ff.; R. S. Storrs, The Puritan Scheme of National Growth (New York, 1858).

[34] Sumner's correspondence with Lieber throughout much of the year 1867 indicates that the Massachusetts senator was making heavy demands on Lieber for an address, "Are We a Nation?" delivered on November 19, 1867, at the New York Men's Republican Union, at Cooper Institute. Sumner made generous acknowledgments; see Works of Charles Sumner (Boston, 1870–1883, 15 vols.), XII, 191–249. See also Sumner's interesting anthology, designed to illustrate the growth of American self-consciousness, Prophetic Voices Concerning America (Boston, 1874).

[35] Lieber to Sumner, August 24, 1867, in Huntington Collection. Cf. Lieber's "Fragments of Political Science on Nationalism and Internationalism," in Miscellaneous Writings, II, 227.

dissimilarities between blacks and whites. "I believe in races as I believe in nations, families, and single brains, but I believe only in certain favorable elements which, under certain circumstances, can produce certain results; and no one can say what certain conditions of geographic and chronologic position, of intellectual succession, &c., &c. will produce." This was in 1850. He hastened to add that since the "Caucasian race" had produced great nations very late in time, such an achievement could not be laid at the door of innate mental superiority: in that case the brain of the Caucasian would have produced great effects before the Hindu and Egyptian brain.[36]

Yet Lieber, in thus eschewing a rigid, doctrinaire conception of racialism, never abandoned his conviction that the "Anglican race" possessed a peculiar gift that distinguished it from every other Teutonic people. Civil liberty made up its "very bones and marrow." The original Teutonic spirit did indeed, he thought, have much of the spirit of "manly individual independence and ungrudged enjoyment of individual humanity," in contrast with the Celtic tendency to be swayed by masses.[37] But the Anglican branch of the "Teutonic race" had succeeded in establishing civil guarantees of these principles. The "Gallican race," on the contrary, seemed peculiarly lacking in this gift.

But, when Napoleon III tried to popularize the idea that the French were a separate Latin race of superior ability, Lieber quickly rejected such a conception. The notion of a Latin race, he wrote, is a "professional error" clutched at by Napoleon as "a very serviceable thing."[38] Lieber had, during the Civil War, protested the southern claim that the people of the Confederacy constituted a race distinct from that of the North,[39] and as he pondered that claim, and the similar one of the French, he sensed at least some of the mischievous implications in racialism. "The word race," he wrote in 1871, "has probably been abused in modern times more than any other." Great and eminent nations such as the Greek and

[36] Lieber to Hillard, April, 1850, in Perry, *Lieber*, p. 245.
[37] *On Civil Liberty and Self-Government*, p. 54.
[38] Perry, *Lieber*, p. 397; see also New York *Evening Post*, August 30, 1871.
[39] *No Party Now but All for Our Country* (Loyal Publication Society, No. 16; New York, 1863), p. 5.

English, he continued, were in fact made up of varied tribes and races, and the whole tendency since the rise of Christianity had been toward greater and greater assimilation. Race concepts, he warned, frequently indicated ignorance or evil purposes.[40] Lieber's views on race seem, in short, to represent a middle stage between the cosmopolitan view of the Enlightenment, which held that race differences are relative to different physical and social environments, and the nineteenth-century view, which insisted on the inherent and abiding differences between races.

To understand the quality of Lieber's nationalism it is important to keep in mind both his class background and his class affiliations. Born into the middle class—his father was an iron dealer—Lieber was wholly sympathetic with it. He had little sympathy for the landed aristocrat and even less for the industrial worker. On the other hand, a "numerous, intelligent and respectable yeomanry" seemed to him an important element in the healthful state of a nation.[41] Lieber also shared the middle-class view of the sanctity of private property; and, as we shall see, his opinions on this subject were closely related to his enthusiasm for nationalism. On his visit to Europe in 1844, Lieber experienced the chagrin felt by all middle-class Americans over the repudiation by certain states of debts to European creditors. "Wherever I go I meet with the insult of silence on my country," he wrote to Sumner. "Unless people are intimate they abstain from talking of America, as we would avoid mentioning a man's mother in his presence when she has forfeited the esteem of the decent."[42] But it is not necessary to dwell too much on Lieber's sensitive awareness of the relation between national integrity in money matters and pride in one's country, nor, even, on the offers he made to men of wealth to write, in return for proper remuneration, popular defenses of property rights.[43]

For Lieber's conception of property had a more profound signif-

[40] New York *Evening Post*, August 30, 1871. See also *Revue de droit internationale*, (1871), III, 458–465.

[41] *Slavery, Plantation and the Yeomanry* (New York, 1863).

[42] Lieber to Sumner, June 2, 1844 (Paris) in Sumner Papers, Letters Received (Harvard University).

[43] Lieber to Samuel Ruggles, February 7, 1843, in Lieber Papers (Library of Congress).

icance than any personal interest in its security might imply. One day—perhaps in 1828—while riding through Connecticut, there came to him a clear vision of property as "the necessary reflex of our individuality in the material world." This might have been shortly after Webster's speech in Cincinnati (1828), in which that great orator declared that property was the creature of government. Such a position Lieber rejected on the ground that property, being "the necessary reflex of our individuality in the material world," must therefore have antedated government. In the course of preparing lectures in political science at South Carolina College, Lieber became more and more convinced of the supreme significance of property.[44] The possession of private property was, in his eyes, indispensable if the individual was to be a true individual. Children, as he noted in a letter to Sumner, want to have a plot of ground, in their parents' garden, that they may call their own. "It is the general *anxiety* of man to be an individual and to individualize everything around him. . . . We must single out one country, from among all countries of the globe, to call ours. The sound, 'My country,' is so delicious,—'my home,' 'my garden,'—because we feel rescued from vague generality, stabilitated; we see our *humanity* reflected."[45]

Such thoughts, together with the threat to property which Lieber sensed in the financial and constitutional "vagaries" of Jacksonism and in the inroads which Utopian Socialism seemed to be making, led him in 1841 to write his *Essays on Property and Labour*.[46] In this book Lieber not only justified property on the ground that it existed before the state and was necessary for the full realization of individuality. He went further and denied that the earth was ever at any time held in common. Thus government could not arrogate what it had not created; but it could, and must, protect property.

[44] Lieber to Sumner, June 13, September 15, 1841, in Huntington Collection.
[45] Lieber to Sumner, August 24, 1837, in Perry, *Lieber,* p. 121.
[46] This book was published by Harper & Brothers in their popular Family Library Series and went through subsequent editions in 1854 and 1856. In several letters Lieber expressed the hope that it might be put in the hands of leading industrialists and bankers.

Among the implications or variations of his theory was the assumption that, as civilization became more complex and as it expanded from the ancient city-state into medieval feudalism and ultimately into modern nations, the large unity of the nation-state became an inevitable prerequisite to the fullest realization of the protection and expansion of property—in short, of civilization itself. Lieber felt that a nation was virtually required to give "ample and unchecked use of the material means and characteristic features which God may have impressed on it."[47] He wrote that *"countries* are the orchards and the broad acres where modern civilization gathers her grain and nutritious fruits." The need of nations for modern industry was clear if one remembered that "national life consists in the gathered sheaves of the thousand activities of men, and that production and exchange are at all times among the elements of these activities."[48]

To facilitate such exchange within a nation, Lieber emphasized the importance of keeping free all the internal channels of communication.[49] If nature fell short in providing "a dignified geography, continuous and well-bound together," the means of communication which God had impressed on the nation's physiography might well be improved by the hand of man. "The more roads and means of communication man adds the more it becomes one country. Canals which unite many rivers, or a network of railways, wedding the distant points to one another, are efficient means to bind together a country as much so as one literature, one history—in some cases more so, in as much as material interests appeal quicker to more minds than intellectual interests."[50]

Such, in broad outline, was the pattern of Lieber's philosophy of nationalism. But the picture is incomplete without some consideration of his attitude toward the relations between nations. Lieber's

[47] Lieber to Ruggles, September 22, 1862, in Lieber Papers (Library of Congress).

[48] "History and Political Science necessary Studies in Free Countries," in *Miscellaneous Writings, I,* 334, 344. See also *Manual of Political Ethics,* p. 189.

[49] *On Civil Liberty and Self-Government,* chap. 9.

[50] Lieber to Ruggles, September 22, 1862, in Lieber Papers (Library of Congress).

nationalism, opposed as it was to "centralization" and "absolute power," was obviously closer to the liberalism of the late eighteenth and early nineteenth centuries than it was to the integral and chauvinistic nationalism of more recent times. Yet he was no pacifist. He repudiated the doctrine of Kant's *Toward Perpetual Peace,* which he regarded as the weakest of the writings of the great philosopher of Koenigsberg;[51] and he similarly deplored the criticisms of war that were made by Sumner, Channing, and Longfellow.[52] "Blood is occasionally the rich dew of History," he wrote in 1844. "Christ proclaimed peace but struggle and contest too."[53] War was necessary, occasionally, not only to effect national unity but also national regeneration. Many nations had, Lieber thought, been "morally rescued by wars, which imparted new vigor to them."[54] Though he did not approve of the Mexican War, yet he thought that by advancing the sphere of Anglo-American civilization it would be instrumental in achieving "the most momentous results in the history of civilization."[55] The Crimean War also met with his approval, and quite naturally he welcomed the Civil War as a struggle for "nationality at a period when the people were not yet fully nationalized, in a political sense."[56] And for the Franco-Prussian War, accomplishing as it did German unification, he had only praise.

But if Lieber's nationalism gave a well-recognized place to war as a normal part of a nation's development and intercourse with other nations, his nationalism was nevertheless sufficiently tempered with a liberal humanitarianism to save it from chauvinism. In fact, Lieber consistently moved toward the doctrine that nations, being interdependent, must collaborate on certain common problems. It

[51] Lieber to Hillard, May 19, 1839, in Huntington Collection.
[52] *Ibid.;* Perry, *Lieber,* pp. 198, 297.
[53] Lieber to Sumner and Hillard, March 16, 1844, in Huntington Collection.
[54] *Manual of Political Ethics,* II, 646; see also *Legal and Political Hermeneutics; or Principles of Interpretation and Construction in Law and Politics* (Boston, 1839).
[55] Perry, *Lieber,* p. 209.
[56] *Ibid.,* p. 271; Lieber to Sumner, August 31, 1864, in Huntington Collection.

is true that, writing in 1838, he rejected the idea of a congress of
nations, which the peace movement was advocating.[57] "Independent national development," he argued, "would be as seriously
interfered with by such a proposed congress of nations as it was for
a long time in the middle ages by the papal power."[58] Moreover, in
view of the fact that our republican "ambassadors" would play a
very subordinate part in any congress of nations, Americans should
be the last, he urged, to advocate such a body.[59]

Yet even with these reservations Lieber was something of an
internationalist. He applied to international relations his cardinal
doctrine in political science: "No rights without their duties, no
duties without their rights." The "patriotic snob" was in his eyes a
contemptible figure; and he believed that nations should take over
from one another institutions, such as common-school systems and
penal codes, if their superiority was patent.[60] As early as 1848 he
urged international adoption of the dollar of the United States as a
monetary unit, of the longitude of England's Greenwich, and of
the thermometer of France. He was a pioneer in promoting international treaties for the regulation of copyrights, immigration,
transatlantic cables, naturalization and expatriation, and contraband. From advocating the settlement of certain types of international disputes by a committee of the law faculty of a neutral
country, he moved toward the idea of a congress of distinguished
jurists for the settlement, and incorporation in an international
code, of debatable questions of national equity.[61] In 1865, in a

[57] Merle Curti, The American Peace Crusade, 1815–1860 (Durham, N. C.,
1929), pp. 55–58, 91.
[58] Manual of Political Ethics, II, 652. Lieber's anti-Catholicism increased
markedly in his later years, largely because he felt that the church was checking
the unification of Germany, but also because, in his eyes, the tenets of papal in-
fallibility and ultramontanism threatened nationalism. Lieber to Fish, April 28,
1872, August 6, 1872, in Fish Papers (Library of Congress); Lieber to Garfield,
March 6, 1869, November 10, 1869, July 6, 1870, in Garfield Papers (Library of
Congress).
[59] Manual of Political Ethics, II, 653.
[60] Lieber to Sumner, February 14, 1838, in Huntington Collection.
[61] Perry, Lieber, pp. 323, 362.

letter to Secretary of State Seward, Lieber proposed the settlement of the *Alabama* dispute by such an arbitral procedure.[62]

By an almost dialectical process, it was in the very midst of the war for nationalism, as Lieber regarded the Civil War, that his interest in international neighborliness was accentuated. Called upon to formulate principles for a military code for the regulation of armies in the field,[63] Lieber was acutely aware of the importance of applying the principles of gentlemanly conduct even toward an enemy.[64] The favorable reception given by foreign jurists to his *Instructions for the Government of Armies of the United States in the Field* still further turned Lieber's mind toward promoting international decency and friendliness through the codification of international law by jurists acting in a private capacity. David Dudley Field (to whom he suggested this idea), together with European jurists with whom Lieber had corresponded, succeeded, shortly after his death, in inaugurating a movement for that purpose.[65]

In 1867 Lieber wrote to his friend Mittermaier that "the great question of this era is the coexistence of many of the leading races or nations, united by the same international laws, religion, and civilization, and yet divided as nations. . . . Among the ancients," he continued, "one state always ruled; but we, the Cis-Caucasian race, are becoming more and more united in one great confederation, binding together all nations."[66] Lieber's lifelong advocacy of free trade—another evidence of his lack of sympathy with anything

[62] New York *Daily Times*, September 22, 1865; *Miscellaneous Writings, II,* 322–329. In a letter of February 10, 1868, to Garfield, Lieber remarked, in referring to his proposal for the arbitration of the Alabama affair, "I say, that it is one of those things which must be said by some one, at some time, for the first time." Garfield Papers (Library of Congress).

[63] For Lieber's part in this, see Brainerd Dyer, "Francis Lieber and the American Civil War," *Huntington Library Quarterly* (July, 1939), II, 449–465.

[64] Lieber to Sumner, September 11, 1867, in Huntington Collection. Lieber, in preparing a new edition of *The Character of the Gentleman* (Cincinnati and Charleston, 1847; Philadelphia, 1864), p. 98, applied his doctrine of the gentleman to international relations.

[65] Lieber to Sumner, February 7, 1865, December 16, 1866, in Huntington Collection; Merle Curti, *Peace or War: The American Struggle, 1636–1936* (New York, 1936), chap. 3.

[66] Perry, *Lieber,* p. 373.

resembling integral nationalism—became more militant in his later years, as, in fact, did his entire conception of the interdependence of nations. "Internationalism is part of a white man's religion, for it is the application of the Gospel to the intercourse of nations," he wrote to Ruggles.[67] Indeed, to Lieber the "divine law of interdependence," applying as it did to nations as well as to individuals, was one of the "original principles or characteristics of humanity" which increased in intensity and spread in action as men advanced.[68]

II

Within this general framework Lieber, in making specific applications of his theory of nationalism, developed a philosophy of American nationalism, which took as its point of departure the assumption that the Americans belonged in an essential way to the "Anglican race." In his book *On Civil Liberty and Self-Government* (1853), he wrote: "We belong to that race whose obvious task it is, among other proud and sacred tasks, to rear and spread civil liberty over vast regions in every part of the earth, on continent and isle. We belong to that tribe which alone has the word Self-Government."[69] But the American branch of the "Anglican race" was more blessed than the English themselves. For they belonged to a nation whose great lot it was "to be placed, with the full inheritance of freedom, on the freshest soil in the noblest site between Europe and Asia, a nation young, whose kindred countries, powerful in wealth, armies, intellect, are old."[70] If the Americans were not made "for a government in which the sway of the law alone is acknowledged, then tell me what nation is or was so?"[71] Remote from the intricate diplomacy of Europe, from the wars toward which we could and should turn our backs, we were peculiarly

---

[67] Lieber to Ruggles, October 8, 1871, in Lieber Papers (Library of Congress).
[68] *Fragments of Political Science on Nationalism and Inter-nationalism*, p. 22.
[69] *On Civil Liberty and Self-Government*, p. 21.
[70] *Ibid.*
[71] *Letters to a Gentleman in Germany, Written after a Trip from Philadelphia to Niagara* (Philadelphia, 1834), p. 32.

free to develop our racial heritage without foreign interference. Only when American sympathies for France in her war with Prussia in 1870 became marked did Lieber feel that artificial means might be necessary to ensure isolation and neutrality in the interest of American nationality: he urged Secretary of State Fish to consider the wisdom, even the necessity, of prohibiting by legislation the sale of war materials to belligerents and the transport of soldiers and contraband on American ships.[72]

Thanks to the isolation which Americans had enjoyed, and to other favorable circumstances, they had, in Lieber's eyes, improved in notable respects on the British in the essential "race qualities" of individual freedom and local self-government. Church and state were strictly separate; the abstract rights of the citizen were more explicitly recognized in America; the absence of a feudal aristocracy had given a more democratic cast to the whole of American polity; and, most significant of all, perhaps, the Americans had succeeded in working out a method by which newly settled contiguous territories were admitted to the established union on terms of absolute equality with the older states.[73] Lieber had only unstinted praise for "the bold idea of engrafting, for the first time in history, the representative principle upon a confederacy,—and thus creating a Union with a complete government, while self-government is left to the States,—and breathing from the beginning the spirit of self-expansion into the whole."[74] The United States, in other words, represented in a striking way Lieber's distinction between nationalization and centralization.

Although Lieber liked to think that Americans were a branch of what he called the "Anglican race," he was, of course, aware of the presence of non-English stocks. His own foreign birth inclined him to a certain natural sympathy with newcomers; he frequently re-

[72] Lieber to Fish, September 17, September 22, October 8, October 26, November 17, and December 30, 1870; Fish to Lieber, October 11, 1870—all in Fish Papers (Library of Congress). See also *Miscellaneous Writings*, II, 310–322.
[73] *On Liberty and Self-Government*, p. 257; *The West, a Metrical Epistle* (New York, 1848), p. 10.
[74] Perry, *Lieber*, p. 284.

ferred, indeed, to the contributions which the foreign-born had made to the land of their adoption. But if on the one hand he thoroughly disapproved of Know-Nothingism,[75] on the other hand he had no sympathy with the continued isolation of foreign groups from the main currents of American life. He spoke out against schools in which German alone was taught,[76] and he reminded his correspondents that he himself had little association with German groups in the United States. He disapproved of the desire of Irishmen to remain Irish at the same time that they became Americans.[77] "There is nothing more dangerous to a country than the dissension of its citizens on the score of national extraction."[78]

Whatever may have been Lieber's theory regarding the essential similarity of races, he wanted the United States to be a white man's country. In 1869 he urged Sumner to support a measure restricting Oriental immigration. Recalling Germany's services in the Middle Ages in driving back the Oriental hordes, he felt that the United States should take action, since "the white race is to rule over the Earth and we are under no obligation to ruin our people by a bastard mixture of Mongolian, Negro and White."[79] And in view of the enormous mass of immigrants from western Europe, many of whom were "communists," Lieber urged the prime importance of national regulation of immigration.[80]

Lieber's position on the role of the Negro in American nationality underwent certain changes. Early in his American career he expressed the hope that the noble white race might not "degenerate into a yellow mongrel breed, such as exists in Brazil and the Portuguese islands along the coast of Africa."[81] When he saw that colonization of the Negroes would not solve the problem, he advocated the creation of a free Negro peasantry as the best means to that end.

[75] Ibid., pp. 278–279; Samuel Tyler to Lieber, July 14, 1855, in Huntington Collection.
[76] Letters to a Gentleman in Germany, pp. 59–63.
[77] Ibid., p. 204.
[78] Manual of Political Ethics, II, 450.
[79] Lieber to Fish, July 1, 1870, in Fish Papers (Library of Congress).
[80] Lieber to Fish, April 3, 1870, June 27, 1872, ibid.
[81] Letters to a Gentleman in Germany, p. 297.

During his residence in the South, he made it clear that he had no sympathy with the abolitionists—he even owned slaves. But he did not defend the institution, and emancipation he welcomed with genuine enthusiasm. On the other hand, he had no high regard for the Negro. In opposing the annexation of Santo Domingo in Grant's administration, he observed that the nation already had enough Negroes.[82] Still, Lieber did not feel that the existence of the black-and-brown minority was an insurmountable obstacle to achieving a true American nationality. In 1868 he had come to the belief that eventually the white race would absorb and sweep away all others in the United States.[83]

Although Lieber's humanitarianism led him to regret the ruthless way in which the white exterminated or brutally pushed back the Indian into the less fertile places in the wilderness, he believed that such a fate was both inevitable and on the whole desirable. Nor did he relish the sentimentalizing of the Indian as a symbol of America. "Poor Indians," he remarked, "first we kill them with brandy, powder and syphilis, and then we put an Indian head on our coins and call men of war after them. The Indian does in no way symbolize America."[84]

In Lieber's conception of American nationalism economic factors bulked no less important than race. In his philosophy of property he found support for two doctrines which he regarded as cardinal in American nationalism. If it was to realize its essence, then authority must be limited; and in the protection of property rights he saw the best means of limiting that "democratic absolutism" which he thought was the only menace to American civil

[82] Lieber to Garfield, December 24, 1870, in Garfield Papers (Library of Congress).

[83] Perry, *Lieber*, p. 385.

[84] Lieber to Sumner, September 2, 1867, in Huntington Collection. Lieber urged Garfield to use his influence to have the Indian head deleted from the penny. Lieber to Garfield, December 15, 1868, in Garfield Papers (Library of Congress). During Lieber's early residence in America, however, he looked with favor on the use of Indian place names. *Letters to a Gentleman in Germany*, p. 245.

liberty. Not merely did he repudiate the Utopian Socialism of the Owenites and the disciples of Louis Blanc, or the even more repellent doctrines of Karl Marx.[85] He went further. He apparently agreed with the Boston Brahmins in thinking that the complaints of the American laboring class were dangerous to the peace and well-being of society,[86] and he was gravely concerned when Justice Lemuel Shaw, of the supreme court of the Old Bay State, recognized the right of labor to organize.[87]

Years later Lieber complimented Sumner for refusing to support Ira Steward's proposal for an eight-hour day, which had been introduced into Congress.[88] The struggle of labor was the more distasteful, not only because it endangered property rights, but also because it questioned the general economic well-being implicit in the very existence of the nation itself. "Never before has a country existed in which industry, honesty, and frugality were so sure of success in acquiring a fair livelihood and an honourable standing in the community as in our own."[89]

Lieber's theory of property had a second implication for American nationalism—the reconciliation which he made between his veneration for property rights on the one hand and "Manifest Destiny" or expansionism on the other. With Chief Justice Marshall and others he believed that "the earth was given to mankind for use; and if it be left wholly unused, it fails to obtain its object."[90] If a nation possessing land seemed unable to use it or to protect it, then "the essential characteristics of property are really lost, and disimpropriation has taken place."[91] While disapproving of the Mexican War, and especially of the methods by which it was pro-

---

[85] Lieber to Sumner, June 13, 1841, in Huntington Collection; Lieber to Fish, July, 1871, in Fish Papers (Library of Congress). Lieber to Ruggles, August 20, 1872, in Lieber Papers (Library of Congress).
[86] William Prescott to Lieber, June 29, 1842, in Huntington Collection.
[87] Lieber to Hillard, August 24, 1842, *ibid.*
[88] Lieber to Sumner, June 25, 1868, *ibid.*
[89] *Essays on Property and Labour* (New York, 1841), pp. 209–210.
[90] *Ibid.*, pp. 146–149. Lieber probably had California in mind.
[91] *Ibid.*, p. 146.

voked, Lieber could, through this theory of efficient utilization of land, justify the absorption of the northern provinces of Mexico. And during the Oregon controversy he wrote to Bunsen that "no power on earth can stop the impulse of a westward emigration of Europeans and Europedes, as soon as they are in America."[92]

Yet Lieber's devotion to the future development of property in backward areas was not unlimited: he opposed the projects for purchasing Cuba without reference to the desire of the Cubans;[93] he bitterly opposed the acquisition of Alaska. On getting wind of a suppressed pamphlet which the State Department had issued on the proposed purchase of Greenland and Iceland,[94] Lieber remarked that he wished he knew some remedy to make the United States ashamed of "island gourmandizing" and of confessing itself "too weak to stand neighbours."[95]

In most respects Lieber's ideas regarding the relation between economic factors and nationalism resembled those of Alexander Hamilton, his great hero and the man for whom he named one of his sons.[96] He could not, however, see eye to eye with Hamilton on the issue of protective tariffs. Lieber, in taking this position, likewise differed from many, though not from all, Whigs with whom he was identified. In the post-Civil War years, when protectionism was dominant, he convinced himself that Hamilton, were he alive, would be a free-trader.[97] And in vigorously opposing the tendency to identify protectionism and nationalism he wrote: "Whether a man be protectionist or free-trader it has nothing to do with his being a true republican and nationalist. Let that question be settled for

[92] Perry, *Lieber*, p. 197.
[93] Phinney, *Lieber's Influence*, p. 74. Lieber, aware that no international lawyer had touched on this subject, wished to oppose, as an American, the European practice of shuffling peoples about without their consent.
[94] Lieber to Sumner, March 26, 1871, in Huntington Collection.
[95] *Ibid.* For Lieber's attitude toward the annexation of Canada see his letter to Fish, June 8, 1869, in Fish Papers (Library of Congress).
[96] For instances, see Lieber to Fish, September 26, 1860, May 17, 1871, *ibid.* On October 3, 1870, Lieber wrote to Fish, "Niebuhr repeatedly said to me that he considered Hamilton far the greatest genius and profoundest statesman America had produced."
[97] Lieber to Fish, September 18, 1870, in Fish Papers (Library of Congress).

itself, but let us not make protection (in my opinion a great folly) a test of patriotism and nationalism."[98]

III

We may now well turn to the task of evaluating Lieber's services to American nationalism, considered as a historical process on the one hand, and as a social philosophy on the other. In many, perhaps most, of the measures which Lieber advocated for consolidating nationalism in America, he was not alone; but he was often a pioneer.

In the early period of the Republic various suggestions had been made by cultural patriots for a national name symbolizing America's unity and distinctive personality, but Lieber did more than anyone else to keep this sentiment alive. The very term, "the United States," he wrote to Gallatin, lacked the cohesiveness that a single name, lending itself to the adjective form, possessed.[99] He told his students that the names *Italia, Deutschland,* and *La France* had been important agents in the realization of national unity in those countries. What a shame, he remarked to Calhoun, that we lacked a name binding up in one sheaf all our patriotic aspirations and devotions, as *England* did for the English, *La France* for the French, and *Italia* for the Italians. What a pity, he continued (in what must have been a very interesting conversation indeed), that no American can signal so magnificent an order as "England expects every man to do his duty." Poets had to use "Columbia" when they were unable to condense "the United States of America"; but "Columbia," alas, had been appropriated by another land! Calhoun replied that we had no name because we ought to have none; we were merely united states, and had no country.[100] Undiscouraged, Lieber

[98] Lieber to Sumner, September 21, 1867, in Huntington Collection. See also Lieber's *Notes on Fallacies of American Protectionists* (New York, 1870). This grew out of Lieber's lecture notes, which in turn were published in three successive numbers of the New York *Evening Post,* and, enlarged versions, by the Free-Trade Society in New York.

[99] Lieber to Gallatin, March 6, 1845, in Huntington Collection.

[100] Lieber to Sumner, September 2, 1867, *ibid.* In speaking of the United States, Lieber, in accordance with custom, used the plural verb. See, e.g., *Letters to a Gentleman in Germany,* p. 169.

used "Windland" in an ode to a prospective canal across Panama. In addition to having a good Anglo-Saxon sound, he observed, the term had been used by our Norse discoverer.[101] Though in his private correspondence Lieber from time to time returned to the theme, he must himself have realized that a national rechristening was out of the question.

Like other cultural nationalists, Lieber also lamented the lack of a distinctively American literature. In *Letters to a Gentleman in Germany* (1834) he adopted the widely current explanations for this failure. Originality was more difficult for Americans than for peoples without a close counterpart, as we had in the English. Moreover, a nation, like an individual, could not at the same time attend to arts and letters and to a thousand things more directly connected with the well-being of life. "The United States have, in some respects, to introduce, sow, plant, and raise what other nations gained slowly in the course of centuries."[102]

But Lieber agreed with cultural patriots in thinking that an international copyright would contribute to the development of a distinctively American literature. In trying to find a publisher for his first American book, he had experienced the difficulty that most Americans experienced unless they were well known: it was much cheaper for publishers to reprint the writing of English authors, to whom, in the absence of an international copyright, they were not obliged to pay royalties. In his pamphlet, *On International Copyright* (1840), and in private correspondence with literary men, with publishers, and with political leaders, Lieber argued that authors who could do so would publish in England, with the result that our own literature would remain in its languishing state. "Some few highly distinguished minds will struggle now and then through these as through other difficulties; but an active, healthy, creative and diffused national literature does not depend upon a few literary or scientific eminences alone, but upon a general state of mental

---

[101] *The West* [and other poems], pp. 22 ff.; Lieber to Sumner, September 2, 1867, in Huntington Collection.
[102] *Letters to a Gentleman in Germany*, p. 169.

activity, purity of taste, and mutual encouragement."[103] In spite of the fact that Lieber met with discouragements in this crusade for international copyright legislation,[104] he did not despair. During the post-Civil War revival of the movement for an international copyright, he again lent his support.[105]

In still other ways the German-American scholar tried to promote the literary independence of his adopted country. He urged publishers to imitate Murray in London, and certain houses in Paris, by liberally rewarding American writers.[106] He did what he could to stimulate American writers to seize on great national events as proper themes for their endeavors. In 1847 he wrote to Samuel Ruggles: "It is sad, that the greatest events happen under our very noses without ever making an American poet sneeze out a potent poem. . . . We make a war, an unjust war. No rhymster sings to inflame the warrior, if he be for the war, or to help the cry against it, if he thinks the war unrighteous—and so a hundred subjects."[107] And in his correspondence with his friends in Boston he frequently regretted that "Our Willises, Longfellows, Bryants—all, all flap their wings to the tunes that come from abroad."[108]

In the interest of national sentiment Lieber also advocated the erection of monuments symbolizing great events in the country's past,[109] and the foundation of a national university. He did not, it is true, envision a university supported by federal funds; but he

[103] *On International Copyright. In a Letter to the Hon. William C. Preston* (New York, 1840), pp. 62–63.

[104] Many publishers opposed the project; Southern free-traders would have none of it; and a certain type of cultural chauvinist feared that it would facilitate the corruption of the American mind! (W. H. Prescott to Lieber, February 10, 1840, and Lieber to Sumner, January, 1866, March 3, 1866, and March 8, 1866, all in Huntington Collection.)

[105] Lieber to J. B. Baldwin, May 31, 1868, in Duyckinck Collection (New York Public Library); Lieber to Fish, April 25, 1871, in Fish Papers (Library of Congress).

[106] *Letters to a Gentleman in Germany,* p. 168.

[107] Lieber to Ruggles, May 2, 1847, in Lieber Papers (Library of Congress). In little more than a month from the time that Lieber wrote this letter, the first of *The Biglow Papers* appeared in the Boston *Courier.*

[108] Lieber to Ruggles, May 2, 1847, in Lieber Papers (Library of Congress). Lieber to Sumner, June 14, 1846, in Huntington Collection.

[109] *Manual of Political Ethics, II,* 163.

longed for an institution "national in its spirit, in its work and effect, in its liberal appointments and its comprehensive basis." What the University of Berlin did for the national spirit when Prussia was humbled by Napoleon, a national university might well do for America.[110] But Lieber's words fell on deaf ears, and when, after the Civil War others promoted the idea, his enthusiasm had waned.[111]

The opponents of Know-Nothingism received from Lieber such help as he could give. To the press he dispatched his attack on Know-Nothingism as a movement destined, if successful, to thwart a true nationality, rather than to promote it.[112] He even smuggled into an article on Mormonism a little sermon on immigrant contributions to American life.[113] Yet after the Civil War, as we have seen, he favored exclusion of Orientals and careful regulation of the admission of European immigrants.

During the secessionist agitation in South Carolina, in 1850 and 1851,[114] Lieber outlined his position in a letter to the president of his college, W. C. Preston, and gave encouragement and at least some guidance to South Carolina Unionists. One of the pro-Union leaders, Benjamin F. Perry, wrote appreciatively of the "great many and most valuable articles" from Lieber's pen.[115] Lieber also prepared an address which, in his absence from the state, was read at a

---

[110] *Miscellaneous Writings*, I, 330–331.

[111] Lieber felt, apparently, that in 1872, when John W. Hoyt, of Madison, Wisconsin, was promoting the idea of a national university, there was little need for it. Lieber to Garfield, April 9, 1872, in Garfield Papers (Library of Congress). Lieber did, however, favor renaming the Library of Congress, and in his correspondence he referred to it as the National Library. Lieber to Garfield, March 16, 1869, December 13, 1870, in Garfield Papers (Library of Congress).

[112] Lieber to Hillard, March 9, 1855, in Huntington Collection; Samuel Tyler to Lieber, July 14, 1855, *ibid.*; Lieber to W. C. Bryant, May 4, 1855, in Bryant-Godkin Collection (New York Public Library).

[113] *Putnam's Monthly* (March 1855), V, 229.

[114] For a discussion of this movement, see N. W. Stephenson, "Southern Nationalism in South Carolina," *American Historical Review* (January, 1931), XXXVI, 314–335.

[115] Benjamin F. Perry, *Reminiscences of Public Men* (Greenville, S. C., 1889), p. 145.

Unionist meeting held at Greenville on July 4, 1851.[116] According to Lieber, this address was copied "the whole extent of our country" and often spoken of as having contributed to the settlement of threatening difficulties.[117] Years later a South Carolinian wrote to him that he had quelled a rising and projected mobbing of Lieber and his family by students and others.[118]

Lieber's arguments during the secession crisis may be briefly summarized. Peaceful separation, he insisted, was impossible, and any war between the states would be one of the bitterest ever recorded. The Union would break into at least three fragments, he feared; and the rapid progress that had thus far marked its career would come to an end.[119] Lieber also reminded South Carolinians that never before had there been a union of free states, cemented by a united representation of the single states and of the people at large, woven together in a true government such as they enjoyed. Secession from that sort of union, he insisted, was equivalent to revolution; and the occasion did not require that. "Situated, as we are, between Europe and Asia, on a fresh continent," he concluded, "I see the finger of God in it. I believe our destiny to be a high, a great, and a solemn one, before which the discussions now agitating us shrink into much smaller dimensions than they appear if we pay exclusive attention to them."[120]

Once the test of nationalism entered the stage of acute civil conflict, Lieber redoubled his energies to promote the cause so dear to him.[121] He did not, of course, suppose that, in a war crisis, a scholar could make the same kind of contribution to nationalism as could be

[116] *Miscellaneous Writings, II,* 125 ff. For an account of the Greenville meeting, see P. M. Hamer, *The Secession Movement in South Carolina, 1847–1852* (Allentown, Pa., 1918), pp. 105–106.

[117] MS. sketch of Lieber's life, by himself, in Duyckinck Collection (New York Public Library).

[118] Lieber to Garfield, March 12, 1869, in Garfield Papers (Library of Congress).

[119] Perry, *Lieber,* pp. 237–238.

[120] *Miscellaneous Writings, II,* 135.

[121] Dyer, "Francis Lieber and the American Civil War," *loc. cit.,* is the best treatment of Lieber's role in that struggle.

performed by men of action.[122] But he summoned the poetic muse, and wrote *A Song of Our Country and Her Flag*. And in drafting the admirable *Instructions for the Government of the Armies of the United States in the Field* he did much to elevate the prestige of the North among European jurists. In public lectures, in private correspondence, and, above all, in the ten leaflets which he wrote for the Loyal Publication Society,[123] he developed his philosophy of American nationalism, strengthened it with new historical documentation, and brought it into the main stream of public thought and feeling.

There is need here merely to show, briefly, how Lieber applied his general philosophy to the crisis. He tried to refute the southern claim to a distinct nationality by disproving the doctrine that the people below Mason and Dixon's line formed a separate race and by insisting on the geographical unity of the country. By an appeal to history he demonstrated, to the satisfaction of many, that political, economic, geographical, and cultural factors had created a true nation, which the rise of an aggressive slavocracy jeopardized, but which it had not destroyed, and must not now destroy.

Through delving into historical records of the colonial and revolutionary era, Lieber became convinced that from the very start the English-speaking colonists had "felt themselves what they soon came distinctly to express themselves to be, a people."[124] The nation was formed, he maintained, not by a formal compact of the people when they entered the Union of the Constitution,[125] but rather it was formed long before, in the hearts and minds of the people. The

---

[122] Lieber put great emphasis on the peacetime contributions of Robert Fulton to American nationalism. *Letters to a Gentleman in Germany*, pp. 44–45. See also *Arguments of Secessionists: A Letter to the Union Meeting Held in New York, Sept. 30, 1863* (Loyal Publication Society, No. 35; New York, 1863) p. 6; and Lieber to Ruggles, September 22, 1863, in Lieber Papers (Library of Congress).

[123] See Frank Freidel, "The Loyal Publication Society: A Pro-Union Propaganda Agency," *Mississippi Valley Historical Review* (December, 1939), XXVI, 364, 369.

[124] *Two Lectures on the Constitution of the United States*, p. 17. Cf. Henry Reed's significant *Two Lectures on the History of the American Union* (Philadelphia, 1856), *passim*.

[125] Webster and other legal nationalists tended to maintain this general position.

colonists had come to a well-marked but almost limitless land at a period when England had achieved nationality and national unity; they brought with them the same language, laws, political concepts, reminiscences, literature, religion, and domestic economy. In the Albany Congress the word "union" was spoken, and from the start of the differences with the mother country the expressions "United America," "one people," "united people," were commonly used. Washington and other leaders, Lieber insisted, spoke of "the people, the nation, the country" in the same sense in which "United Italy" was at the very moment being used.[126] In short, historical forces had created a nation. The whole tendency of modern history required the existence of nations. The South was no nation. Such was the doctrine that Lieber did so much to publicize.

Once the war was over, Lieber crystallized these arguments in his pamphlet *Nationalism*.[127] While not unappreciated abroad, its chief influence was in the United States. President Theodore Woolsey, of Yale, who revised Lieber's *On Civil Liberty and Self-Government* (1875) and in many respects was a disciple of the German-American scholar, developed some of Lieber's ideas regarding the relations between nations.[128] President Daniel Coit Gilman, of Johns Hopkins, also came under his spell.[129] Lieber's writings attracted young John Burgess to New York in the hope of studying with him;[130] and, while this proved impossible because of pecuniary considerations, there is much in the nationalistic theory of Burgess that is close to Lieber's thought.[131] Public men as well as scholars were impressed by *Nationalism*. Horace Binney, a prominent Penn-

[126] *No Party Now but All for Our Country; Arguments of Secessionists; Amendments of the Constitution Submitted to the Consideration of the American People* (New York, 1865).

[127] *Miscellaneous Writings*, II, 221 ff. The Italian publicist, Alexandra Stefani Garellio, referred to Nationalism as "the Golden Tract." See also J. C. Bluntschli's "Introduction," in *Miscellaneous Writings*, II, 7–14.

[128] See Theodore Woolsey, *Political Science; or, The State Theoretically and Practically Considered* (New York, 1877).

[129] D. C. Gilman, "Francis Lieber," *International Review*, X (April, 1881), p. 342.

[130] J. W. Burgess, *Reminiscences of an American Scholar* (New York, 1934), p. 70.

[131] See, especially, *idem, Political Science and Comparative Constitutional Law* (Boston, 1890–91, 2 vols.), I, 1–47.

sylvanian, regarded it, not as a "fragment," but as "the Philosophy of the History of Civilization";[132] and Judge M. Russell Thayer, of Philadelphia, wrote that it contained "within a very small compass a greater amount of political philosophy and a more condensed statement of the general truths derived from historic experience than was perhaps ever before embraced within the same space."[133] James A. Garfield considered *Nationalism* to be a "Missionary Tract" and gladly distributed it in Congress and elsewhere.[134] It was likewise appreciated and used by Charles Sumner, while Hamilton Fish thought highly of it.

Lieber did not, of course, father all the ideas in the pattern of nationalistic thought which he expressed and promoted. Nor did his exposition of nationalism meet with the approval of all who spoke as American nationalists. For his doctrine of Americanism was not that of the most democratic elements in the country. On the other hand, it was not altogether typical of that of the most conservative groups. It stood, so to speak, midway between the natural-rights philosophy on which much of the early American nationalistic thought was based and the more integral, flag-waving "one hundred percentism" of a later day. It postulated not merely a legal and constitutional but also an organic conception of nationalism. Unlike the great expositions of American nationalism which many of the outstanding nationalists made, it related nationalism to sociological and cultural forces.

Moreover—and this is important—Lieber's doctrine of nationalism, emphasizing as it did rights and duties alike, was, consciously or unconsciously, functional to the basic interests of the middle class. And the United States in fact, and still more in theory, was what the Old World called "middle class." It is because Lieber's doctrines were so congenial to the northern middle class in its struggle against the planting aristocracy that the significance of his theories becomes the more marked. But it is equally noteworthy

---

[132] Garfield to Lieber, Dec. 15, 1868, in Garfield Papers (Library of Congress).
[133] "Biographical Discourse," in *Miscellaneous Writings*, I, 33.
[134] Garfield to Lieber, Jan. 6, 1869, in Garfield Papers (Library of Congress).

that Lieber's doctrine of nationalism, hostile as it was to what he called the "democratic absolutism" emanating from attacks on property by "communists" and by labor, continued to be functional to middle-class interests after Appomattox. Such considerations explain, in the last analysis, Lieber's importance in the history of nationalistic thought in America, and in the struggle for nationalism itself.

6

Human Nature
in American Thought:
The Retreat from Reason
in the Age of Science[1]
(1953)

THE century from 1860 to the present has marked a steady retreat from reason. This retreat has recently become headlong, so
that at present we are living in a new age of faith. But at the beginning of the century, in 1860 let us say, reason was still en-
throned in the United States. In the 1860's the traditional Christian
approach was still dominant, and continued to be, for that matter,
in the succeeding decades. Orthodox doctrine taught the reality of
original sin, but it also taught men to believe in their ability to
struggle against sin and in the posibility of redemption. In an expanding Christian circle the idea of the malleability of human
nature, of its potentialities for good, was finding fresh emphasis;
and in this circle the idea was coming to be held that sin is social

---

[1] An article on the same general topic, and dealing specifically with "The Age
of Reason and Morality, 1750–1860," appeared in the *Political Science Quarterly*
for September, 1953. The two pieces inaugurated the Gino Speranza Lectures at
Columbia University.

rather than individual in character, and that the Christian effort must concentrate on reforming society. Christian ideas about human nature also squared with age-old proverbs: people accepted the maxim, "You can't change human nature," but they also quoted the conflicting proverb, "As the twig is bent, so the tree inclines."

On a more sophisticated level men still largely subscribed to the faculty psychology which Professor Thomas Upham of Bowdoin College had done so much to popularize. This assumed a duality of body and mind. The body was the seat of those base impulses which to the orthodox meant original sin. But the mind was made up of capacities classified under the faculties of understanding, feeling, and will. Through the will man could rule his baser impulses and translate his innate moral ideas into action. Properly disciplined by early formal training, reason and will could enable individuals to eliminate traditional shortcomings in themselves and in society. Thus the academic scheme of human nature represented a synthesis of Christianity and the Enlightenment.

Such optimistic views of human nature were firmly entrenched in American thought of 1860 despite some dissident notes. These ideas had so long been dominant in the thinking of leading Americans that by that time they were commonplace even among the masses. They were reflected in dime novels, in the popular women's magazines, and in Fourth of July orations.

It is not strange that so dominant a philosophy of human nature was very little affected by a tremendous event in 1859, the publication of Darwin's *The Origin of Species*. This did provoke a lively response as the years passed, particularly in intellectual circles. But it did not at first cause even intellectuals to doubt *their* ability to get at *the* truth. Not for perhaps fifty years did this doubt even begin to be a serious one in their thinking—not indeed until William James and John Dewey spoke so plainly that they had to listen. No wonder that the retreat from reason was a very slow one.

Just as the traditional formulations about human nature continued after 1859 to enjoy wide credence, so did the social "sciences" associated with these formulations. Economics, political science, sociology, and history continued to appeal to the older ideas about human nature for validity. Even as late as the turn of the twentieth century the academic social studies were for the most part formal, rational, and highly schematic. Each one, as synthesized by eminent writers, postulated universal and unchanging laws—laws comparable to those governing the mind of faculty psychology or the physical universe in Newton's system. These laws, discovered by the use of reason, were all highly reasonable and abstract. And they were well cloaked with moral virtue.

It is possible to comment only briefly on these formal and rationalistic social disciplines. The classical and neoclassical economics assumed that the individual acts rationally, and that reason leads him to avoid pain and seek pleasure. It also assumed that the economy is governed by abstract and unchangeable laws of supply and demand. It further assumed that any complete economic equality as between individuals is out of the question—it does not, for one thing, square with the inequality of endowment of individuals. Neither, so the neoclassical economy held, does it square with universal economic laws. But on the other hand, if these laws are obeyed, then a reasonable equilibrium between desires and satisfactions can be counted on. The way is open to economic progress if not to economic utopia.[2]

In the field of political thought we again find the assumption of a system governed by certain laws of nature. According to these laws, formulated in the seventeenth century and analogous to Newton's laws of gravitation, every individual possesses inalienable rights to life, liberty, and property. Government exists to protect the individual in these rights. It cannot properly interfere with their natural operation by favoring the weak and improvident at the ex-

[2] See Rexford Guy Tugwell, "Human Nature in Economic Theory," *Journal of Political Economy* (June, 1922), *XXX*, 317–345; A. J. Snow, "Psychology in Economic Theory," *Journal of Political Economy* (August, 1924), *XXXII*, 487–496; and C. E. Ayres, "Fifty Years' Development in Ideas of Human Nature and Motivation," *American Economic Review*, 26th supplement (March, 1936), 224–236, 250–254.

pense of the strong and capable. To do so would deny to the latter their natural rights to liberty and property. The national sovereign state can, however, use its police powers in war to protect the natural rights of its citizens when these are menaced by aggressors beyond the national boundaries. Such was the prevailing synthesis of political science familiar to our grandfathers in the 1870's and 1880's and, in a sense, to our fathers on the threshold of our own century.[3]

In the sphere of social relations, the sociology of three-quarters of a century ago was coming to terms with the nineteenth-century doctrine of evolution in a greater degree than had the sister disciplines of economics and political science. But sociology was also formal and rationalistic—theoretical and schematic in its conception of absolute laws. These permitted the able and ambitious to climb the social ladder; but if one failed to take advantage of the ladder, or slipped in the effort, he must be content with his status. The social laws also included the acceptance by women of their limited rôle. So too the inferior races must accept their inferiority. But in each case there was room for improvement—within the proscriptions set by nature.[4]

At the very time that the formal, moralistic, and rational synthesis of the social studies was achieved, new and revolutionary developments had begun to challenge the dualistic faculty psychology with its emphasis on an innate rationality and morality in human nature. In America it was not a scientist but a poet who first proclaimed an entirely naturalistic and monistic view of man. Walt Whitman rejected all antitheses between body and soul and identified morality with obedience to nature's law of the organic unity of man.[5] Such evil as the Good Gray Poet saw in "flippant people

[3] Max Lerner, "The Political Theory of Charles A. Beard," *American Quarterly* (Winter, 1950), II, 303–331.

[4] Albion Small, "Fifty Years of Sociology in the United States 1865–1915," *American Journal of Sociology* (May, 1916), XXI, 721–864.

[5] For an interesting discussion, see R. D. O'Leary, "Swift and Whitman as Exponents of Human Nature," *International Journal of Ethics* (January, 1914), XXIV, 183–201.

with hearts of rag and souls of chalk" he laid at the door of man's refusal to accept the unity of body and soul. But few took Whitman's startling and shocking message very seriously.

If at first a similar hostility greeted kindred ideas blown to our shores by the new scientific currents, in the long run these proved telling. In 1867 Edward Livingston Youmans called attention to the progress that had been made, chiefly abroad, in the scientific study of human nature. He pointed to the implications of the physiological discoveries of Sir Charles Bell and Dr. Marshall Hall, of the far-reaching theory of Sir Charles Darwin, and of the application by Helmholtz and others of the techniques of physics to the study of sensations.[6] Other Americans discovered the pioneer work of Wundt in the laboratory study of mental activity. In later decades, careful observations and controlled experiments, especially in relation to the behavior of animals and young children, showed the continuity of animal and human behavior. All this was, of course, in line with the theory of organic evolution.[7]

One highly significant result of the development of biology in the later half of the nineteenth century was the more specific content given to the hitherto loosely used term instinct.[8] A German Darwinian, Preyer, elaborated a list of specific instincts which he applied to an analysis of child and adult behavior. In America William James listed some fifty instincts, which his pupils Thorndike and Woodworth still further extended. The discoveries of the geneticists, Mendel, Weismann, Morgan, and others, led to a sharpened and more precise analysis of instincts in purely biological terms. In time it became evident that many of the so-called instincts were in truth not inherited mechanisms but rather acquired patterns of behavior. But before this became fully evident many psychologists, including James and, especially, G. Stanley Hall, taught

[6] Edward Livingston Youmans, "On the Scientific Study of Human Nature," in *The Culture Demanded by Modern Life* (New York, 1867), pp. 373–411.

[7] See Gardner Murphy, *Historical Introduction to Modern Psychology* (New York, 1949), especially chaps. 8, 10, 11, 13, and 14; and A. A. Roback, *History of American Psychology* (New York, 1952), Part II.

[8] Edward Chace Tolman, "The Nature of Instinct," *Psychological Bulletin* (March, 1923), XX, 200–218.

that inherited patterns of behavior provided the natural if not the inevitable foundation for the subordinate role of women and of the backward races, for war, and for competitive capitalism.[9]

The darker view of human nature which in the earlier Age of Reason and Morality had found only such exceptional literary exponents as Hawthorne and Melville was now buttressed both by the new Darwinian emphases and by incoming literary currents from abroad. Half-whimsically, half-seriously, Mark Twain held man up to scorn for pretending to a morality denied the higher animals. The satirist went so far in *The Mysterious Stranger* as to dub man "such an unreasoning creature that he is not able to perceive that the Moral Sense degrades him to the bottom layer of animated beings and is a shameful possession."[10] Dr. Oliver Wendell Holmes wrote his "medicated novels" in which he made a sweeping use of the mechanistic and unconscious factors in human behavior. His proto-Freudian essay, "Mechanism in Thought and Morals," discussed these on the scientific level.[11]

Conservatives who opposed the program of feminists, pacifists, and socialists declared, "You can't argue with an instinct." When Henry George asked Edward Livingston Youmans what could be done about the political corruption and the selfishness of the rich in promoting it, the disciple of Darwin and Spencer replied: "Nothing! It's all a matter of evolution. Perhaps in four or five thousand years evolution may have carried men beyond this state of things."[12] The same conviction that selfishness, competition, and struggle, based on an instinctive nature, governed social relations was reflected in the Middletown of the 1930's: "the strongest and best

[9] Merle Curti, *The Social Ideas of American Educators* (New York, 1935), chap. 12.

[10] Samuel L. Clemens, *The Mysterious Stranger and Other Stories* (New York, 1922), p. 50. See also the *Autobiography*, ed. Albert B. Paine (New York, 1924, 2 vols.), II, 248.

[11] "Mechanism in Thought and Morals" was given as a Phi Beta Kappa address at Harvard in 1870 and is to be found in *The Works of Oliver Wendell Holmes* (Boston and New York, 1892, 13 vols.), VIII, 260–314. For a modern psychiatrist's comments on Holmes' fiction, see Clarence P. Oberndorf, *The Psychiatric Novels of Oliver Wendell Holmes* (New York, 1943).

[12] Henry George, *A Perplexed Philosopher* (New York, 1892), p. 136 n.

survive—that's the law of nature after all—always has been and always will be."[13]

But you would be left with a very false impression if you supposed that the newer biological study of human nature did nothing more than to buttress faith in the inevitability of war, racial and sex inferiority, economic competition, and the *status quo* generally. In undermining the older view of human nature as innately rational and moral, the new psychology did not close the doors entirely to the traditionally American faith in meliorism. In the functionalist phase which the new psychology in the United States assumed under the leadership of James, Mead, and Dewey, mind was thought of as the capacity of the organism to adapt itself to situations, to solve problems. The traditional concept of motivation and learning was rejected for the more realistic one of the adaptation of the organism to changing situations through problem solving.

In John Dewey especially the new views about human nature reinforced the optimistic faith in man's capacity to shape his future in ways that seemed desirable and good.[14] It is worth noting that Dewey developed his views in the first two decades of the twentieth century when the movement for social, political, and economic reform was at high tide. At the very turn of the century he argued that all concepts of human nature are, as it were, politically determined. The theory that human nature does not and cannot change was, he insisted, a view functional to and prevalent in aristocracies. The democratic scheme of human nature emphasized thinking as problem solving and living as a coöperative social enterprise in which experience was reconstructed on ever more satisfying levels, individual and social. In other words, far from conceding that the new psychology struck a blow at the old faith in man's capacity for progress and democracy, Dewey held that it actually opened new avenues to those objectives. His view of human nature was at its

[13] Robert S. and Helen Merrell Lynd, *Middletown in Transition: A Study in Cultural Conflicts* (New York, 1937), p. 407.

[14] For a discussion of Dewey's psychology in relation to the American environment, see Curti, *Social Ideas of American Educators,* chap. 15, and *The Growth of American Thought* (New York, 1951), pp. 557 *et seq.*

core essentially American in its emphasis on mind-in-use and on man's ability to make adjustments in a changing environment which he himself could direct. "True psychology," he declared, "is itself a conception of democracy."

In rejecting dualism, in questioning the sweeping scope so many psychologists gave to instincts and to imitation in learning, above all in repudiating the idea of mind as fixed structure, Dewey advanced a democratic and one may say an American conception of human nature. Some now think he was too optimistic, but one must nevertheless note that much empirical investigation in school, clinic, industry, and mass communication supports his thesis. And in the current programs for the study and improvement of human relations we have an impressive tribute to his theory of human nature.[15]

Dewey represented not only a retreat from the earlier rationalistic conception of the autonomous individual. He also in a sense represented a qualification of the emphasis of the early scientific studies of human nature in terms of biology and physics. In supplementing this emphasis with a consideration of man in his social context, Dewey supported the cultural anthropologists. Many of these shared his optimistic views about the potentialities of human nature. For cultural anthropologists questioned the assumption that all the traits common to western civilization represented absolute laws governing all human behavior everywhere. On the contrary, careful scientific investigations of many primitive peoples seemed to indicate that competition and aggression, presumably universal traits, scarcely exist in certain cultures. Moreover, far from regarding women as mentally inferior, some peoples assumed that women are more highly endowed with intelligence and other desirable traits than men. And it was something of a shock to learn that just as we looked down on primitive peoples as innately inferior to us, so they regarded us as innately inferior to them. If we spurned the long-haired Kaffirs as little more than baboons, they regarded our

[15] Gordon W. Allport, "Psychology and the Fourth R," New Republic (October 17, 1949), CXXI, 23–26.

almost bald pates and our inability to get along in their forests as proofs of innate inferiority.[16]

The implications of all this gave a much larger sphere to culture than to biology in explaining complex characteristics of collective behavior; undermined the assumption that universal economic, political, and social laws govern all peoples; and postulated a relativism in discussions of human nature. Also if culture is more important than biology in many hitherto unsuspected spheres, the way is open to an enlarged and reinforced faith in the possibility of uprooting man's exploitation of man, war, and other customs assumed to rest on inborn characteristics.[17]

These emerging ideas of human nature rested not only on the functional psychology and the pragmatic instrumentalist philosophy of James and Dewey and on cultural anthropology. They also drew support from and gave support to vigorous nonconformist and protest movements on the political, social, and economic stage in the era of progressivism and the new freedom. Also related to the newer ideas about human nature and to protests against the *status quo* was a new approach to social, economic, and political problems. The breakdown of the older, rationalistic, schematic conception of human nature inevitably weakened the various syntheses of the social studies that had drawn support from the traditional rationalistic conception of human nature.

Equally important was the fact that in the later decades of the nineteenth century and in the first decade of our own, the pressure of industrial and urban problems became so great that social scientists began to study these problems empirically. Field surveys, case histories, and, above all, quantitative or statistical techniques rev-

---

[16] David Bidney, "Human Nature and the Cultural Process," *American Anthropologist*, n.s. (July–September, 1947), XLIX, 375–399; Ross L. Finney, "Culture and the Original Nature of Man," *Journal of Applied Sociology* (March–April, 1927), XL, 339–343.

[17] William F. Ogburn, *Social Change with Respect to Culture and Original Nature* (New York, 1922); Charles A. Ellwood, "The Modifiability of Human Nature and Human Institutions," *Journal of Applied Sociology* (May–June, 1923), VII, 229–237; and Devere Allen, "Human Nature: Perennial Excuse for War," *World Unity Magazine* (October, 1930), VII, 83–94.

olutionized the older rational social studies by imbuing them with both empiricism and faith. Economists now concerned themselves no longer with studying abstract economic principles or laws which they applied to imaginary problems, such as Robinson Crusoe's classical economic behavior on a lonely island. They turned rather to specific, fact-finding studies of price behavior, of depressions, and of actual economic institutions such as corporations, labor unions, and coöperatives; for these were now seen to influence economic activity in ways that failed to correspond to the older ideas about economic law.[18]

Skillful advertising technicians, appealing to sex, prestige, and desire to conform, proved that demand could be vastly expanded. One advertisement pictured a hopeful, hard-working businessman bent over his papers as he weighed a new investment versus a household demand. The caption read, "No use balancing your books if your wife can't balance a teacup." Experiments in paying higher wages for a bigger output upset older ideas about the iron law of wages. Friction between labor and management often yielded to insights gleaned from the new knowledge about human nature.[19] This emphasis on the application to specific problems of the new insights reinforced the faith both in man's power to shape his economic future and in the democratic belief that the poorest need not always be with us.

And there were similar changes in political studies. Empirical investigations of concrete problems proved that it was possible greatly to improve administration and efficiency in a democracy. Other studies suggested that lawmaking is the result of various pressures of interested groups rather than of any use of abstract reasoning. Laws came to be increasingly regarded not as timeless, unchanging absolutes, but as instruments for adjusting in varied ways

[18] This is discussed by Louis Wirth in his essay on the social sciences in Merle Curti (ed.), *American Scholarship in the Twentieth Century* (Cambridge, 1953).

[19] Ordway Tead, *Instincts in Industry* (Boston and New York, 1918), and *Human Nature and Management* (New York, 1929); Milton Nadworny, "Scientific Management and Labor, 1900–1940: An Historical Study," Ph.D. thesis, University of Wisconsin, 1952.

to changing human needs. All this strengthened the belief that, however great the difficulties, men are not governed by absolute political and economic laws, but that economic and political phenomena are far more complex and relative, and therefore more malleable, than had been assumed.

These implications are even more striking when we turn to the rising empirical studies of crime, delinquency, and other social problems. The new theories of human nature suggested that aberrant behavior may be more largely the result of conditioning, of the impact of specific and unfortunate experiences and situations, than of faulty will power or deficient reasoning. In proving the direct relation between unfortunate environment and crime and delinquency, and in demonstrating the useful potentialities of counseling, social workers still further strengthened the belief that man need not helplessly submit to a fate he cannot control.[20] New knowledge about the relation of inadequate nutrition or of deficient glandular activity or of harrowing childhood fears to mental illness revolutionized attitudes in this sphere. And the teachings of the cultural anthropologists and, in later years, of the social psychologists about the cultural as opposed to the biological bases for differences among men encouraged Negroes and their white champions in their fight against discrimination.[21] Psychologists proved that women possess as a group quite as high intelligence as men and have potentially quite as varied interests, and such findings reinforced the democratic movement to enlarge the opportunities of women in every sphere—educational, political, economic, and social.[22] It came to be recog-

[20] Pioneer studies include William Healy, *The Individual Delinquent* (Boston, 1915); American Academy of Medicine, *Physical Basis of Crime* (Easton, Pa., 1914); and Carl A. Murchison, *Criminal Intelligence* (Worcester, Mass., 1926). See also Arthur E. Fink, *Causes of Crime: Biological Theories in the United States 1800–1915* (Philadelphia, 1938).

[21] For example, Franz Boas, *The Genetic Basis for Democracy* (New York, 1939); T. R. Garth, *Race Psychology* (New York, 1931); and Otto Klineberg, *Race Differences* (New York, 1935).

[22] The pioneer study was Helen Bradford Thompson [Wooley], *The Mental Traits of Sex* (Chicago, 1903). Other significant investigations are reported in Beth L. Wellman, "Sex Differences," in *A Handbook of Child Psychology* (Worcester, 1933), pp. 626–649; and Quinn McNemar, *The Revision of the Stanford-Binet Scale* (Boston and New York, 1942), pp. 42–54.

nized that the Victorian authority Havelock Ellis quoted was wrong in regarding the suggestion that women possess sexual feelings as "a vile aspersion." The current Kinsey report speaks to this point!

The conception of human nature associated with the name of John Dewey has continued to be applied in many fields of human relations. But currents of thought in many ways quite opposite have gained increasing vogue. I have already called attention to the pessimistic overtones of the hereditarian emphasis on instincts—to the weight given to biology in the nature-nurture controversies. The early efforts to measure intelligence also seemed to run counter to the traditional view that all men possess rational faculties in a relatively high degree.[23] But before commenting on the sweepingly antirationalistic and antidemocratic interpretations given to the testing movement, I must recall to mind the gloomy overtones implicit in the teachings of Freud.

Freud's message had already been heralded, at least in part, by the pioneer work of the Boston psychiatrist, Dr. Morton Prince. This too-often neglected American emphasized the large role of the unconscious, of repression, and of conflict in mental aberrations. He welcomed Freud, who visited the United States in 1908.[24] Freud's teachings became increasingly familiar in the era after World War I. Without using the experimental techniques and the controlled observations of the objective psychologists, the Freudians developed a theory of human nature which, in emphasizing the importance of sex, contributed to a better understanding of motivation and behavior. This was particularly to the point in view of the traditional neglect of sex in the early faculty psychology and even in the great *Principles* of William James.

The newer views about the nonrational factors in behavior were abundantly illustrated in the First World War, an event which both in itself and in its aftermath did much to shake the older con-

[23] For a discussion of this, see Curti, *Social Ideas of American Educators*, chap. 14; and David Spitz, *Patterns of Anti-Democratic Thought* (New York, 1949).
[24] Morton Prince, *The Dissociation of a Personality* (New York, 1905), and *The Unconscious* (New York, 1914). See also William S. Taylor, *Morton Prince and Abnormal Psychology* (New York, 1928).

fidence in the inevitability of progress. In this country intellectuals were shocked to see evidences of sadism and cruelty on the battle-field and in the prison camp. The widespread sense of catastrophe, futility, and defeat was expressed in a cartoon which pictured a baboon contemplating an endless sea of soldiers' graves and saying, "If this goes on we will have to start all over again!" On another level thoughtful men and women were horrified to see how readily a highly charged emotional war propaganda was stimulated and how quickly a frightening mass hysteria resulted. What lay in store in the 1950's was anticipated at the trial in 1917 of fifteen professors at the University of Nebraska for alleged pro-Germanism on the most flimsy testimony, and the senseless persecution of countless citizens whose German-sounding names suggested guilt by association. Even more shocking than all this was the way in which the war forced almost everyone to take the recital of wholesale slaughter without turning a hair. All these things illustrated grimly enough the newer revelations about the irrationality of the human make-up.[25]

In the years that followed the First World War new evidences of irrationality weakened still further the older confidence in the ability of an essentially reasonable and moral human nature to shape a future of freedom, democracy, and peace. Propaganda was organized on a huge scale and used not only by advertising men and pressure groups. Some political leaders who had formerly trusted "the people's will" now began to see that those in power could call on the skillful techniques of the public-relations specialists and other experts to sway large masses of human beings. Grave doubts increased as to whether the people are rational and moral, whether the people are really always right. The psychological testing done during the war seemed to indicate so low a general intelligence that some jumped to the conclusion that the average person is simply too dumb to perform the functions of citizenship with any competence. Even when more critical psychologists demonstrated the inadequacy of the first tests and the errors in interpret-

[25] Merle Curti, *Peace or War: The American Struggle 1636–1936* (New York, 1937), chap. 8.

ing them, the idea of the average dumbness remained—and bolstered the doctrine of the elite as preached on the one hand by the eugenicists and on the other by the new humanists of the Irving Babbitt and Paul Elmer More persuasion. Many climbed on the bandwagon of Henry Mencken and echoed his gibe that democracy is, in view of the low IQ of the masses, only boobocracy. These ideas did not die even when psychologists pointed out that the IQ was only an arbitrary measure, needing still more careful analysis, and not even fixed in any individual.[26]

The faltering record of the League of Nations did not do much to keep alive a confidence that man can uproot war. It did not add to the peace of mind of thinking people either, when social scientists demonstrated the emptiness of mere verbal professions of peace, such as personal pledges never to fight—or even the Kellogg-Briand Pact. In the 1830's Professor Thomas C. Upham of Bowdoin College had argued that if only the peoples would insist that their rulers renounce war, peace would be at hand. Ironically, now in the 1930's they were insisting, but peace seemed farther away than ever.

In the 1930's the new revelations about the irrationality of men were even more shockingly illustrated. The inhuman atrocities committed by Fascists and Nazis against their fellow men weakened the belief that it is possible to control men's social behavior intelligently for truly social ends. Reports of purges in the Kremlin began to blast the earlier roseate predictions of well-known American authorities that in eliminating competition and insecurity the Soviet experiment was creating a happier version of human nature than western man had known.[27] I need hardly add that the experiences of the postwar world have confirmed the growing doubts—the tension and fears, the uncertainties and anxieties associated with the atom bomb and the cold war are all too much with us. One ex-

[26] See again Spitz, *Patterns of Anti-Democratic Thought*, especially chap. 7.
[27] For example, E. C. Lindeman, "Is Human Nature Changing in Russia?" *New Republic* (March 8, 1933), LXXIV, 95–98; Frankwood E. Williams, "Can Russia Change Human Nature?" *Survey Graphic* (March, 1933), XXII, 137–142; C. Dreher, "Collectivism and Human Nature," *Harper's Magazine* (September, 1934), CLXIX, 489–491. Cf. Max Eastman, "Socialism Doesn't Jibe with Human Nature," *Reader's Digest* (June, 1941), XXXVIII, 41–49.

ample, which will be easily recalled, is symptomatic of the waning faith in man's ability to shape his social destiny into moral and rational channels. I refer to the articles in *Collier's Magazine* for October 7, 1952. The story, told by our distinguished playright and biographer, Robert E. Sherwood, and a galaxy of well-known writers, describes the Third World War—*the war we did not want but could not prevent.* This shocking profession of inability to direct our future as we want it to be was indeed not quite all-inclusive and absolute. For even the *Collier's* writers envisaged the reconstruction of a defeated Soviet Union in accordance with dominant American ideas about freedom and comfort—including a style show in the Kremlin to give Soviet women the fashions they have been unhappily pining for these thirty-odd years! But if some faith survives in our ability to shape our future at least in part, the picture is indeed very different from that associated with the doctrine of human nature widely held in the Age of Reason and Morality and in the first phase of the intellectual revolution of the early twentieth century.

For it is clear that we are in a period of reaction against the promises of the functional conception of human nature that resulted from the application of scientific methods to the study of behavior. That reaction is evident in the virtual disappearance of the more than century-old peace movement: to advocate peace today in any except the officially sanctioned way is to court the charge of subversiveness. The reaction is also seen in the insistence of psychoanalysts and of leaders of women's education that it was all quite wrong to suppose that women are the equals of men in their emotional and intellectual equipment. These spokesmen deny that women have as varied powers and interests as men. They ascribe mental conflicts to the efforts of women to assume responsibilities in the big world hitherto assumed only by men. Many indeed have bade farewell to feminism.[28]

[28] For example, Helene Deutsch, *The Psychology of Woman: A Psychoanalytic Interpretation* (New York, 1944); and Ferdinand Lundberg and Marynia Farnham, *Modern Woman:The Lost Sex* (New York, 1947).

The break with the early twentieth-century intellectual revolution can also be seen in the current reaction against progressive education and in the emphasis in many circles on discipline and formal training.

In the field of race relations there have indeed been continued signs of improvement—of efforts to implement in practice the scientific testimony to the equal potentialities of all races. Despite these gains there is still a wide gap between our knowledge and our practice, as the dynamite bombings in many southern localities and evictions such as that in Cicero, Illinois, painfully remind us.

Unfortunately it is impossible to stop with these instances of the current reaction against the nineteenth-century confidence in reason and morality and against the seemingly better-grounded scientific view of human nature that in the early decades of the twentieth century helped create so promising a social science. For the reaction is also apparent in the readiness of legislatures, administrative agencies, and courts to curtail civil liberties and academic freedom. A free discussion of competing ideas, we are told, jeopardizes our security. The reaction is to be seen further in the reliance on verbal oaths of loyalty. These hardly square with the findings about motivation and behavior or with much we have presumably learned from social science.

Above all, the new temper is seen in what appears to be a characteristic attitude on the part of college students and other youth: a conscious and unconscious quest for security. Sometimes this takes the quite possibly harmless form of overreliance on expert counseling and guidance. This is the heyday of the psychiatrist. Yet one thoughtful psychiatrist recently remarked that some time the psychiatry of today may well be regarded as no less childish than medieval alchemy now seems to us. More significantly, the search for security seems to be indicated in the emphasis on conformity—on not sticking your neck out. Underneath it all is, one gathers, a feeling of powerlessness to do much except to gaze on what well may be impending disaster and to take such comfort as one can in the small, the immediate, the concrete things, in just getting along and just holding on. No longer are people shocked or greatly excited about a world of violence and catastrophe.

The mood seems to be one in which freedom is regarded as too negative to be satisfying—despite our verbal professions—that indeed freedom imposes too great a burden of anxieties in a perilously uncertain world. In the nineteenth century the great value attached to individual freedom—a value functional to so much elbow room and to such wide and varied opportunities—was complemented by the habit of forming and joining voluntary associations. Thus men and women escaped in at least some degree the loneliness that individualism often meant. We still have our voluntary associations. But, though the crowds are bigger than they were in the Age of Reason and Morality—if they are not lonelier—one must now think at least twice before running the risk of possible guilt by association! Man himself may not be obsolete, even in a world of incalculable and perhaps uncontrollable instruments of destruction. But in some quarters the feeling prevails that freedom and the will to use it for social reconstruction are more or less obsolete.

Finally, the reaction against the intellectual revolution of the later nineteenth century and the early twentieth may perhaps also be seen in the distrust in many circles of the scientific method itself as an instrument for guiding men out of chaos and darkness into peace and light. Perhaps it is another irony of American history that the scientific methods and techniques to which we owe so much can also be used to incite hysterical emotion and to make man's destruction of humanity more efficient. Thus in the amazing atomic age the retreat from reason has led many to abandon faith in science. No substitute, no new faith, has as yet been found which seems completely to fill the gap left by the retreat from reason. Neither neo-Thomism nor neoörthodoxy has swept the country. May, perhaps, the future historian conclude that the dominant faith of our time is the religion of nationalism—the American way? This of course is not a new faith. It goes back to our colonial experience. It was nourished by the Enlightenment and by its romantic aftermath. It was consolidated and sharpened as the nineteenth century ran its course. Yet nationalism now seems to have fewer competing loyalties than ever before.

All this suggests that the exponents of the newer theories of human nature and of the empirical approach in the social sciences expected too much, too soon. Many feel that science has been a god, and a false one no longer to be trusted to establish goals and to determine values by which man is to live; hence the tendency of many to seek for security in authoritarian philosophies or orthodox religious faith. Hence the tendency of others to turn their faces against the unresolved conflicts of our time and to find solace in the arts. Hence the tendency of still others to despair of man's faith in his ability to bring about that which ought to be, to give way rather to the dark and hopeless cult of irrationality, or to brood on the rediscovery and implications of the problem of evil. Hence the renewed faith in American nationalism, and renewed opposition in many quarters to internationalism.

Time, of course, may prove that the current reaction against both the surviving heritage of the Age of Reason and Morality and the intellectual revolution of the last part of the nineteenth century and the early years of our own is only temporary. Certainly the historian may properly suggest that this may be the case. If so, the historian of the future will attach less importance to the reaction than do many thoughtful men and women today. It is of course natural for those who came to maturity in a world of depression, war, and prospects of war to expect little—to expect *too* little, to reconcile themselves too easily to an acceptance of what is and what seems likely to be. It is also understandable that many of my generation whose hopes have been dimmed by mankind's crucifixion in the past quarter of a century should share the view so common apparently among younger people in this country and in so many others. But I for one am convinced that this is not the part either of realism or of wisdom. Or of sound historical perspective. For, should the world crisis persist, should fear and suspicion and hatred and reliance on force continue to be man's chief outlet, then we may be sure that we shall have to face crises that will shake the world—and events that may quite possibly destroy civilization.

Each of us, whether he knows it or not, has some kind of a world view, vague and inarticulate, or clear and expressed. Each must take some stand in the current crisis. Not to take one is, in effect, to take one.

My own general approach to the problems of our time, based in some part on my study of changing concepts of human nature, may have some interest. I believe that we should make room in our outlook for tested knowledge about human nature and social behavior. But if we are wise we shall also provide for the revision of that knowledge—for what we now know, or think we know, is not the last word. And I am equally convinced that we should find out how to make more constructive use of the knowledge we have. For the gulf between traditional American values and professions and actual individual and social behavior seems to be ominously widening. We can of course say that the ideals so generously and eloquently expressed in the American experience assumed too much and must be pared down. But let us not pare down too much! For if we do, we confess our bankruptcy. We also confess that we do not choose to take our stand with those great and bold spirits, of other lands as well as our own, those great and bold spirits, known and unknown, recorded and unrecorded, who have helped develop the higher values of civilization and who have struggled for their realization. The American phase of that struggle has been especially full of promise, not only for Americans, but for millions of men and women the world over.

In other words, we can not separate ourselves from the past; and we may still choose what aspects of the past we cherish and in cherishing will try to advance. And in any long historical perspective we may still find exciting and exhilarating the great ethical values that man has developed and the rich esthetic gifts and potentialities he has evidenced. If we would be truly realistic, I think we must temper our recognition of man's biological limitations with an appreciation of his great achievements, in the field of social and political thought as well as in natural science and technology. And, of great importance in these times, I believe we must try to understand and in the best sense appreciate other cultures and systems —even those in conflict with our own. Moreover, I think we should make a truly experimental and sustained effort to think and to act in ways likely to encourage a similar understanding and tolerance of us on the part of others. Finally, I think it is possible to choose whether one wants to express what I have been saying in the symbols of the Christian vision of man's weakness and of his ability to progress toward redemption; or whether he wants to put it in the humanistic and naturalistic terms that American thought about human nature and social values also includes.

I know, of course, how hard it is, especially at this time, to formulate a clear outlook on the world, an outlook that seems to be both realistic and idealistic in terms of what we know about human nature and about the ideals and values America has received, succored, modified, and created. But we are heirs of an American experience that has cherished new beginnings and sustained a faith in our capacity to direct our fate along rational and humane paths. In the words of a great historian, once a teacher in this university, we may conclude:

Long the victim of material forces, man had, by taking thought, made himself the master of wind and wave and storm. May he not, by taking thought . . . make himself the master of his social destiny? Perhaps not; but as the human mind is greater than the waterfall which it compels or the lightning's flash which it confines, so the control of human destiny is a nobler object than the search for material power. Even though every door be slammed in our faces, still we must knock.[29]

[29] Charles A. Beard, *The Economic Basis of Politics* (New York, 1947), p. 3.

7

Dime Novels and the American Tradition (1937)

THE ballad and the folk song have long been recognized as important keys to the thought and feeling of a people, but the dime novel, though sought by the collector and deferred to in a general way by the social historian, is dismissed with a smile of amusement by almost everyone else. Neither the folk songs nor the dime novels were actually created by the plain people of America. But in their devotion to these modes of expression, they made them their own. The dime novel, intended as it was for the great masses and designed to fill the pockets of both author and publisher, sought quite naturally the lowest common denominator: themes that were found to be popular, attitudes that met with the most general approval, became stereotyped. Moreover, the dime novel, reflecting a much wider range of attitudes and ideas than the ballad and the folk song, is the nearest thing we have had in this country to what is now so much discussed, a true "proletarian" literature, that is, a literature written for the great masses of people and actually read by them.

Although a study of our dime novels alone cannot enable anyone to determine what are the essential characteristics in the American tradition, it can contribute very materially to that end. Sooner or later, almost certainly, the industrious researchers who have

mined so many obscure lodes of American literary expression will
turn their attention to these novels and all their kin. Let no one
think, however, that the salmon-covered paperbacks once so eagerly
devoured by soldiers, lumberjacks, trainmen, hired girls, and adolescent boys now make exciting or agreeable reading—even for the
historian, much as their social and historical implications may interest him. As for the crowds who get their sensational thrills today
from the movies and the tabloids, I fear that they would find these
hair-raisers of an earlier age deadly dull.

Before considering the relation of the dime novel to the American tradition and its importance to the historian of ideas and feelings, it may be well to call attention to the immediate forerunners
of the five- and ten-cent paperback with its lurid cover illustration,
which so shocked middle-class prejudices that small boys from
"good" families had to read this "trash" in haystacks or attics. It has
long been associated with the names of Erasmus and Irwin Beadle.
But contrary to a general impression, the dime novel did not
spring full-grown from their minds when in 1860 they published
Malaeska: the Indian Wife of the White Hunter, the first of the
famous series that ultimately netted the Beadles and their humble
employee, George P. Munro, over thirteen millions of dollars. For
at least twenty years before *Malaeska* was released from the press
the dime novel had been in the making. Such publishers as Gleason
in Boston, Stratton and Barnard in Cincinnati, Peterson and
Graham in Philadelphia, and DeWitt and Davenport and Robert
Bonner in New York had begun as early as the 1840's to issue, for
a quarter and occasionally for even less, paper-covered novelettes
full of sensation, mystery, romance, and blood-and-thunder. Long
before 1860, Emerson Bennett's melodramatic adventure stories of
the West, "Ned Buntline's" rowdy and jingoistic romances of sea
pirates, Joseph Holt Ingraham's sensational and sentimental tales,
and the deep purple creations of George Lippard had demonstrated
that there was a market among the masses for the kind of products
that the Beadles were to turn out in large quantities. Nor was the
rise of this proletarian literature a uniquely American phenomenon:

enterprising publishers in this country sometimes pirated whole series of English equivalents, the "shilling shockers."

The pre-Civil War cheap literature for the masses and the dime novel, which grew out of it, ministered to diverse needs. No doubt, the chief function of this "subliterary" fiction was to supply a general demand of the common people, who were becoming reading-conscious as a result of the movement for free public schools and the rise of the penny press. In the Jacksonian democracy of the time, the ordinary man, aware of his political weight, quite naturally turned to the type of reading which recognized his worth as an individual and gave him a sense of importance in the world. It is also true, of course, that cheap literature provided the farmers, lumberjacks, and canal men with diversion. Then too, country folk were moving in great numbers to the miraculously growing towns, and even in the city, for all its novelty, the necessarily hard life of the common people tended to become humdrum. In the exciting, melodramatic action of the yellowback, they found vicarious adventure, an escape from everyday routine. Above all, through these novels people could gain a renewed faith in the desirability of self-reliance and the possibility of achievement, which their authors extolled.

This cheap fiction, ministering to the needs of humble folk, emphasized certain popular themes and values. It is not too much to say that one of the leading features of the dime novel, as of our cheap literature in other forms before the Civil War, was its promotion of the spirit of adventure, or, to use a more recent term, rugged individualism. A great deal of the popularity of the yellowback lay in its exaltation of favorite American types of the day—the adventurer or the frontiersman—as opposed to the people who led sheltered lives. Whether the hero makes good and achieves success and renown on a privateer or on a whaler, in the big city or on the frontier, he invariably does so through his shrewdness, his pluck, his dogged courage and determination, his individual prowess. The confidence man is outwitted, the wicked speculator is brought to bay, the frontier rascal, the outlaw, and the desperado, the cad and the dandy, the female impostor—all these are over-come by the sheer force of rugged individualism and courageous exploits.

Even when there is a crying social evil, the remedy is never found in a social attack on the problem but rather in single-handed effort. Thus, for instance, in *The Maid of Wyoming, or, the Contest of the Clans,* a Beadle novel of 1866, John Bradbury resorts to direct action to keep the Yankees from taking up land in the rich valley and, in doing so, displays an ambition for wealth and do-minion over his fellow man which leads his daughter to turn against him and to support the newcomers. Her encouragement of the hero helps to bring out his inborn talents as a leader and to win the day for the principle of a community of freeholders rather than one of tenants and proprietor. In another novel, about the dastardly practices by which a Chicago mercantile firm was swindling certain of its own partners, we find that the trouble was at length ended not by legal action or some other type of social attack, but by the heroism of two men—Jack Bledsoe, a Westerner of sterling cour-age, and Joe, a street boy with a shrewd mind and a heart of gold. Similarly, the heroine in *The Country Cousin* was warned on set-ting out for New York that she must, in that den of wickedness, rely on herself alone if she was to escape being devoured by the lions.

In the dime novels dealing with the American Revolution—a surprisingly large category—the popular ideal of the self-made man was portrayed with as much vigor as in the stories of the Wild West and the big city. The brave-hearted blacksmith Simon Hunt, the hero of *Cedar Swamp,* found his reward for the sacrifices he had endured for his country's cause. Years afterward, at a military reunion, blacksmith Hunt was introduced as "the Hon. Simon Hunt"—upright, clear-headed, self-educated statesman. William Eyster, the author, observed that "the States, just escaped from despotism and reckless rulers, needed just such men to assist in their counsels."

Thus the American faith in rugged individualism and in bold-spirited struggle against unfavorable circumstances was abundantly reflected in the dime novels. These novels, particularly those of the frontier, spreading as they did like a forest fire over the land, provided vicarious adventure to stay-at-homes and at the same time confirmed Americans in the traditional belief that obstacles were to be overcome by the courageous, virile, and determined stand of the individual as an individual.

The dime novel not only idealized and promoted the spirit of adventure and individualism; in good Jacksonian fashion it also exalted the humble man as opposed to those born with a silver spoon in their mouths. The cult of the plain people, already well on the way toward its flowering before the Beadles began in 1860 to publish their ten-cent thrillers, was exemplified again and again in the tons of paperbacks turned out by that enterprising firm and its competitors, George Munro, Street and Smith, and the lesser fry. Writing for the masses, it was, of course, entirely natural that the newspapermen, teachers, and freelancers who did hack work for the dime-novel publishers should express sympathy for the underdog. The plain folk—the humble farmer, artisan, hunter, or cowboy—were frequently idealized and sentimentalized.

The democratic implications of the dime novels are legion. Though in some of them good blood might in the end be discovered in a hero or heroine who had throughout the book seemed to be of obscure birth, this was by no means a general rule. In the stories of the American Revolution, to take a popular type, the struggle for independence is frequently interpreted as a contest between the colonial aristocrats and the plebeians. This is especially surprising since the conventional treatment of the War for Independence in the Peter Parley and the McGuffey schoolbooks, to say nothing of the great majority of Fourth of July orations of the time, gave little hint of the fact that the Revolution was a social struggle.

A recurrent situation in the dime novel of the Revolution shows a humble patriot maid rejecting a Briton or a Tory who, on seeking her hand, assures her that he could offer her wealth and position. So Bessie, the heroine in *Mossfoot the Brave,* dismissed with ridicule the aristocratic Tory from his languishing position at her feet. "Mr. Swinton," she said, "we are plain farmers here, and do not understand fine speeches, especially from people who regard themselves as high above us in social rank. Probably among those of your own class a compliment of that kind—for I suppose you intended it to be meant as a compliment—might meet with approval, but it is lost on me."

The condescending Tory treatment of plain people was again and again crudely satirized in order to bring out the democratic fashion in which patriots dealt with those in a lower social scale. Nat Blake, the henchman and tool of the Tory villain Robert Atnee, in *The King's Man,* was much wronged by his master, but he knew his place. "Oh, I forgot myself," he returned on one occasion when he might have seemed a bit too forward in his suggestions. "You are the gentleman, I am the scoundrel. 'Tis you who plan; I am the tool to execute." Contrast this with the frank, kindly, and democratic way in which patriotic Americans, of whatever rank, are represented as treating artisans, farmers, and servants, and it becomes clear that the writers of these books saw in the American Revolution a democratic movement, in part, designed to supplant the rule of a privileged colonial aristocracy.

But the most striking democratic implications which the dime-novel writers ascribe to the American cause appear in the favorite theme of its emancipation of the rank and file from the grinding overlordship of feudal masters. In *Dauntless Dick,* for example, the bold privateer ultimately married well and became thoroughly respectable because the changes in his environment which followed success in the Revolution brought out the innate excellence which had been "cruelly and unjustly withheld" by the circumstances of provincial society. Indeed, the idea that the Revolution freed new human energies previously confined by an entrenched aristocracy is illustrated again and again in the emphasis put on the birth of a democratic society with the success of American arms. In one tale, John Paul Jones, who has been brutally scolded by the Earl of

Selkirk, father of his sweetheart, for having the plebeian effrontery to take an interest in his daughter, is made to reply: "My lord, farewell. . . . You may think that there are no gentlemen but those born in the purple. Before many years are over, my lord, you will see a nation of gentlemen arise across the ocean, that never knew a lord. To that nation I go; and you, my lord, who supported the stamp duties, will live to see the fairest jewel of the British crown wrenched from it by the hands of those whom you call plebeians. I shall be among them, my lord." And so he was, keeping his promise to make his name ring all through England as a name of fear.

Nor did the American Revolution, in the eyes of dime-novel writers, fail to liberate the obscure woman, who, along with the men, rose from the ranks to positions of importance. One of them tells the story of Deborah Sampson, born of poor and inferior parents, who had as an indentured servant learned to read tolerably well. Donning soldierly attire, she fought unsuspected in the ranks until sickness led to the discovery of her secret. Her name, we read, became venerated as that of a self-made woman whose great gifts the War for Independence had released for a great cause.

The same idealization of the plain people and the same disparaging of the enemy as uppity and exclusive may doubtless be found in the dime novels dealing with the Civil War, for in those I have sampled by Northern writers the Boys in Blue are pictured as democratic, the Rebs in Gray as haughty and aristocratic. The clash between the proud and the humble was certainly exploited by the writers of all these romances in order to heighten conflict and action. But they may very well have felt that the novels would also have a greater appeal to the trainmen, lumberjacks, servant girls, and bargemen who were their chief purchasers at railway bookstalls and newsstands if the aristocracy were made as unattractive as possible, if democracy were glorified by being identified with patriotism and, as was invariably true, with the happy ending. The amazing success of George Lippard's novels of the Revolution, which interpreted the struggle from a similarly radical, democratic point of view, was no doubt recalled by the Beadles and their corps of writers who followed him. However, it is not improbable that the democratic attitude of these authors rested on genuine conviction quite as much as it did on any mercenary calculation.

There is no way of determining the extent to which this democratic social and political interpretation of the Revolution affected the millions who read the novels. Perhaps there was little serious influence; doubtless the main impression made was the momentary excitement or diversion. In any case, the conception of the Revolution as a class movement, as a great struggle between democracy and aristocracy, which was implicit in these best-sellers, did not, apparently, persist, unless such an image of the struggle begun in 1776 lingered on in some "underground" way, or in types of expression not yet studied. It would seem more likely that the picture of the Revolution as a social struggle did not survive after the dime novel was replaced by newer commercial ventures for the absorption of leisure. Conceivably it was whittled away by antithetical influences and propaganda. But that is another story.

The dime novel not only idealized the adventurous life of the self-made man and exalted the lowly; it also exalted the American people above all others. Some of the creators of our cheap literature for the people, men like Sylvanus Cobb, Jr., and Edward Z. C. Judson, were aggressive champions of the Know-Nothing movement and regarded themselves as divinely commissioned to uphold "Americanism." Indeed, no very wide acquaintance with the Beadle imprint, or with that of the Munros and of Street and Smith—the most prolific purveyors of this cheap literature—is necessary to indicate that it was a factor, and probably an important one, in the development of American patriotism and nationalism. In emphasizing the uniqueness and the superiority of American scenery, institutions, and, especially, American character, the dime novels must have enhanced national pride and patriotic devotion in the minds of their masses of readers.

The frontier, for example, was glorified and idealized as a distinctively American phenomenon. Of course, it was a highly colored picture of the West which hack writers painted for Easterners through the almost endless succession of stories about Texas Rangers and cowboys, Nevada miners, California vigilantes, and Montana bad men. But through this medium the West entered into the consciousness of a large number of Americans and became for the first time a living reality. It was thought of as peculiarly American. Endowed as it was with the spirit of adventure and romance, manly courage and female virtue, this image of the West was an engaging one. It is not at all unlikely, furthermore, that the recent concern of the historian, critic, and novelist with the frontier as a factor in American development is related to the interest which Emerson Bennett, "Ned Buntline," and Edward Wheeler, the creator of Deadwood Dick, aroused in their youthful readers in the sixties, seventies, and eighties.

The novels for the people likewise expressed and probably promoted American nationalism by the prevailing attitude of the authors toward the Indian, the Negro, and the immigrant. In the romances dealing with the successive frontiers the Indian was generally pictured neither as a noble savage nor as a merely backward racial type, but as an innately primitive, stubborn, treacherous, and vindictive barbarian, destined to give way to a superior race. The Negro was sentimentalized but described as definitely inferior to the white man. And, in general, newcomers seem to have been less favorably treated than the native-born old American stock.

By familiarizing a public that read little and traveled less with a considerable body of the legend and history of their country, the dime novels still further promoted the spirit of nationalism; and they did this in such a way as to leave small doubt regarding the superiority of America to all other countries. George Lippard, in his *Legends of the American Revolution* (1847), created and popularized many a patriotic myth to which the public clung tenaciously. The editor of a somewhat later popular series of dime tales declared:

The reader will long linger over these pages thrilled by the consciousness that the scenes so vividly brought before him are a real, a living, abiding part of our existence as a people. The "storied Rhine" and "classic Italy" are laid and overlaid thickly with traditions which give a vague interest to soil, ruin, mountain and sky. We, also, have our traditions—different in kind, but of wild and marvellous interest—and the day shall come when the banks of the fair Ohio, the blue Muskingum, the picturesque Albany, the noble Mississippi, shall be trodden by reverent feet, while the thoughts of the traveler speed back to the days of the lurking red-man and the bold ranger. It is no mean duty of the chronicler to treasure up the threads of a thousand little facts, and weave them into a web which shall perpetuate them for the future.

Of all the dime novels designed to inspire patriotism, no group was more important than that dealing with the American Revolution, the most popular topic of the historical romances. Indeed, this struggle provided more titles, apparently, than did urban life, or than any single theme save the frontier itself. At least thirty-two authors tried their hands at Revolutionary stories, and of the two thousand dime and half-dime novels in the Huntington Library— one of the richest collections in existence—upward of eighty are on this subject. All through the 1860's, the Revolution was, in fact, the favorite theme. This is the more interesting in view of the widely accepted interpretation of the Civil War as "the second American Revolution." That war called forth a mass of literature to stimulate patriotism by making the War for Independence live again in the imaginations and hearts of those fighting, as they saw it, to save the independence that had been won by their forefathers at Concord, Lexington, Saratoga, and Yorktown. Hundreds of thousands of soldiers in the northern armies during the Civil War must also have been quickened in loyalty to the Stars and Stripes, in their willingness to undergo privation and sacrifice, by the lessons of patriotism and sacrifice inculcated by the "thrillers" which Beadle and Company were said to have tied up like bales of hay and shipped to the front. Light and compact, these little books could easily be carried in a knapsack and "swapped" in camp, hospital, or prison. In 1862, in announcing a new story of the American Revolution by the popular writer N. C. Irons, the publishers observed that "the leading characters are persons of historic truthfulness, rendering the novel a fine transcript of those times of great sacrifices and noble aspirations. It is one of Mr. Irons' finest historical romances; and, in these stirring days when the Old Continental spirit is being reawakened, it will give particular satisfaction to the readers of fiction."

Although the Centennial Year, 1876, called forth another crop, new preoccupations, such as the putting down of the Indians and the fighting of the bad men in the Far West, dominated the minds of novel writers. Still, scattered titles on the American Revolution appeared until well into the nineties, when the heyday of the dime novels themselves had passed. Even after the turn of the century, a new series, The Liberty Boys, continued the tradition.

The authors who exploited the Revolution for their romances varied considerably in their acquaintance with the historical material with which they dealt. Many revealed the most scanty knowledge of their country's early history; but others, such as O. J. Victor, Elizabeth Oakes Smith, John Neal, and especially Charles Dunning Clark, a journalist of Oswego, New York, were fairly at home in it. Clark, who took the pen name "W. J. Hamilton," was a local historian of the country about Oswego, and his specialized knowledge stood him in good stead in the services rendered to the Beadle publishing house. Even the best authors like Clark and A. J. H. Duganne, a philosophical radical, who had contributed to the Fourierist periodical *The Harbinger*, were naturally far more interested in plot, action, romance, and mystery than in the social, political, and philosophical implications of the Revolution itself. Yet it is not difficult to reconstruct from them a picture of the Revolution which must have been fairly well established in the minds of habitual readers of the dime and nickel novels. This can be done partly by taking into account the explicit pronouncements of characters, partly by studying what is implicit in situations and, above all, the everyday behavior of the hero, the villain, and their copartners. The picture of the Revolution which thus emerges is not only a very interesting one but also has a special significance in relation to the version of the American Revolution which was current in the writings of standard historians of the time.

The dime novels dealing with the Revolution, like those concerned with the frontier and with city themes, obviously owe a good deal to their cheap and sensational predecessors. Of the writers for the masses before the time of the Beadles, an impressive number, including Benjamin Barker, Henry A. Buckingham, Park Clinton, Sylvanus Cobb, Jr., Newton Mallory Curtis, and others, struck off romances of the Revolution. But no one did more to celebrate the birth of the nation than Daniel Thompson, the Vermont lawyer whose *Green Mountain Boys* became a sort of folk novel, and George Lippard, the eccentric Philadelphia lawyer who scandalized the well-born and the well-established by his sensational revelations of "the upper ten and the lower ten thousand."

The popular Revolutionary novels that came both before and after the Beadles began their publications in 1860 appealed to a much wider public than did the somewhat more refined romances on the same period, from which the writers for the people took many cues. Between the brittle paper covers of these now rare best-sellers of a century and less ago, one can find, unmistakably, reflections of James Fenimore Cooper, Lydia M. Child, Charles Fenno Hoffman, William Gilmore Simms, and John Pendleton Kennedy. The relationships between "highbrow" and "lowbrow" literature must be better understood before we can attack one of the major problems in American culture, that of the transit of ideas, attitudes, and tastes not merely from Europe to America, and from one locality to another, but also from one cultural and class level to another. In structure and in their interpretation of the Revolution, the more genteel novels had many features in common with their humbler and more popular contemporaries and with the later Beadle dime stories of the struggle for independence. Both the more "highbrow" and the "lowbrow" stories emphasized adventure, action, mystery; both associated patriotism with physical attractiveness and courage; both found their conflicts in the struggles of Whigs and Tories and the depredations of Indians allied to the British cause. In the one as in the other, bloody encounters, hairbreadth escapes, abductions of heroines, and thrilling naval or military engagements are the order of the day. In both there is conflict between patriotism and selfishness; in both virtue generally triumphs over adversity.

But there are noticeable differences. The dime novels, unlike many of the more "highbrow" forerunners, almost always end happily. True, the very first of the Beadle series has a sad ending, but one searches in vain for anything resembling the tragedy of *Amelia, or, the Faithless Briton* (1798), a gruesome story in which the heroine, betrayed by a handsome but dissipated and worthless British officer, poisons herself. Nor is there any parallel in the dime novels to James McHenry's *Meredith, or the Mystery of Meschianza* (1831), a more complex but no less stark tragedy.

Other differences, apart from the shorter length and cheaper price of the dime novel, are differences of degree. The books for the masses are more exciting, more melodramatic. There is more blood, and more thunder, in them. The action is swifter; the descriptive details that weighed down the Revolutionary romances of Cooper and Simms are left out. The dime novels are even more moral than their lofty counterparts, and these were indeed moral enough! Characters are more wooden and incredible; conceptions of human nature, absolutistic and crude. All this may mean that popular taste craved such unrealistic treatment, but it may also be attributed to the fact that the authors who catered to it were poor writers turning out their products mechanically.

Of greater importance, from the social point of view, is the fact that in the cheap novels the Revolution itself is interpreted with more highly colored and jingoistic patriotism and more militant democracy than in the "literary" fiction. They resemble in this respect both the Fourth of July orations which had such a vogue during the boyhood of the writers of the dime series and the earlier spread-eagle romances of the Revolution, for which George Lippard was, above all others, responsible.

Without exception these dime novels encouraged their readers to believe in the inevitability of the war. None but the most critical could doubt, after reading four or five of these books, that liberty could have been won and secured only by bloodshed. No mention is ever made of England's divided mind on the colonial question or of the possibility of any solution other than the appeal to arms. "In all history," says one of their heroines, "it is recorded that the price of liberty is blood and never is this envied boon yielded by the grace of rulers. It is wrested by the sword, and so fatal is usually the struggle that the sweets which freedom give to life are rarely enjoyed by those who win them." This is quite typical of the way in which they built up the idea that the Americans were justified in appealing to the sword.

For the most part, responsibility for the Revolution was laid at the door of the King and his tyrannical interference with the liberties and property of his American subjects. Frequently heroes spoke bitterly and harshly of the monarch. "Dearest Agnes," says Felix Temple to his tender-hearted, beloved Agnes Falkland, "no other currency will redeem us from the King of England's tyranny than blood. He is rapacious as the Hindoo Olin, and demands human sacrifices of unconditional servitude."

In the black-and-white picture which upheld the complete justice of the American cause there was no place for honest or idealistic dissent, as may be seen from the treatment of Quakers. No Friend, in any of the novels, stood stoutly by his convictions. Even the most consistent, like Onadiah Prim, after expressing stern disapproval of the trade of soldiering, gave succor to wounded Americans. Many, like Stoddard Franklin, a young Quaker preacher, actually took up arms in defense of home and kindred when they were threatened by the deadly Indian allies of the British.

In his interpretation of the Revolution as a spontaneous uprising of the true and the bold and the righteous, the dime novelist did not for a moment suggest that they met with no opposition from their fellow countrymen. On the contrary! The conflict necessary for the proper rendering of melodramatic action was easily found in the strife between Patriot and Tory. One discovers in the dime novels of the Revolution, and in the earlier fiction for the masses which George Lippard wrote, a picture of bitter civil war which seldom found expression in the school texts or other non-fictional treatments of the struggle. Thus in some respects these novels presented the Revolution more accurately than did the sober histories of Botta, Marshall, Hildreth, and Parson Weems.

With few exceptions, the Tory is portrayed in a way to inculcate disdain and hatred. He is frequently courtly, debonair, smooth-tongued; he is always haughty and un-American. Often he is a dark, sinister character. In most cases he is motivated by mercenary principles. Timothy Turner, the villain in *Cedar Swamp,* sells the British his "very soul and body for paltry gold," while others build their fortunes on the iniquitous slave trade, or, like David Marks, on the unscrupulous exploitation, through moneylending, of honest and simple farm neighbors. Now and then a Tory appears as a worthless vagabond, but more often King George's men are utter swine, despicable beyond words. Of this type is Chester Dingley, the stout, red-faced, pompous villain who tries to win the hand of lovely and brave Edith Alston, only because he is convinced that her father's magnificent estates will become his as soon as His Majesty's troops are victorious and the rebel properties are confiscated for the benefit of the loyal. Some of these wretches are even more brutal. More than one who has captured the lover of a patriot heroine forces her to choose between marrying the captor whom she despises or seeing her beloved executed as a spy. In the rare instances when a British officer is endowed with some of the qualities of a hero—Marcus Goodheart in *Maid of Esopus* is a lonely example—the American heroine in the end chooses the patriot hero. Thus the pattern which identified the victory of true love with the ultimate triumph of patriotism is not broken.

In contrast with the Tories, American patriots are pictured invariably as most engaging and superior. Among them we find no rascal, no brute, no Judas. For the most part, upholders of the American cause are good, simple folk, honest farmers, or sturdy artisans—possessed of all the homely virtues, like the heroes of many modern proletarian novels.

While in a few novels of border warfare those allied with the patriot cause are guilty of unseemly violence and depredation, it is the British and the Tories, with their Indian allies, who are responsible for the worst brutalities. The burning of homes; murder, confiscation, violence, rapine; plundering, imprisoning, hanging by wholesale—these are the work of the British and their Tory henchmen. The whole point of John Neal's *The White-Faced Pacer* is the contrast in the inhuman treatment accorded by the British to Nathan Hale and the decency shown by the Americans to Major André. No one who based his judgment—as thousands must have done—on a reading of the dime novels dealing with the events of '76 and subsequent years would doubt that the Americans were kindly and humane as well as righteous, or that the British and Tories were with few exceptions vindictive and cruel as well as mistaken and tyrannical.

The patriotic spirit of these dime novels was of an elemental sort such as adherents of the slogan "My country right or wrong" could accept. It identified patriotism not with love of the land itself, not with a definite tradition and a common goal, but with vague, generalized concepts such as "liberty" and "right." This unthinking type of patriotism was just the kind that played a part in the heated relations with England which accompanied and followed the Civil War, relations which showed marked improvement only at the very end of the century. Even though it is impossible to put one's finger on any definite connection between the dime-novel patriotism and the clamor for war with England on so many occasions, it is not unreasonable to assume that there was such a connection.

In illustrating the subliterary interpretation of American patriotism and nationalism, the Revolutionary dime novels deserve emphasis. No doubt a study of the formidable output celebrating the Civil War would reveal a somewhat similar brand of patriotism. Any thoroughgoing study of the American tradition as cherished by the masses of the people calls, of course, for consideration of subliterary fiction of all periods. Dime novels could also be profitably read in order to determine attitudes toward other problems in our cultural history, as, for example, popular notions of "book-learning," foreigners, "inferior" races, wealth, and "success." Certainly the student of social and intellectual history who tries to understand the transit of ideas from the more favored to the less favored must examine the dime novels. These fragile, rare, and highly fugitive books will be useful likewise to anyone interested in proletarian literature. They must be taken into account particularly by those interested in the democratization of culture and the commercialization of leisure, in the rise and reinforcement of our traditions of adventure and rugged individualism, in the development of class consciousness, and in the growth of American patriotism and nationalism.

PART III

America
Reaching Outward

8

The Reputation of
America Overseas,
1776–1860 (1949)

IN DRAFTING the Declaration of Independence the fathers, imbued with "a decent respect for the opinions of mankind," submitted their view of things to a "candid world." But this official effort to promote the American case overseas did not become a precedent. While the government was at no time wholly blind to foreign views of American policy, only in great crises such as the Civil War and World War I did it take the trouble to give the world our side of the story.

In our own time the more thoughtful and articulate part of the population has been disturbed at the misconceptions and even distortions of American institutions, values, and objectives that have prevailed in other countries. With an eye to hemispheric solidarity the government, just a decade ago, undertook to correct some of these images by tentatively embarking on an official program not only of defending its policies but also of explaining the American

NOTE. I wish to thank Kendall Birr, Frederick Jackson Turner research assistant at the University of Wisconsin, for his help in collecting material on certain topics dealt with in this paper.

way of life to our southern neighbors. In the throes of global war and its aftermath the program was broadened. But neither the Congress nor any influential section of the public has been keen about official explanations of American life and objectives to the peoples of other lands. This is the harder to understand in view of the treasure and thought other leading powers have lavished on their cultural-relations programs, all of which have in truth been conceived as instruments of national policy. It is the more curious that Americans have been largely indifferent in this sphere inasmuch as they have led the world in modern advertising techniques.

The time is surely at hand to consider the reasons for this state of affairs. The present essay, limited to the first eighty-five years of our national history, is an exploratory study, designed in part to call attention to some of the problems in this field that cry for investigation. It is also, in a sense, another chapter in the history of American patriotism. In addition, it is a contribution to a larger study of the images that peoples in other parts of the world have held of the United States. It is further hoped that this essay, exploratory and tentative though it is, may throw some light on the nature of American civilization in world perspective.

I

The nation started its independent career confronted by Old World prejudices against and misunderstandings of American institutions which even the greatest of the colonial agents, Benjamin Franklin, had been unable to dispel.[1] Throughout the era of the French Revolution and Napoleon, conservative Europeans saw in the United States a successful defiance of established authority and an experiment with republican and equalitarian principles dangerous to the established order in the Old World. The United States, Frederick von Schlegel declared in 1828 in a lecture at the Uni-

---

[1] For example, *A Conversation between an Englishman, a Scotchman, and an American* (London, 1770). This has only recently been identified as a piece by Franklin. For Franklin's habit of writing anonymously, see Verner W. Crane, *Benjamin Franklin, Englishman and American* (Baltimore, 1936), pp. 106–108.

versity of Vienna, had been for France and the rest of Europe "the real school and nursery of all these revolutionary principles."[2] The bitter anti-Americanism of British conservatives who spoke for the established order has in part been described.[3] The fear and jealousy of such conservatives was ill-concealed as late as the Civil War. Even after the triumph of northern arms, Cambridge University, having no mind to feed "American self-conceit," turned down a British offer of an endowed lectureship to deal with the history, literature, and institutions of the United States. The fact that Harvard was to name the incumbent was an additional reason for the rejection, inasmuch as that institution was regarded as badly tainted with Unitarianism.[4]

Even when English leaders of thought and policy were not ill-disposed toward America, their ignorance was often astounding. "Indeed, so little is known in Europe of the people of the United States," wrote an American critic of England in 1802, "that it would be necessary, if you would describe them, to affirm, with no little assurance, that they are white as other people, that they live in houses, that they boil and roast their meat, and that they speak the English language, at least as well as they do in Devonshire."[5] In 1818 a young American scholar reported that Southey, like "everybody else in Europe," was "totally ignorant of the character and spirit of the people and the genius of its institutions."[6] Ten years later Jared Sparks, while breakfasting at the house of Lord Brougham, discovered that not only his host but also J. S. Mill was "extremely misinformed" about the United States.[7]

[2] Frederick von Schlegel, *The Philosophy of History* (New York, 1841, 2 vols.), II, 272.

[3] Robert E. Spiller, *The American in England During the First Half Century of Independence* (New York, 1926); Richard H. Heindel, *The American Impact on Great Britain, 1898–1914* (Philadelphia, 1940), p. 292.

[4] *Anglo-American Times*, March 24, 1866; H. B. Learned, "The Thompson Readership: A Forgotten Episode of Academic History," *American Historical Review* (April, 1918), XXIII, 603–608.

[5] William Austin, *Letters from London* (Boston, 1804), p. 5.

[6] *Life of Joseph Green Cogswell as Sketched in His Letters* (Cambridge, Mass., 1874), p. 90.

[7] Herbert B. Adams, *The Life and Writings of Jared Sparks* (Boston and New York, 1893, 2 vols.), II, 60.

On the Continent, ignorance was even more marked. A few examples that could easily be multiplied many times must suffice to illustrate the point. In 1810 Europeans clung to utterly disproved notions regarding the inferiority of American climate, soil, fish, beasts, birds, plants, and men. "These absurdities," wrote an American defender, "appeared engraved with the stamp of knowledge and authority; their circulation was general and accredited; and it is amazing how current they continue to this day, notwithstanding the proofs that have successively adduced themselves of their falsification and baseness."[8] As late as the mid-century, John L. Motley discovered that almost no European had ever heard the name of Daniel Webster; few if any realized that the federal form of government made it impossible for the President to decree the abolition of slavery; and the great majority of the educated knew and cared nothing about the men of the United States or its politics or its condition. Only among the lower classes, to whom America was a place to escape from "the monotonous prison house," was the United States an object of curiosity and interest.[9] What Motley reported was similarly observed by other American travelers.[10]

Throughout the first half of the nineteenth century and beyond, prejudice against America continued to be widespread among the upper classes. It was if anything deepened by their disapproval of the great emigration and by the repudiation of debts on the part of several American states. A few examples must illustrate the theme. In 1800 a Swede, one Kierulf, who had returned from a transatlantic sojourn with an inveterate hatred of the republic, wrote essays meant to wean away European admirers from the American heresy. When challenged, he brought suit in both Hamburg and Berlin against those who dared take issue with him. "You see," wrote one of his critics to an American correspondent, "that you have terrible enemies in Europe."[11]

[8] Charles Jared Ingersoll, *Inchiquin, the Jesuit's Letters* (New York, 1810), pp. 164–165.
[9] George W. Curtis (ed.), *The Correspondence of John Lothrop Motley* (New York, 1889, 2 vols.), I, 147–148.
[10] James Freeman Clarke, *Eleven Weeks in Europe* (Boston, 1852), p. 50.
[11] William C. Lane (ed.), "Letters of Christopher D. Ebling," in *Proceedings of the American Antiquarian Society*, n.s. (1925), XXXV, 346–347.

Indeed, that was no exaggeration. Despite the fact that Charles Botta's friendly history of the American Revolution ran into many editions, only one Italian journal reviewed it and that one spoke of it in harsh terms. The regime of Louis XVIII forbade the circulation in France of the *North American Review*.[12] In Spain the censor for some time oddly regarded *Rip Van Winkle* as an attack on King Ferdinand![13] More understandably, Spanish authorities in the colonies of the New World spared no pains to keep wandering citizens of the United States from scattering copies of the Declaration of Independence and the Constitution.[14] The Reverend Philip Schaff reported in 1854 that many respectable men of high culture, especially in Austria, spoke only with contempt of America, which they regarded as "a grand bedlam, a rendezvous of European scamps and vagabonds."[15]

As late as the threshold of the Civil War, the study of American history and political institutions was apparently proscribed in all the continental universities save those of Switzerland. In 1858 Luigi Filippi, professor of history at Naples, was imprisoned by Ferdinand II for declaring to his students that George Washington was a great man whose example might be worthy of emulation. At about the same time, Dr. Carl Retslag, professor at Rostock, was allegedly given a two-week prison sentence for substituting a lecture on American institutions for one on Danish affairs. The King of Prussia and the Emperor of Austria-Hungary were reported to have refused permission for the establishment of chairs of American history at Berlin, Prague, and Vienna. Michelet's removal from his professorship in Paris had some relation, no doubt, to his pointed references to the American Revolution and to the inferences he drew from it. The doors of the Sorbonne closed to Edouard Laboulaye when he announced a lecture on the American Constitution.[16]

[12] Adams, *The Life and Writings of Jared Sparks*, I, 285; II, 93.

[13] John De Lancey Ferguson, *American Literature in Spain* (New York, 1916), p. 3.

[14] Harry Bernstein, *Origins of Inter-American Interest 1700–1812* (Philadelphia, 1945), pp. 79–80.

[15] Philip Schaff, *America. A Sketch of the Political, Social, and Religious Character of the United States* (New York, 1855), p. vii.

[16] *Appleton's Journal* (April 12, 1873), IX, 494.

II

If America had its foes in Europe, it also had friends. Champions of humanitarianism, liberalism, and democracy found in America a great inspiration and argument. The influence of the American Revolution on Mably, Condorcet, Herder, Goethe, Schiller, Wieland, Klopstock, and others has been well documented.[17] Long before the mid-nineteenth century American writers enjoyed wide popularity not only in Great Britain but on the Continent as well.[18] And in Great Britain proponents of reform, especially among the Chartists, cited the example of the United States in arguing for the measures close to their hearts.[19] Indeed, the inarticulate masses, according to the testimony of more than one American traveler, looked to the United States not only as an asylum to which to escape, but as a symbol of freedom and the poor man's paradise.[20]

In the sympathetic attitude of liberal leaders and the rank and file in Europe is to be found a reason for general American indifference toward the calumnies of conservatives and the widespread ignorance and misunderstanding of American institutions and values. To many it seemed sufficient that Europeans were correcting misinformation and promulgating proper views of American institutions. The labors of these men have never been adequately evalu-

[17] Beatrice M. Victory, *Benjamin Franklin and Germany* (Americana-Germanica No. 21, Publications of the University of Pennsylvania; Philadelphia, 1915); Michael Kraus, "Slavery Reform in the Eighteenth Century," *Pennsylvania Magazine of History and Biography* (January, 1936), LX, 54; Carl Wittke, "The American Theme in Continental Literatures," *Mississippi Valley Historical Review* (June, 1941), XXVIII, 3–26. See the studies of Gilbert Chinard, particularly *L'Amérique et le rêve exotique dans la littérature française au XVIIe et au XVIIIe siècle* (Paris, 1934).

[18] William B. Cairns, "British Republication of American Writings, 1783–1833," *Publications of the Modern Language Association* (March, 1928), XLIII, 303–310; Frederick Saunders, Progress and Prospects of America (New York, 1855), p. 21; Clarence Gohdes, *American Literature in Nineteenth-Century England* (New York, 1944).

[19] G. D. Lillibridge, "American Images in Great Britain 1820–1840," unpublished master's thesis, University of Wisconsin, 1948, and work in progress.

[20] Samuel G. Goodrich, *Recollections of a Lifetime* (New York, 1857, 2 vols.), II, 481; Clarke, *Eleven Weeks in Europe*, p. 50; Curtis, *Correspondence of John Lathrop Motley*, I, 147–148.

ated. They included Dr. Christopher D. Ebeling, Hamburg teacher, book collector, and gazetteer,[21] and several less well-known German editors and publishers of short-lived papers devoted to American materials,[22] Samuel T. Coleridge in England,[23] Sarmiento in Argentina,[24] and Sen Ki-yu in China.[25] But their story must be told elsewhere. In still other ways foreigners took some responsibility for presenting their compatriots with a more discriminating view of various aspects of American life. From England, France, Germany, and the Scandinavian lands came investigators commissioned by their governments to study American libraries, schools, prisons, the jury system, commercial policies, and internal improvements.[26] We may be reasonably sure, whatever further study of this neglected field reveals, that in limited circles at least the reports of these inquirers increased the understanding and appreciation of certain aspects of American civilization.

We must not overlook the vast array of books written by travelers to the United States. Many, to be sure, were ill-informed, prejudiced, and even hostile; but others were reasonably accurate in their information, while a few offered illuminating evaluations of

[21] See introductory notes, Lane, "Letters of Christopher D. Ebeling," American Antiquarian Society, Proceedings, 1925.

[22] For example, Atlantis, 1826–1827; Columbus, 1827-1832; Atlantische Studien, 1853–1857; Atlantis, 1854–1855, the files of which have been consulted. See also Thomas C. McCormick (ed.), Memoirs of Gustav Koerner 1809–1896 (Cedar Rapids, 1909, 2 vols.), I, 411–412, for a discussion of Westland, no file of which has been discovered.

[23] Adams, The Life and Writings of Jared Sparks, II, 130; Samuel T. Coleridge, The Table Talk and Omniana (London, 1923), pp. 132, 165, 208.

[24] Domingo Faustino Sarmiento, Viajes en Europa, Africa i America (Santiago, 1849–1851); Allison W. Bunkley (ed.), A Sarmiento Anthology (Princeton, 1948), pp. 5 ff.; Madaline W. Nichols, "A United States Tour by Sarmiento in 1847," Hispanic American Historical Review (May, 1936), XVI, 190–212.

[25] Foreign Relations 1867, I, 452–453, 512.

[26] Edward Livingston to Francis Lieber, May 19, 1833, Lieber Papers (Huntington Library); Sir Thomas Wyse, M. P., report in Publications of the Central Society of Education (London, 1838, 2 vols.); P. A. Siljestrom, Educational Institutions of the United States (London, 1853); J. L. Tellkampf, Essays on Law Reform, Commercial Policy, Banks, Penitentiaries in Great Britain and the United States (2nd ed., Berlin, 1875), pp. 187 ff.; Gunnar J. Malmin (ed.), America in the Forties. The Letters of Ole Munch Raeder (Minneapolis, 1929).

American institutions and life.[27] We need to explore more thoroughly the continental analyses of this type and to study their reception and influence in Europe. There is also much yet to be learned, despite existing monographs,[28] from a careful study of the 330-odd British travel books known to have been written before 1860. Finally, much work remains to be done in the emigrant guidebooks written and published in Europe by Europeans; while some of these, covertly designed to discourage immigration, were full of distortions, yet others were fairly informative manuals.[29]

The limited and sporadic efforts of European friends of America to develop a more reliable image of the United States did not in itself explain the failure of Americans themselves to develop a vigorous defense of their civilization. For one thing, most intellectuals throughout the first three-quarters of the nineteenth century tended to look on Europe as the fountain and seat of culture and to regard American achievements in all save material things as relatively inconsequential. Again, those who did look with pride on the nation's progress in political institutions and economic development were imbued with an unqualified faith in the doctrine of progress which led them to assume that in time the American example would automatically and imperceptibly conquer Europe. Hundreds of instances of this sort of reasoning might be cited. But the *Southern Literary Messenger* spoke for a multitude of prophets: "Already have the rotten and antiquated foundations of every despotic and exclusive institution of the Old World been silently undermined by the influence and example of self-government exhibited by the United States, and they only await a coming shock

[27] For example, Frederick von Raumer, *America and the American People* (New York, 1846); Philarète Chasles, *Anglo-American Literature and Manners* (New York, 1852); Michael Chevalier, *Society, Manners and Politics in the United States* (Boston, 1839).

[28] Jane Louise Mesick, *The English Traveler in America, 1785–1835* (New York, 1922); Max Berger, *The British Traveler in America, 1836–1860* (New York, 1943); and Allan Nevins, *America Through British Eyes* (New York, 1948).

[29] For example, Richard Holditch, *The Emigrant's Guide to the United States* (London, 1818); and *A Letter from a Tradesman Recently Arrived from America* (London, 1835).

to crumble into ruin."[30] Even the collapse of the revolutionary movement in 1848–1849 did not entirely dispel this fond illusion.[31]

III

In turning to the efforts of Americans themselves to present, not only to Europeans but to their southern neighbors and to the Orient, an appreciative picture of the institutions, objectives, and values of the United States, it is important to ask what interests and motives these defenses of American civilization represented. In some instances the personal motives back of the efforts are obvious; in others they can be discovered, if at all, only by further study of relevant private papers. In the case of the missionaries it is clear that religious motives predominated. Other champions of the American cause to peoples overseas were acting largely on patriotic or economic motives, or a combination of the two. However, the body of thought in the defense can best be presented here with reference to dominant arguments rather than in terms of the particular situation with which they were associated.

The first move in the American defense, resting largely on patriotic grounds but also in part on personal pique at the unfairness with which American writers had been reviewed in the British literary journals, was to question the motives and competence of British travelers in the New World. It was pointed out that few if any who came in the first quarter of the nineteenth century were men of literary distinction. The credulousness and the tendency of these travelers to generalize on the basis of a single experience were fully uncovered. Again, foreign reliance on the reports of immigrants was attacked. By accepting uncritically reports of disgruntled immigrants, in most cases "the very chaff of Europe," British critics only demonstrated, it was claimed, their utter lack of discrimination. It was, furthermore, common to indict the indicters by asserting that they feared the competition of American commerce and

[30] *Southern Literary Messenger* (July, 1842), VIII, 6.
[31] See the author's article, "The Impact of the Revolutions of 1848 on American Thought," in a forthcoming issue of the *Transactions of the American Philosophical Society*.

the example which successful republican institutions offered European radicals.[32]

Another approach was to write books on England for English readers in which, in effect, the pot called the kettle black. British calumnies on American institutions, character, and culture were matched, if not neutralized, by citing instances of British shortcomings: of corruption in church and state; of an idle aristocracy living on the fat of the land while farmers and town workers eked out a wretched existence; of profiteering in the illegal slave trade; of crime, misery, beggary; of swindling, forgery, and larceny; of medical, mechanical, and culinary quacks.[33]

In the bitter literary war, champions of America declared that if English letters could boast greater triumphs than the United States, at least there was no snobbish literary aristocracy in the new country.[34] In due time, moreover, America would show what it could do in writing books. Meantime a stout patriot insisted that if Americans were not yet capable of writing books of theory, they contrived to anticipate in practice the contents of those produced abroad—several years before their appearance! "When your writers present us with their systems, we are prepared to pronounce on their merits, for we have already tested them."[35]

One American defense deserves special attention. Robert Walsh's *An Appeal from the Judgments of Great Britain respecting the United States* was published at Philadelphia in 1819 and at London a bit later. Walsh, a Catholic of means, a book collector, a scholar, and a critic, wished "to repel actively, and, if possible, to arrest, the war which is waged without stint or intermission, upon our national reputation."[36] It was folly, he went on, to hope that

[32] James K. Paulding, *The United States and England* (New York, 1815), pp. 20–21; James Athearn Jones, *A Letter to an English Gentleman* (Philadelphia, 1838), pp. 18, 24.

[33] James K. Paulding, *A Sketch of Old England, by a New-England Man* (New York, 1822), *passim;* Royall Tyler, *The Yankee in London* (New York, 1808), *passim;* William Austin, *Letters from London, passim.*

[34] Jones, *A Letter to an English Gentleman,* pp. 35 ff.

[35] *Ibid.,* p. 42.

[36] Robert Walsh, *An Appeal from the Judgments of Great Britain respecting the United States* (Philadelphia, 1819), p. vi.

the British might assign some bounds to their attacks as long as Americans forbore recriminating in kind. So, having solicited aid from leading Americans, he dug up books and pamphlets and brooded over the information he found. Replying sharply to specific British travelers' diatribes, documenting British political and commercial jealousy of the United States, defending the colonial cause and the Revolution, laying at the door of England most of the blame for the existence of slavery in America, Walsh spared no pains, negatively and positively, in defending American civilization.

Both American and British periodicals at once responded. Writing in the *North American Review*, Edward Everett declared that Walsh was justified in recriminating against slander. "It is not only lawful for us, but it is our bounden duty to repel it; and we should deserve the abuse which has been heaped upon us, were we so insensible to the value of the national reputation as to leave it unrefuted."[37] Jefferson, Madison, John Adams, John Quincy Adams were only a few of the well-known Americans who rushed congratulations to the doughty Philadelphian. The Pennsylvania legislature passed a joint resolution of commendation and purchased a copy of the *Appeal* for each member. In England Walsh's book was, of course, bitterly attacked in the leading periodicals. But it was read in high circles and, according to report, not without good effect.[38]

Others continued the literary war. Egotistical and swashbuckling John Neal of Maine invaded England determined to prove that the British would read an American book, or at least an American article, despite Sydney Smith's famous question, "Who reads an American book?" Neal succeeded in persuading some of the leading literary journals to accept articles that at least mildly defended American writers and Presidents.[39]

[37] *North American Review* (April, 1820), X, 349.
[38] Sister M. Frederick Lochemes, *Robert Walsh: His Story* (Washington, 1941), chap. 6.
[39] John Neal, *Wandering Recollections of a Somewhat Busy Life* (Boston, 1869), pp. 245 ff., 339. See also Fred Lewis Pattee (ed.), *American Writers. A Series of Papers Contributed to Blackwood's Magazine* (1824–1825) by John Neal (Durham, N.C., 1937).

Cooper's *Notions of the Americans*, published in 1828, was an even more spirited defense of American institutions. A goodly company of American students, authors, and travelers in England tried, consciously and unconsciously, to answer English criticism of their country by giving evidence of good breeding, sympathy with British culture, and their own kinship with it. Thanks to such men as Emerson, Longfellow, Hawthorne, and others whose books enjoyed no little popularity in England, a more cordial attitude toward America was gradually promoted.[40]

Not, apparently, until Lowell's famous essay of 1869, "On a Certain Condescension in Foreigners," did an American man of letters with skill and wit try to set the British straight on American objectives, institutions, and character. The *Atlantic Monthly* essay of 1869 had none of the militant, vitriolic tone of Walsh's *Appeal*. Urbane, appreciative of the richness of England's literature and of our own indebtedness to it, "A Certain Condescension" nevertheless made the point that England must learn to look on the Americans, not as an inferior brand of their own kind, not as a nation of Shylocks, but as a new powerful force in the world.[41]

IV

Meanwhile a different approach to the problem of advancing a more just European appreciation of American life and character had been exemplified in the efforts of a group of Americans to present in as objective a way as possible basic facts about the American economy and culture. The pioneer was David B. Warden, born in Ireland, trained at the University of Glasgow, and a teacher, author, and book collector in several American communities before entering the diplomatic service in 1804. For a decade as secretary to the American minister and as consul in Paris, Warden

[40] Spiller, *The American in England, passim;* Townsend Scudder, "Emerson's British Lecture Tour 1847–1848," *American Literature* (March, May, 1935), VII, 15–36, 166–180.

[41] The essay, which appeared in the *Atlantic Monthly* for January, 1869, is in *The Writings of James Russell Lowell* (Boston and New York, 1890, 11 vols.), III, 220–254.

devoted a great part of his energy to spreading knowledge about the United States and in defending the democratic experiment by letting the facts speak for themselves. He continued to do so in his years of retirement in the French capital.

In the preface of his *Statistical, Political, and Historical Account of the United States,* published in Edinburgh in 1819, Warden paraded, as accurately as possible, the history, geography, and topography of his adopted country; its rich mineral and other resources; the rapid growth of agriculture, commerce, and population; the rising standard of living; and the prevailing security of life. The role of widely disseminated knowledge in America, the significance of the separation of church and state, and the abolition of feudal privileges were all duly set forth. Detailed descriptions of every state followed. A French version of this remarkable work, extended by new volumes at various intervals between 1826 and 1844, together with still other comparable publications, did not exhaust the energy and devotion of Warden to the cause that had become all-important in his life.[42]

Yet when Samuel Goodrich took up his duties as consul at Paris in 1851 he found a general ignorance of the United States. Had Warden's volumes been ignored? In any case, Goodrich modestly followed the path he had hewn. To meet the constant requests for information from officials, bankers, merchants, and writers, Goodrich brought out *Les Etats-Unis d'Amérique,* a volume which, he reported, was favorably received. "There is, indeed," Goodrich commented, "a great and growing interest in our country all over Europe, and it seems to be the duty of American officials abroad to take advantage of their opportunities to satisfy and gratify this curiosity by furnishing, in a correct and accessible form, the kind of information that is desired."[43]

Although John Howard Payne, the first American actor to win

[42] Warden developed, in part, his conceptions of the consular functions in *The Origin, Nature, Progress, and Influence of Consular Establishments* (Paris, 1813). See *Chronologie Historique de l'Amérique* (Paris, 1826–1844, 10 vols.). Warden's papers are in the Library of Congress and the Maryland Historical Society.

[43] Goodrich, *Recollections of a Lifetime,* II, 481.

recognition in England, and Jared Sparks, editor, historian, and in time to come president of Harvard, believed that the defense of America in England might best be furthered by the establishment of a newspaper devoted to American affairs, neither was able to bring this about.[44] Only in 1866 was the *Anglo-American Times* established. But George Palmer Putnam, influenced in part no doubt by Warden, brought out in London in 1845 his *American Facts*. This collection of "plain, unadorned notes, relative to the progress and present condition of the United States," tried to set the British right about many things: their distorted conviction that all the states had dishonestly repudiated their debts; that it was impossible to be both an American and an honest man (facts and figures were mustered to prove the contrary); that Americans were the only piraters of foreign books (Putnam demonstrated that at least 382 American books had been reprinted in England in a ten-year period without reference to the interests of their authors); that however lamentable slavery was, it did not prevail everywhere, that many Americans condemned it and labored for its abolition, and that even where it did exist the picture was not as dark as the abolitionists claimed. *American Facts* further compared expenditures for public education in the two countries and concluded that Boston, a city of 90,000, spent more in this field than did the whole of England.

Open to question was Putnam's effort to prove that four-fifths of the crime, poverty, and disorder of which England made such a point in her indictments of America was to be laid at the door of the immigrants who had come to America in the last three decades.[45] All in all, however, *American Facts* was a striking achievement. It provided Americans in England with ammunition to defend their country if they were so minded; and Putnam was surprised at its sale and reception outside the American colony. George Hillard, a Boston lawyer who knew something of the situation, wrote to Putnam that he had "earned a title to our gratitude"

---

[44] Adams, *The Life and Writings of Jared Sparks, II,* 130; G. Harrison, *John Howard Payne* (Philadelphia, 1885), pp. 133 ff.

[45] George Palmer Putnam, *American Facts* (London, 1845), pp. v, 15–17, 85–87, 153–154, 247.

by his "manly and spirited defense of us, and, God knows, need of defenders."[46]

One of the most significant defenses of American civ that can properly be related to patriotic motivation was that which the Reverend Philip Schaff made in his Berlin and Frankfort lectures in 1854. Schaff was a German immigrant, a church historian, and a theologian of standing. Taking as his point of departure the prevalent conviction in Europe that American life was honeycombed with materialism, radicalism, and sectarianism, rocks on which the union was destined sooner or later to founder, Schaff, admitting many of the shortcomings of his adopted land, nevertheless emphasized the soundness and vitality of its life. Putting into a larger perspective the issue of slavery by indicating its complexity; pointing out that materialism was not alien to Europe and that the abundant resources of America quite naturally accentuated it; emphasizing the enthusiastic and practical spirit of American philanthropy; arguing that disgraceful rowdyism was in no sense a necessary or even an important attribute of democracy; balancing the evils of sectarianism in this country with the vitality of its religious life; pointing to the unity in the very diversity of the peoples making up the country—through all these arguments Schaff indeed made a profoundly cogent defense of America. Europe, he concluded, would be wise to give up its conviction that the republic was on the threshold of dissolution. It would be well advised to take note of the growing influence of the United States in Latin America, Africa, Asia, and in Europe itself; for the young giant had much to offer a comfortless Old World wasting itself away in wars and revolutions.[47]

v

Not entirely unrelated to the predominantly patriotic motive in efforts to explain American institutions was the zeal among evangelical Christians for extending into Europe what were regarded as

[46] George Haven Putnam, *George Palmer Putnam* (New York, 1912), p. 58.
[47] Philip Schaff, *America. A Sketch of the Political, Social and Religious Character of the United States, passim.* See also David S. Schaff, *The Life of Philip Schaff* (New York, 1897), pp. 145–146.

characteristically American conditions for the spread of the true Gospel. In 1842 the Christian Alliance was formed to work, in the words of one close to it, for the extension of "the glorious principles of the American Revolution" into Europe. "It is to spread abroad at once freedom in religion and freedom in the state."[48] Four years later Americans participated in the formation in London of the Evangelical Alliance, which stood for the essential principles of the Christian Alliance. No account, however brief, can omit the mention of two outstanding leaders in this movement. Edward Kirk, an agent of the American Board of Commissioners for Foreign Missions, made his first trip to Europe in 1837 to study conditions, to lecture, to preach; he took part in the formation of the Evangelical Alliance; in 1857 he opened the first American church in Paris. This valiant exponent of what he regarded as the American principles of separation of church and state, and of complete religious equality and freedom, discovered an obstacle to his mission in European criticisms of slavery and race prejudice. He could only explain as best he could and warn his fellow Americans against the inconsistency of trying to spread American principles of religious freedom abroad while Americans kept the Negro in chains at home.[49] Like Kirk, Robert Baird went abroad to work for an American evangelical approach to religion, for separation of church and state, for complete freedom of conscience, and for temperance. Associating with monarchs and peasants alike, this Presbyterian divine was, in the words of a contemporary admirer, admirably fitted by his intimate knowledge of the United States to be "the accurate expounder of American Institutions abroad." His democracy was in truth an exemplification of the humanity and Christian love that "acts more than it talks" and that expresses American con-

---

[48] David Mears, *Life of Edward Norris Kirk, D.D.* (Boston, 1877), p. 202.

[49] *Ibid.*, p. 105. For European interest in the antislavery movement, see Charles Edward Stowe, *Life of Harriet Beecher Stowe* (Boston and New York, 1889), pp. 189 ff.; Frank J. Klingberg and A. H. Abel, *A Side-Light on Anglo-American Relations, 1839–1858* (Lancaster, Pa., 1927); and Dwight L. Dumond and Gilbert H. Barnes (eds.), *Letters of Theodore Dwight Weld, Angelina Grimké Weld and Sarah Grimké, 1822–1844* (New York, 1934).

cepts of political and religious freedom as part of "the progress of the age."[50]

The great missionary movement which Latourette and others have studied was, of course, primarily religious in its purpose. But the missionaries were not only ambassadors of God; they were also agents of American civilization. The Mormons, whose publications appeared in Liverpool, Geneva, and elsewhere,[51] glowingly pictured life in Deseret, spread considerable knowledge about, and aroused a good deal of interest in America as well as in the Church of Jesus Christ of the Latter-day Saints. During the three decades before the Civil War when missionaries were wedging their way into the indifferent or hostile lands of eastern Asia, frequent bickerings, misunderstandings, and clashes occurred. But at the same time, as Tyler Dennett has pointed out, every friend made was also a friend of the nation that sent the missionary to "relieve suffering, teach the illiterate, and enlighten the superstitious."[52]

The missionary impact,[53] together with that of the businessman, elevated the United States to a relatively high place in the estimation of Asiatic peoples. A few examples must suggest the story. Elijah Bridgman published in Chinese in 1838 a *Brief Geographical History of the United States*. This, which was republished on later occasions, introduced Chinese readers to American institutions, social customs, education, religion, literature, and the system of national defense. Many American textbooks were translated into Chinese under missionary auspices.[54] Before the Civil War, American missionaries, as agents of the native governments, as directors of hospitals, as teachers, and even as professors in higher institu-

[50] Charles Holden, "Robert Baird," *Pulpit Portraits* (New York, 1848), VIII, 170, 174–175.

[51] Files of the *Millennial Star*, published in Liverpool, and of *Étoile du Déseret*, issued at Paris, are rewarding sources.

[52] Tyler Dennett, *The Democratic Movement in Asia* (New York, 1918), p. 4.

[53] See, among secondary studies, George H. Danton, *The Culture Contacts of the United States and China, 1784–1844* (New York, 1931); Tyler Dennett, *Americans in Eastern Asia* (New York, 1922); and Kenneth Latourette, *A History of Christian Missions in China* (New York, 1929).

[54] Alexander Wylie, *Memorials of Protestant Missionaries to the Chinese* (Shanghai, 1867).

tions of learning, were, in the words of William Seward, advancing "the American system, in which philosophy, politics and morals, as well as religious faith, are taught with just regard to their influences in social and domestic life."[55]

Other possible ways of influencing Chinese opinion were devised. At least as early as 1860 the suggestion was made by an American missionary, with the approval of the American legation in China, that the surplus from the Indemnity Fund of 1856–1857 be used to establish an institution of higher learning at Peking in which Americans might be trained in Chinese and Chinese in American studies.[56] Although this came to nothing, it bore some relation to the decision of the Chinese government in 1872 to send boys to America for their education.[57]

American missionary efforts were not, of course, confined to the Far East. By the time of the Civil War the foundations had been well laid for many educational enterprises in the Near East, including one that was to develop, on the model of a New England college, into an institution in which an effort was made to demonstrate, in American fashion, that peoples of different national backgrounds may learn to live amicably together.

If actions speak louder than words, American philanthropy, which interpenetrated missionary enterprises, began even before the mid-century to operate on a secular level. Here we can merely refer to the relief of hunger-stricken Ireland at the height of the potato famine[58] and to the munificence of George Peabody, American banker in England, in providing some years later for a pioneer housing project for London's very poor.[59] The impulses back of

[55] William H. Seward, *Travels Around the World* (New York, 1873), p. 104.

[56] *House Report*, No. 113, 45 Congress, 3 Session, pp. 5 ff.; *Diplomatic Correspondence of the United States*, 1862, pp. 843 ff.; *Diplomatic Correspondence*, 1864, Pt. 3, pp. 346–347.

[57] Yung Wing, *My Life in China and America* (New York, 1909), p. 183.

[58] Robert B. Forbes, *An Interesting Memoir of the Jamestown Voyage to Ireland* (Boston, 1890). For an earlier example of a different type of American philanthropy abroad, see Benjamin Count Rumford, *Essays, Political, Economical, and Philosophical* (Boston, 1798, 2 vols.).

[59] *Report of the Centennial Celebration of the Birth of George Peabody* (Cambridge, Mass., 1895), p. 35.

these and similar enterprises, the attitudes of Americans toward them, and the impact they made on the outer world, especially on prevailing ideas about America, deserve further study.

VI

Economic considerations often played a large part in activities designed to help shape foreign images of the United States. A case in point is the literature intended to guide the emigrant. To be sure, some of this was in a genuine sense disinterested. Franklin's *Information to Those Who Would Remove to America* (1783), for example, was inspired by a desire to be helpful in a very practical way.[60] This was likewise true of the later guidebooks sponsored by emigrant-aid societies.[61] But some emigrant guidebooks were prepared by Europeans with an economic or religious interest in discouraging folk from leaving the old country; it is not hard to imagine what a grim picture of America these presented to the people of the old countries. Still others were put out by shipping interests, European and American, and by American land-speculating companies. After 1845 some of the western states, eager to increase their population, sent abroad, to attract immigrants, commissioners well armed with various kinds of propaganda, including guidebooks.[62] In general, the guidebooks representing such interests not only painted America in glowing terms but emphasized the great advantages of those regions to which it was hoped to attract

[60] Albert Henry Smyth (ed.), *Writings of Benjamin Franklin* (New York, 1905–1907, 10 vols.), VIII, 603–614. See also Thomas Cooper, *Thoughts on Emigration in a Letter from a Gentleman in Philadelphia to His Friend in England* (London, 1794).

[61] For example, *Report of the Executive Committee to the Board of Directors of the Emigrant's Friend Society* (Philadelphia, 1848); circular of the Irish Emigrant Society, "To the People of Ireland" (New York, 1844), in *Wiley & Putnam's Emigrant's Guide* (London, 1845), pp. 136–141; D. R. Thomason, *Hints to Emigrants* (Philadelphia, 1848).

[62] Theodore C. Blegen, "The Competition of the Northwestern States for Immigrants," *Wisconsin Magazine of History* (September, 1919), III, 4–11; W. L. Jenks, "Michigan Immigration: State Policy on Induced Immigration," *Michigan History Magazine* (January, 1944), XXVIII, 69–70, 75–82; Marcus L. Hansen, "Official Encouragement of Immigration to Iowa," *Iowa Journal of History and Politics* (April, 1921), XIX, 161–170.

immigrants. Virtually all the guidebooks included, with varying degrees of accuracy and inaccuracy, detailed information about the several states: soils, climates, land policies, public improvements, and facilities for worship and education.

What picture of American civilization emerged from those emigrant guidebooks which were well disposed toward the coming of certain types of people? The prospective immigrant was generally urged to remember that, while America provided plenty of work at good wages and abundant cheap land, success depended on a willingness to work. America, as Franklin had put it, was a land of labor where it was no disgrace to toil with one's hands and where birth was far less important than skill in useful enterprise. "Comfortable subsistence," declared a typical later statement, "is enjoyed everywhere, unless prevented by peculiar misfortunes, or by vice."[63] The right to enjoy the fruits of one's labor was emphasized time and again: no well-defined class lines, no tithes, no exorbitant taxes, it was argued, interfered with that right.

Something was written about religious freedom and lack of censorship and military conscription, though all these bulked less large than the economic attractions. Occasionally the emigrant guidebooks, especially those sponsored by the benevolent societies, discussed the ways in which slavery was likely to affect an immigrant who settled in the South; and some reviewed fairly the question of nativist prejudices against newcomers.

Of particular interest were the analyses of American character. In the more discriminating manuals allowances were made for sectional variations. Most writers emphasized the self-reliance, enterprise, devotion to work, practical ingenuity, and inventiveness of the American stock. If the Americans were eager to accumulate wealth, they were ready to spend it on comforts, and in times of calamity their generosity was outstanding. If Americans were less concerned than Europeans with the imaginative arts, they cherished the dissemination of general and useful knowledge. Above

[63] S. H. Collins, *The Emigrant's Guide to the United States of America* (Hull, 1830), p. 27.

all, independence, a democratic outlook, and a spirit of give and take were deemed preëminent characteristics.[64]

If the emigrant guidebooks need further study, this is even more true of immigrant letters. Often, of course, these described hardships, failures, and disappointment. But in greater number they also emphasized successes; sometimes they glowed with enthusiasm. One who knew the lower classes of Europe well wrote in 1848: "Those who have come over and tasted the sweets which our blessed country affords, in comparison with what they enjoyed in the Old World, have exerted all their influence and employed all their resources to induce their friends who remained behind, to essay the voyage."[65] When immigrant letters enclosed remittances, we can be sure that their eloquence was all the more persuasive.

In great degree economic factors, associated with those of patriotism, explain the bold efforts of traders in Latin America in the early years of the nineteenth century to arouse enthusiasm for the United States. Philadelphia merchants as early as 1793 were sending American revolutionary literature into Cuba. In 1802 William Shaler and Richard Cleveland explained to the citizens of Valparaiso how greatly the United States had profited from independence and republican institutions; they left Spanish translations of the Declaration of Independence and the Constitution. This they also did in Mexico and Cuba.[66] A Chilean priest complained of this sort of activity: "They make their entry, and praising their own country and condemning the colonial government subject to Spain, they shamelessly offer all the aid of their great power to those people who wish to shake off the yoke of legitimate and just domain."[67] Belief that the establishment of republics promised trading ad-

[64] In addition to the guidebooks cited, representative are Daniel S. Curtiss, *Western Portraiture and Emigrants' Guide* (New York, 1852); John Reagan, *The Emigrants' Guide to the Western States of America* (Edinburgh, 1852); and Calvin Colton, *Manual for Emigrants to America* (London, 1832).

[65] *Christian Union* (July, 1848), I, 395.

[66] Richard J. Cleveland, *A Narrative of Voyages and Commercial Enterprise* (Cambridge, 1843), p. 174; Roy Nichols, "William Shaler, New England Apostle of Rational Liberty," *New England Quarterly* (March, 1936), IX, 71–96.

[67] Quoted in Bernstein, *Origins of Inter-American Interest,* p. 82.

vantages was, of course, an obvious motive on the part of these merchant missionaries of American institutions; but who shall say that they were not also patriotic?

The considerations of business (and art) explain how Europe gradually became familiarized with many aspects of American life. Between 1837 and 1852 George Catlin was exhibiting his paintings of Indian chieftains, villages, and ceremonials, thus giving Europeans a more reliable impression of the aborigines than prevailing notions afforded.[68] In 1843 the Virginia Minstrels introduced a new picture of Negro life, song, and dance to Britishers. The show aroused little interest, but, in due time, other minstrel shows fared better.[69] The famous Hutchinson family sang to British audiences of American slavery and abolitionism, of the rights and wrongs of women, and of the evils of drink and the joys of temperance, thus dramatizing American reforms.[70] Before the Civil War had been long under way, the Beadle dime novels introduced to English readers new vistas of thought about the plantation and the Wild West.

VII

But the most striking image of America that emerged in the fourth and fifth decades of the century reflected the great technological advances of which the country boasted. Wells with a new type of patent cloth that won the praise of Lord Brougham; Johnson with his improved cotton textile machinery, his gasometer, and his superior daguerreotype; Selich with his wood screw machine; Wheelright with his strange but useful gadgets and improvements; Perkins with a machine for making a new type of cut nails, and another for engraving steel plates, by which a new era in engraving was introduced; Perkins again with his extraordinary steam gun—

[68] United States Magazine and Democratic Review, n.s. (July, 1842), IX, 44–52; George Catlin, Notes of Eight Years' Travels and Residence in Europe (New York, 1848, 2 vols.).

[69] Carl Wittke, Tambo and Bones (Durham, N.C., 1930), pp. 27, 46, 53.

[70] Philip D. Jordan, Singin' Yankees (Minneapolis, 1946), pp. 120 ff.; Carol Brink, Harps in the Wind (New York, 1947), passim.

these were only a few of the American triumphs in technology that by 1840 impressed England.[71] In Paris, in the fateful year 1848, Hoe arrived to demonstrate the miraculous new rotary press.[72] In Egypt, Mehemet Ali sent George Gliddon back to America to bring cotton gins in order that the culture of the promising staple might be encouraged.[73] Meantime in Latin America, William Wheelright was developing along Yankee lines the port facilities of Valparaiso and installing gas and water works. Edward August Hopkins was introducing American steamship facilities into Paraguay and Argentina. Allan Campbell was building railways in both Argentina and Chile.[74] Other engineers and promoters helped these pioneers in developing new images of the United States in the minds of Latin Americans—a story that still awaits adequate study.

In the pre-Civil War period the most dramatic demonstration of the growing power and importance of American technology took place at the London Crystal Palace in 1851, the first of the great modern international exhibitions. The Americans arrived penniless, for their government, unlike the authorities in other countries, turned over to private enterprise the business of showing our wares to Europe. The London press indulged in sarcastic remarks regarding the sorry display Brother Jonathan was likely to make.[75] But George Peabody did what Congress refused to do: he dug into his pockets and brought up $15,000 to enable his fellow Americans to put on an impressive exhibit of Colt revolvers, Bond spring governors, Hobbs' unpickable locks, Goodyear rubber goods, and McCormick's marvelous reaping and mowing machines.[76]

[71] *The Beacon*, n.s. (October 10, 1840), I, 374.
[72] Robert Hoe, *A Short History of the Printing Press* (New York, 1902), p. 12; *Southern Literary Messenger* (March, 1849), XV, 178.
[73] J. C. Nott and George R. Gliddon, *Types of Mankind* (Philadelphia, 1854), p. xxxv; George R. Gliddon, *A Memoir on the Cotton of Egypt* (London, 1851), and *Appendix to the American in Egypt* (Philadelphia, 1842).
[74] There is a brief summary of these activities in Domingo Faustino Sarmiento, *North and South America. A Discourse* (Providence, 1866).
[75] Phebe Hanaford, *The Life of George Peabody* (Boston, 1870), pp. 78–79; *An Account of the Proceedings at the Dinner Given by Mr. George Peabody* (London, 1851).
[76] D. Eldon Hall, *A Condensed History of the Organization, Rise, Progress and*

The significance of the American participation in this great technological show for shifting the emphasis in European images of American civilization and for challenging Americans to defend that civilization in positive and concrete ways has never been appreciated. The London press, changing its tune, paid tribute to the superiority of the American exhibits: John Bull, the journals in effect declared, must sit up and take notice.[77] In reporting on the impression of the American machines a Louisianian spoke for many others in declaring that the United States had triumphed in industry; had discovered how the power of machines might release men from drudgery, multiply his capacities for producing, enhance his comforts, and quicken his enjoyments.[78]

Benjamin Pierce Johnson, whom the governor of New York appointed to represent that state at the exhibition, reported that "the influence of our exhibition has been far better upon the world, has more powerfully demonstrated the peculiar advantages of our free institutions, in the development of the energies of the people, than could have been done if the government had made a large appropriation." For the American exhibits, Johnson continued, proved the energy, skill, and ingenuity of the citizenry. "The character of our articles were such as to show to the world that we worked for the great masses, not for the luxurious and privileged few." If our displays were not equal to the splendid European articles aimed to minister to human pride, they demonstrated the superior status of our great laboring and middle classes; they proved that in the United States genius, industry, and energy find no barriers to their career.[79]

Completion of the Great Exhibition of the Industry of All Nations (Redfield, N.Y., 1852), chap. 4; *The Journal of the Great Exhibition of 1851* (London, 1851), pp. 71, 117, 141, 182–183, 198, 215–230. The American government did provide the frigate *Lawrence* to convey the exhibits to London.

[77] *The Writings and Speeches of Daniel Webster* (National Edition, Boston, 1903, 18 vols.), *XIII*, 444.

[78] Charles T. Rodgers, *American Superiority at the World's Fair* (Philadelphia, 1852), pp. 5–6.

[79] Benjamin P. Johnson, *Report of Benjamin P. Johnson, Agent of the State of New York, Appointed to Attend the Exhibition of the Industry of All Nations* (Albany, 1852), pp. 13–14, 153–163.

In the post-Civil War period the American exhibits at the international expositions became highly eloquent arguments not only for the superiority of American technology but for the material blessings that technology was putting at the doorstep of the masses. From this point on, European images of American civilization began to shift, and Americans tended to rely more and more, in promoting an understanding and appreciation of American civilization, on material rather than on idealistic and humane arguments. But this is another story.

VIII

The refusal of Congress in 1849 and 1850 to appropriate subsidies for the American exhibitors in London suggests in part an adherence to laissez-faire theories. Yet the record of the federal government in promoting an understanding abroad of American life and institutions was not entirely a negative one in the first three-quarters of the national history. In Latin America, particularly, official effort was made to explain the institutions, policies, and values of the United States. Joel Poinsett, minister to Mexico, issued in 1827 in Spanish a pamphlet replying to a manifesto of the Vera Cruz legislature which denounced the United States government. The minister declared he had never taken part in the internal affairs of Mexico, "unless to advocate, in a Republic, on every fitting occasion the superiority of a republican form of government over all others, to explain the practical benefits of the institutions of the United States and the blessings which his countrymen have enjoyed and still continue to enjoy under them, be considered an interference with the internal concerns of this country."[80] Poinsett had, nevertheless, enabled several York-rite lodges to be chartered after the Yankee model, and he did, in bidding the Mexicans farewell, urge them to follow the example of their northern neighbors in matters affecting political institutions.

[80] William R. Manning, *Diplomatic Correspondence of the United States concerning Independence of the Latin-American Nations* (New York, 1925, 3 vols.), III, 1663–1668.

Poinsett was not alone in such a conception of the duties of American diplomats. Henry M. Brackenridge wrote President Monroe that it was within our power to help shape the character of nations destined one day to take an important role in world affairs; and he lost no chance to remind the Latin peoples that they too might enjoy the prosperity and success of the United States by imitating her example. To that end he distributed in Buenos Aires copies of the United States Constitution and did what he could to develop cultural contacts.[81] Although desire to foster cultural relations played a negligible part in the decision to dispatch Lieutenant James Gillis in 1849 to set up an observatory in Santiago, his scientific labors in Chile exemplified not merely the interest of the United States in trade and navigation, but in the foundation sciences as well.[82]

The most significant example of government concern with the expansion of American influence in the world was, of course, the Perry expedition to Japan in 1853–1854. Although there had been contacts of a sort between the two countries for more than a half-century, Perry's success in opening Japan to the commercial and cultural influences of the United States through boldness, threats, and persuasiveness was one of the outstanding diplomatic achievements of the nineteenth century. Among the purposes of the expedition was that of demonstrating American theories, inventions, and techniques to the Japanese. The tact and skill of our first diplomatic representative, Townsend Harris, who persuaded the Japanese that his countrymen were less aggressively selfish than other nationals, created a favorable image of the United States and paved the way for continued American impacts on Japan.[83]

[81] Henry M. Brackenridge, *South America. A Letter on the Present State of That Country to James Monroe* (Washington, 1817), pp. 24, 34; *Voyage to Buenos Aires, Performed in the Years 1817 and 1818 by Order of the American Government* (London, 1820). The former was written while Brackenridge was a member of a commission to investigate political conditions in South America. See Claude M. Newlin, "Henry M. Brackenridge," *D.A.B.*, II, 543.

[82] *House Executive Document*, No. 121, 33rd Congress, 1 sess.

[83] *Narrative of the Expedition of an American Squadron to the China Seas and Japan* (Washington, 1856, 3 vols.); S. W. Williams, "A Journal of the Perry

In Europe, American diplomatic representatives did not in general feel any such responsibility as did Warden and Goodrich to correct misinformation about their country and to promote an appreciation of it. Nathaniel Niles, Harvard trained and a physician of some note, did, it is true, propose to the State Department during his second assignment to the court of Sardinia (1848–1850) the exchange, free of duty, between Italy, Switzerland, and the United States of cheap editions of the literature of each country, in order to promote a better understanding of the national cultures.[84] It is noteworthy that Niles, who was thus something of a pioneer in proposing a two-way intercultural program, did not feel charged to defend republican principles and values in the normal course of his diplomatic labors.[85]

In fact, a major complaint of a group within the Democratic party, which in the early 1850's took the name "Young America," was that the diplomatic corps truckled too much to the monarchical courts and failed to represent vigorously enough republican principles and values.[86] Parke Godwin of the New York *Post* spoke for this group in declaring, in 1853, that America had failed deplorably to make more than a slight impression on the thought of the world. Urging his country to play a global role, deviating by no jot or tittle from fidelity to democratic principles at home and abroad, Godwin further insisted that the government promptly help to arrest all foreign schemes of aggression and give active support to republics and to struggling nationalities. Only in this way could America help Old World liberals understand that our kind of liberalism was not theirs, no mere vague recoil from despotism, but a positive,

Expedition to Japan," *Transactions of the Asiatic Society of Japan* (1909), XXXVII; Allan B. Cole (ed.), *A Scientist with Perry in Japan. The Journal of Dr. James Monroe* (Chapel Hill, 1947). See also M. E. Cosenza, *The Complete Journal of Townsend Harris* (New York, 1930).

[84] Nathaniel Niles to Secretary of State Clayton, March 30, 1850 (Turin), Department of State Archives, Sardinia.

[85] Niles to Rives, May 12, 1849 (Turin), William Rives Papers (Library of Congress). The Niles manuscripts are also at the Library of Congress.

[86] Merle Curti, "Young America," *American Historical Review* (October, 1926), XXXII, 34–53.

dynamic enhancement of all that is best in life. It was hardly likely, Godwin concluded, that the United States in the near future would become involved in a war by reason of such a policy. But if it should, "in what more just or magnanimous battle could a great people emerge? . . . It would not be a strife for territory . . . nor for the subjection of weak dependents, but a glorious struggle for liberty, justice, and humanity."[87] Here was anticipated the time when many Americans would accept such an interpretation of the national mission to expound the American scheme of civilization to the world.

Thus we have the picture the United States offered for consideration to the world before the Civil War nearly tore the nation apart. By that time all the major patterns of thought about us, all the main envisagements or images of us as a nation and a people which were to compete for acceptance in later times, had begun at least dimly to emerge. Indifferent though most of our people were to the images we presented to the world, there they were, whether faithful or not to the actualities of American life, reflecting pictures of the United States, its shortcomings, its strengths, its values, its ways of life.

[87] Parke Godwin, *Political Essays* (New York, 1856), pp. 106 ff., 127.

9

"Young America" (1926)

WHEN a slogan comes to be used commonly by politicians, editors, and diplomats it may be assumed that it expresses a set of ideals and emotions of some significance. "Young America" was such a slogan. Its adoption by an important group in the Democratic party during the election of 1852 was a political gesture that received serious attention at home as well as abroad. Since foreign powers are not always in a position to determine how deep the realities behind a gesture may be, it is the more important to evaluate the gesture and to determine its relation to the national psychology. The purpose of this paper is, first, to describe and evaluate the movement Young America, with special reference to its foreign policy and activities; and, second, to indicate the relation of the movement to national self-consciousness in the years following 1850.

The idea of a Young America seems first to have been formulated in a commencement address by Edwin de Leon at South Carolina College in 1845.[1] He observed that as there was a Young Germany, a Young Italy, a Young Ireland, so there might well be a Young America. For "nations, like men, have their seasons of infancy, manly vigor, and decrepitude." The young giant of the West, America, was pictured as standing at the full flush of "exulting

[1] Edwin de Leon, *The Position and Duties of Young America* (Charleston, 1845).

manhood," and the worn-out powers of the Old World could not hope either to restrain or to impede his progress. If there was to be a Young America, then the new generation, the young men of America, would have to express their faith in the glorious destiny of the country, by seizing political power to hasten the fulfillment of that destiny.

Such ideas were not new. From the time of Benjamin Franklin and Philip Freneau,[2] Americans, for the most part, had been convinced that their country had a distinctive mission to perform—the introduction of a new and better political order in the world. If there was one idea to which Americans as such could subscribe, it was the conviction that their country, as the only large democracy in the world, had the best possible form of government. Philosophers like Emerson and poets like Whitman expressed this idea in terms only more refined than those of popular Fourth of July orators. Our republican and democratic institutions and ideas were held to be unique. The opportunities America afforded made her the symbol of the future and of progress, for she was free from the inequalities and handicaps of the Old World.[3] The problem of determining how the historic mission of America might best be advanced occasioned multiple interpretations. This was natural, for a new country in which a national culture had not given unity to diverse regions rarely expresses a well-developed national self-consciousness.

To Young America direct and immediate participation in the affairs of the world was the indisputable formula of procedure. The time, in their eyes, was thoroughly ripe for the realization of the American mission. Success in the Mexican War, easy and cheap, had acted like an intoxicant. It engendered a jingoism which de-

[2] Albert Smyth (ed.), *The Writings of Benjamin Franklin* (New York, 1905, 10 vols.), *VIII*, 416; F. L. Pattee (ed.), *Poems of Philip Freneau* (Princeton, 1902, 3 vols.), I, 66 *et seq.*

[3] *Journals of Ralph Waldo Emerson* (Boston and New York, 1909–1914, 10 vols.), X, 84; "The Young American" (1844), in *Nature, Addresses and Letters* (Boston, 1892), pp. 343–372; and Walt Whitman, *Gathering of the Forces, 1846–1847* (New York, 1920, 2 vols.), I, 28 (editorial in the Brooklyn *Eagle*, November 24, 1846).

manded even more grand accomplishments! This urge for participation in world affairs found little expression because the country was absorbed in internal problems growing out of the war.

When, however, the European revolutions of 1848 had been crushed by reactionary governments, there was occasion for action. How could Americans, conscious of their mission to advance their superior institutions, be content with mere example? Despotism needed an immediate lesson. Indeed, if the distinctive institutions of America were to be secure from the advancing menace of autocracy, the task was not only clear but demanded immediate performance.

The year 1852 offered an admirable opportunity for a discontented group of young men within the Democratic party to adopt this phrase "Young America" as a slogan and a rallying cry. The enthusiasm Kossuth was arousing indicated that the country might be ready to assume an active role in championing the revolution which that Hungarian declared must shortly break out. The New York *Herald* declared that the cause of Hungary was a trump card which, skillfully played, might win the White House.[4] Webster, Whig Secretary of State, attended the congressional banquet given Kossuth on January 7, 1852, being led in part by a desire to repeat the popular success of his Hülsemann letter.[5] It seemed to Hülsemann, Austrian chargé, that Webster's speech, candidly recognizing the justice of Hungarian independence and expressing a wish to see that independence accomplished, signified an intention to quit the Cabinet and to found his candidacy for the Whig nomination on an alliance with Kossuth.[6] This was likewise the opinion of the

[4] New York *Herald*, January 15, 1852.

[5] *Writings and Speeches of Daniel Webster* (National Edition, Boston, 1903, 18 vols.), XVI, 588; XVIII, 502.

[6] Hülsemann to Schwarzenberg, No. 3, Letter A, January 8, 1852, "Rapports de l'Amérique 1852" (Haus-, Hof-, und Staatsarchiv, Vienna). Hülsemann was instructed that it was impossible for the Austrian government to maintain diplomatic relations with Webster (Schwarzenberg to Hülsemann, February 4, 1852). The Cabinet in Vienna feared that the United States would be entrapped by Kossuth's schemes (Schwarzenberg to Hülsemann, November 25, 1851). The temporary break in diplomatic relations occasioned by Hülsemann quitting Washington was healed because of Austria's reluctance to antagonize a power whose

Prussian minister-resident, Baron von Gerolt.[7]

As early as December, 1851, it had been plain that the Senate would be the stage for discussions regarding the expediency of assuming a more vigorous position in the interest of European republicanism. Senator I. P. Walker of Wisconsin (Democrat) announced on December 16 of that year that "the country must interpose both her moral and her physical power" against the interference of one nation in the affairs of another in violation of public law and morality. He maintained that the country ought to be ready, if necessary, to fight for Hungarian freedom.[8] On January 20, 1852, Cass of Michigan introduced into the Senate a resolution to the effect that the United States had not seen nor could they again see, without deep concern, the intervention of European powers to crush national independence.[9] Cass, although repudiated by the leader of Young America as an "Old Fogy,"[10] could not have represented that group more effectively than by his earnest plea for the adoption of the resolution. The country, urged Cass, must not remain a "political cipher." The world must know that there are "twenty-five millions of people looking across the ocean at Europe, strong in power, acquainted with their rights, and determined to enforce them."[11]

Although the support of the Cass resolution came chiefly from the Mississippi Valley, Stockton of New Jersey urged active, physical force in behalf of struggling republics.[12] Nor was the measure supported merely by members of the Democratic party. For example, while Seward urged that the moral argument was sufficient for a protest against Russia's intervention in Hungary, he seized

---

desire for intervention in Europe was feared (Buol-Schauenstein to Hülsemann, May 11, 1852).

[7] Gerolt to the King of Prussia, No. 13, I, 1, 132, March 30, 1852 (Geheimes Staatsarchiv, "Washington 1852," Berlin).

[8] *Congressional Globe*, 32nd Cong., 1 sess., pp. 105 *et seq.*

[9] *Ibid.*, p. 310.

[10] The *Lantern* (comic weekly, New York) (Feb. 14, 1852), I, defined, with much humor and gusto, an "Old Fogy" as a superannuated officeholder.

[11] *Congressional Globe*, 32nd Cong., 1 sess., p. 310.

[12] *Ibid.*, pp. 438 *et seq.*, February 2, 1852.

the occasion to point out the commercial advantages to be derived from the triumph of the republican idea in that country.[13]

The chief opposition to the resolution came from the Whigs, but they were joined by every southern Democrat with the exception of Soulé of Louisiana. The arguments advanced indicated that the Cass resolution aroused both sectional and class opposition. An interference with the affairs of Europe would furnish Europeans with an excuse to intervene in our domestic problems.[14] An active foreign policy would necessitate an increased concentration of power in the federal government.[15] The secret of our prosperity and greatness, it was held, lay in our policy of isolation. A departure from it would not unite the country, as certain Democrats maintained. Indeed, the sectional character of the debates was pointed to as evidence that the very discussion of a new foreign policy was weakening still further the bonds of union.[16]

This opposition plainly came from the more prosperous and conservative regions. Clemens of Alabama appealed to the established commercial interests, picturing a foreign war on "mistaken humanitarian grounds" as bringing disaster to the manufacturing interests of New England, the agriculture of the West, and the cotton plantations of the South, since markets would be closed and our commerce subjected to seizure.[17] A test vote indicated that the South, whether Whig or Democrat, opposed any change in our foreign policy, while Iowa, Illinois, Wisconsin, and Indiana formed an almost solid block in favor.[18]

These discussions in Congress, together with the Kossuth excitement, furnished ample stimulus for the launching of the movement calling itself Young America. The greater part of the nerve and energy of the movement was supplied by George N. Sanders. This picturesque figure, a volatile Kentuckian, served from 1844 to the

[13] *Ibid., Appendix,* pp. 787, 143, March 1, 1852.
[14] *Ibid.,* pp. 551 *et seq.* Senator Cooper of Pennsylvania, April 28, 1852.
[15] *Ibid.,* pp. 531–532. P. Ewing of Kentucky, April 21, 1852.
[16] *Ibid., Appendix,* p. 551. Senator Cooper, April 28, 1852.
[17] *Ibid.,* p. 179, February 7, 1852.
[18] *Ibid.,* p. 186. Test vote, January 2, 1852, to lay a memorial for intervention on the table.

outbreak of the Civil War as a wire-puller and spokesman for the
group in the Democratic party whose battle cry was "expansion
and progress."[19] Sanders's rhetoric was that of the promoter of
grandiose business projects to be realized by jingoism. At the same
time his faith in the liberal institutions of his country and its mission to extend them was apparently genuine. His querulousness
and dubious financial operations had alienated him from the older
members of the party.

The personnel of the group associated with Sanders was not entirely definite, but it may be said that it represented, in general,
frontier sections of the country.[20] Stephen A. Douglas of Illinois
was popularly reputed to be the soul of the movement.[21] His colleagues in Congress, James Shields and William Richardson of
Illinois, were also leading spirits in the group. Others were William
Corry of Cincinnati,[22] Robert J. Walker, formerly of Mississippi,[23]
William R. Smith of Alabama, William Polk of Tennessee, and

[19] Sanders did not share Calhoun's opposition to the annexation of Oregon,
Calhoun to Sanders, February 3, 1844, in Political Papers of George N. Sanders
(New York, 1914), a sale catalogue presenting extracts from many letters that did
not pass from the sale to the Library of Congress. The writer has recently found,
in a little-known biographical encyclopedia of Kentucky, evidence that Sanders
may have played an important part in the agitation over the annexation of Texas,
in being indirectly responsible for the famous letter which helped to lose Clay
the Presidency. According to William Corry, a friend of Sanders, he organized
a meeting at Ghent, Kentucky, during the campaign of 1844, which passed resolutions favoring the annexation of Texas, and appointed him chairman of a
committee to correspond with the candidates regarding their respective positions
on that question. Clay's Raleigh Letter, Corry says, was in response to a query
from Sanders's committee. Biographical Encyclopedia of Kentucky of the Dead
and Living Men of the Nineteenth Century (Cincinnati, 1878), p. 538.

[20] John L. O'Sullivan, T. de Witt Reilly, and Tammany Hall represented an
eastern group closely associated with Young America.

[21] In his speech at the congressional banquet in Kossuth's honor Douglas made
a pompous and bombastic speech defying the crowned heads of Europe, at the
same time declaring himself willing, under certain circumstances, to use military
force to secure Hungarian and Irish self-determination. New York Herald, January 10, 1852.

[22] In Cincinnati the Nonpareil represented Young American sentiment.

[23] Walker had suggested the possible desirability of an alliance of the United
States and England against autocracy at a Kossuth dinner at Southampton, England, which he attended as American consul. Hülsemann to Schwarzenberg, No.
31, November 17, 1851.

E. C. Marshall of California.[24] But regardless of whether the particular members of the group came from frontier regions or not, it
is clear that the group as a whole represented frontier ideals.[25]
Among these was the typically frontier interest in the future development of capitalism. "Great, powerful and rich as are the
United States," said Marshall, "they must become greater, more
powerful, more rich."[26] The *Democratic Review,* which with
Sanders as editor became the organ of Young America in January,
1852, argued that if republics were established in the heart of
Europe, reciprocal free trade, which was assumed as an inevitable
result, would enormously enhance our commerce and provide
markets for surplus produce.[27] Naïve indeed were these candid ad-
missions. At times, however, they were veiled with idealistic sentiments. The general American conviction of a mission to extend free
institutions, and thus to promote a better world order, was remembered and appealed to. It is significant that these idealistic sentiments, bombastically and pompously expressed, were as genuine
elements of American self-consciousness as the materialistic ones
linked with them.

This materialistic aspect of Young America was most ably expressed by Pierre Soulé during the Senate debates on Cass's resolution criticizing Russian intervention in Hungary. "What, speak of
isolation!" exclaimed Soulé. "Have you not markets to secure for
the surplus of your future wealth?" It was therefore in Soulé's eyes
"our own interest, and if not our interest our duty, to keep alive
. . . that reverence for the institutions of our country, that devout
faith in their efficacy, which looks to their promulgation through-

[24] These men were spokesmen for Young America in the House of Representatives.

[25] The advocacy of homestead legislation was an example of this tendency.
George Evans had named his paper devoted to furthering homestead legislation
Young America! (New York, 1846–1849). The New York *Herald* warned Young
America that it must be "up and doing" if it did not want the Free-Soilers to steal
this part of its program. Established capitalistic interests of the East were naturally
opposed to "western railroad stock-jobbers" unless they themselves were in control.
New York *Herald,* May 20, 1852.

[26] March 19, 1852. *Congressional Globe,* 32nd Cong., 1 sess., pp. 383 *et seq.*

[27] *Democratic Review* (July, 1852), XXXI, 40.

out the world as to the great millennium which is to close the long chapter of their wrongs."[28] This vigorous plea indicated the sympathy of the southern Mississippi Valley with the program of an active foreign policy in behalf of republican institutions abroad. Just as the established vested interests feared the disastrous effects of a policy of intervention, so interests capable of potential development demanded participation in world affairs to secure commercial advantages.

The appeal which Young America made to many Virginia Democrats may be explained by this emphasis on a future development of capital. Virginians, conscious of their agricultural decadence, were making efforts to stimulate industry and commerce as well as agriculture.[29] Hence such Virginians as R. M. T. Hunter, James A. Seddon, and John Daniel of the Richmond *Examiner* were favorably disposed toward Young America.[30] The old alignment with the complacent Calhoun Democrats was not an entirely desirable one. The projects of Maury[31] and George Law's plans for the development of direct steamship lines from Norfolk to Europe might obtain substantial advantages from the program of Young America. Indeed, Law was the chief financial support in the concrete efforts Young America was to make.

Still another factor in the force of Young America's appeal for intervention in behalf of European republicanism was the presence of large numbers of newly arrived immigrants in the United States, who, for the most part, were friends of republicanism at home. Tammany Hall, with its foreign complexion, ratified, as early as October, 1851, the Young American principle of "no more neutrality, active alliance with European republicanism throughout the world." William Corry, one of the most vehement partisans of

---

[28] March 22, 1852. *Congressional Globe,* 32nd Cong., 1 sess., Appendix, pp. 349 *et seq.*

[29] See C. H. Ambler, *Sectionalism in Virginia* (Glendale, Calif., 1910), *passim.*

[30] C. H. Ambler (ed.), *Correspondence of R. M. T. Hunter* (Washington, 1918), pp. 127, 136.

[31] M. F. Maury, *The Amazon and Atlantic Slopes of South America* (Washington, 1853). Virginia was expected to profit from newly opened-up commerce in South America (1853).

Young America, addressed Tammany with a speech which might well be taken as the platform of Young America.[32] The fact that large numbers of these newly arrived foreigners settled in the West was another reason why that section was the heart of Young America. The New York *Herald* professed to believe that the Young American crusade for intervention rested on a mere desire on the part of Western politicians to win votes.[33] Although it is difficult to evaluate the degree of truth in this charge, there is evidence that such ambitions influenced in part the behavior of the group adopting the slogan "Young America" as a battle cry.[34] But whatever part the desire to win German votes played in shaping the interventionist politics of the Westerners in Congress, there was unquestionably a close relationship between the expansive, missionary republicanism of the German exiles and the philosophy of Young America.[35]

Thus Young America as a recognized political group began its activities in 1852, with special interest in coöperation with European republican movements. Naturally individual members of the group had before that time been active in furthering similar ideas. The leader, George Sanders, had been personally concerned in

[32] New York *Herald*, October 23, 1851. Corry's correspondence with Joseph Holt (Joseph Holt Papers, Library of Congress) indicates prodigious activity in behalf of Young America.

[33] New York *Herald*, February 5, 1852.

[34] See, for example, Thomas McCormack (ed.), *Memoirs of Gustav Koerner* (Cedar Rapids, 1909, 2 vols.), I, 591, 545, 577, 599, 588; T. C. Blegen, "The Competition of the Northwestern States for Immigrants," *Wisconsin Magazine of History* (September, 1919), III, 3–29; F. I. Herriot, in *Deutsch-Amerikanische Geschichtsblätter* (1912), XII, 404; William Hense-Jensen, *Wisconsin's Deutsch-Amerikaner* (Milwaukee, 1900–1902, 2 vols.), I, 229–230; Moritz Busch, *Wanderungen zwischen Hudson und Mississippi im Jahre 1851 und 1852* (Tübingen and Stuttgart, 1854), p. 85; Ernest Bruncken, "Political Activity of the Wisconsin Germans," *Wisconsin Historical Society, Proceedings*, 1901, p. 191; Kate A. Everest, "The Germans in Wisconsin," *Wisconsin Historical Collections*, XII, 300.

[35] See, for example, T. S. Baker, "America as the Political Utopia of Young Germany," *Americana Germanica* (1897), I, 86; Richard Riethmüller, "Walt Whitman and the Germans," *German American Annals* (March, 1906), IV, 92; Julius Goebel, "A Political Prophecy of the Forty-Eighters," *Deutsch-Amerikanische Geschichtsblätter* (1912), XII, 462; Karl Heinzen, *Der Pionier* (Boston, 1853–1879).

certain dealings with European revolutionaries and had thus attracted the suspicious attention of representatives of the established governments. Sanders had associated himself with George Law in a notorious musket deal. By act of Congress the War Department offered for sale 114,000 muskets antiquated by the adoption of the new percussion lock. Sanders went to Europe to dispose of these arms to the revolutionary leaders, some of whom he must have met during his participation in the siege of Paris the previous year.[36] Before arrangements could be made the revolutions were crushed.[37] But the problem of disposing of the muskets continued to occupy Sanders's attention. He frankly admitted that the only possible purchasers were the European republicans, and he defended the right of private citizens in a neutral country to sell arms to belligerents.[38] Perhaps this vested interest whetted Sanders's enthusiasm for a new revolutionary outbreak in Europe. Hülsemann, the Austrian chargé, feared the influence which Law and Sanders exerted on Congress "through intrigues and bribery."[39] This uneasiness increased when the announcement was made that Kossuth had purchased part of the muskets.[40] Rumors indicated that, by his order, secret shipments of powder and arms were being prepared in New York.[41] There seems to have been no more truth in these rumors than in those which had disturbed the Austrian representative during the spring of 1850.[42]

[36] Henry Labouchere to Lord Northbrook, April 23 (no year), *Political Papers of George N. Sanders.*

[37] Letter from Sanders to the New York *Herald,* February 12, 1852.

[38] *Ibid.*

[39] Hülsemann to Schwarzenberg, No. 20, February 21, 1852.

[40] *Ibid.,* No. 31, Letter A, April 25, 1852.

[41] *Ibid.*

[42] Hülsemann caused some nervousness in the Austrian Imperial Cabinet by reports, in 1850, that expeditions were fitting out in New York for the Adriatic and Naples, with the purpose of inciting the Hungarians and overthrowing the Hapsburg monarchy (Hülsemann to Schwarzenberg, No. 11, March 15, 1850; Schwarzenberg to Hülsemann, April 1 and 14, 1850). The intuitions of the Prussian minister resident, Baron von Gerolt, that these expeditions were intended for filibustering in Cuba, proved correct. Gerolt to the King of Prussia, No. 5, March 18, 1852.

It is true, however, that Sanders was making rash promises to Kossuth. The Hungarian had urged that the aid of a Democratic government in the spring of 1853 would be too late. Thereupon Sanders vouchsafed his readiness and ability to purchase "the best and fastest going steamer in the United States mercantile marine" and to place it at Kossuth's disposal, armed, manned, and equipped. Kossuth observed that this offer was the most significant one which had been made and one which, if realized, would alone make his American visit entirely successful.[43] Kossuth was soon disillusioned since Sanders failed to secure financial support.[44]

The world knew little of these projects, and Sanders's enthusiasm was too great to be limited to clandestine and uncertain channels. His zeal took the form of championing the nomination of Stephen A. Douglas as the Democratic candidate for the Presidency. Douglas appealed to a group of younger men in the party who, like Sanders, had not enjoyed the spoils of office, and who were thoroughly discontented with the domination of the Old Fogies. The ritual of the Democratic party had come to be more important than its spirit.[45] There was need of an evangelistic revival. Hollow complacency was not enough to maintain the party machine intact. Leadership in the party had long enough been in the hands of the Old Fogies. This was the keynote of the articles which Sanders began to print in the *Democratic Review,* an organ long representing the more progressive wing of the party, and of which he became editor in January, 1852. He insisted that the party must have a man for the Presidency who realized that our national integrity had long enough been prostituted to foreign governments; that our flag and our armaments must no longer subserve the whims of foreign tyrants.[46] The Old Fogy Democrats, J. C. Breckinridge and General

[43] Kossuth to Sanders, January 27, 1852 (Pittsburgh), *Political Papers of George N. Sanders.*
[44] Kossuth to Sanders, July 11, 1852. Letter in private collection of Mr. John H. Gundlach, St. Louis.
[45] R. G. Nichols, *The Democratic Machine, 1852–1854* (New York, 1923), pp. 223, 224.
[46] *Democratic Review* (January, 1852), XXXI, 2.

W. O. Butler of Kentucky, and especially Marcy and Cass,[47] were "superannuated wire-pullers," living in the shadows of great men, mimicking their gestures, words, bows. Without progressive ideas upon which to base its actions or to attract support, Old Fogyism had been forced to rely on subterfuges, corruptions, schemes in utter antagonism to democracy and the true national interests of the country. The program of Young America was drawn with rhetorical splendor. Sectional and party discord were to be healed through a progressive foreign policy, which included the principle of American intervention on the side of the struggling republics in Europe.[48]

Everyone knew that Sanders, in writing these articles, had Stephen A. Douglas in mind. Douglas's defiance of the crowned heads of Europe and his eloquent if vague declarations in favor of the self-determination of all oppressed nationalities, together with his liberal promises of patronage, marked him as the natural leader of Young America.[49] He had denounced the Clayton-Bulwer Treaty as "truckling to Great Britain" and thus won the support of Tammany and the Irish vote. His advocacy of homestead legislation, western railway interests, the Oriental trade, and the acquisition of Cuba appealed to the frontier interest in an expectant development of capitalism.

The connection between Douglas and Sanders had begun in 1851. Douglas had at first great confidence in Sanders's judgment, and in April, 1851, wrote that he was glad his plans were approved by him.[50] "I profit more by your letters than any I receive,"

[47] Cass aroused the hostility of Sanders because of the nepotism which had kept the son of Cass at his post in Rome when his refusal to recognize the Roman Republic in 1848 had seemed a "betrayal" of republicanism. Sanders also maintained that Cass had shown himself subservient to Louis Philippe in his *France, Its King, Court and Government* (New York, 1848). *Democratic Review* (May, 1852), XXX, 456.

[48] *Democratic Review* (January, February, March, 1852), XXXI.

[49] New York *Herald*, January 10, 1852; *Illinois State Register*, February 5, 1852; *Congressional Globe*, 32nd Cong., 1 sess., p. 70; Nichols, *The Democratic Machine*, p. 114.

[50] Douglas to Sanders, April 11, 1851 (Washington). *Political Papers of George N. Sanders.*

wrote Douglas.[51] In December, 1851, Sanders asked Douglas for
money with which to purchase the *Democratic Review*. Therefore
the later denials which Douglas made as to any knowledge of
Sanders's plans were mere falsehoods. "I appreciate the service you
are rendering me and the importance of the movement, and will
do all in my power," Douglas wrote on December 28, 1851, promising at the same time to try to raise the money if it were absolutely
necessary.[52]

Douglas soon discovered the danger in the course Sanders was
pursuing in the *Democratic Review*. In a letter of February 10 he
reminded Sanders that from the beginning he had opposed the
policy of bitterly attacking other Democratic candidates.[53] But the
March and April numbers of the *Democratic Review* bristled with
denunciations of the Old Fogies and shouted the cry "Young America." On April 15 Douglas wrote another long letter to Sanders,
begging him to give up the course he was following and emphasizing the injury that had been done by the assaults on the candidates for the nomination. "If these attacks are repeated my chances
are utterly hopeless, and I may be compelled to retire from the
field and throw my influence in favor of one of those whom the
Review strives to crush."[54]

The course of Sanders in the *Democratic Review* unquestionably
injured the cause of Douglas.[55] The affair was discussed in the

[51] *Ibid.*, July 12, 1851 (Chicago); also R. M. T. Hunter to Sanders, May 9,
1851, Sanders Papers (Library of Congress).
[52] Douglas to Sanders, December 28, 1851 (Washington), in Gundlach Collection (St. Louis). J. Addison Thomas, a friend of Marcy, informed his chief
on January 27, 1852, that the *Review* had been bought by a friend of Douglas.
Marcy Papers (Library of Congress), XXII.
[53] Douglas to Sanders, February 10, 1852 (Washington), Gundlach Collection
(St. Louis).
[54] Douglas to Sanders, April 15, 1852 (Washington), Gundlach Collection
(St. Louis). The *Lantern* cartooned Sanders with a *Democratic Review* banner
slaying "Old Fogies," with the "Little Giant" in mortal terror, begging him to
stop. (May 22, 1852), I, 20.
[55] B. F. Angel to Marcy, March 11, 1852 (Washington); Thomas H. Hyat to
Marcy, February 26, 1852; A. Campbell to Marcy, March 12, 1852; L. Shephard
to Marcy, December 15, 1852; Thomas Carr to Marcy, February 3, 1852. Marcy
Papers (Library of Congress), XXII.

House of Representatives, Richardson of Illinois attempting to prove that Douglas had had no connection with Sanders and the *Review*. But Breckinridge of Kentucky pointed out that Douglas had recommended the journal to the country after he had read its articles condemning the Old Fogies.[56] The damaging effect of these discussions, together with other factors, made Douglas's hope for the nomination less buoyant. In the Baltimore convention his active supporters could not achieve the necessary majority, though his ninety-two votes showed that his strength lay in the Mississippi Valley and California.[57]

Although Young America had occasioned alarm among the Whigs as well as among the Democrats,[58] the nomination of Pierce had a quieting effect. The New York *Herald* considered Pierce a "discreet representative of Young America."[59] The *Democratic Review* made the best of the situation by urging that since Pierce was a new man, he was quite capable of becoming all that the *Review* had urged.[60] During the summer Douglas, in campaigning for Pierce, appealed to the Young American sentiment.[61] Edmund Burke succeeded in persuading Dr. Hebbe and a Mr. Flinchmann, both influential among the German population, to campaign for Pierce. "The grand ideas which are the most potent in the election," Burke wrote to Pierce, "are sympathy for the liberals of Europe, the expansion of the American republic southward and westward, and the grasping of the magnificent purse of the commerce of the Pacific, in short, the ideas for which the term *Young America* is the symbol."[62] Kossuth wrote a circular to the German clubs and societies virtually urging them to support Pierce.[63]

[56] *Congressional Globe,* 32nd Cong., 1 sess., Appendix, pp. 299, 420, 711–714.
[57] Allen Johnson, *Stephen A. Douglas* (New York, 1908), p. 206.
[58] New York *Herald,* March 25, 1852; Edward Stanley in the House of Representatives, June 14, 1852. *Congressional Globe,* 32nd Cong., 1 sess., Appendix, p. 707.
[59] New York *Herald,* June 10, 1852.
[60] *Democratic Review* (June, 1852), XXX, 491.
[61] New York *Herald,* September 11, 1852.
[62] Edmund Burke to Franklin Pierce, June 14, 1852. Pierce Papers (Library of Congress), III.
[63] *Deutsch-Amerikanische Geschichtesblätter* (1917–1919), XVII–XIX.

Although Young America had not nominated its candidate, the party platform incorporated many Young American ideas. This platform advocated "the full expansion of the energies of this great and progressive people," and the *Democratic Review* interpreted the meaning to its own satisfaction.[64] The platform moreover resolved that "in view of the condition of popular institutions in the Old World, a high and sacred duty is devolved with increased responsibility upon the Democracy of this country." The New York *Herald* looked to the Pierce administration for the promotion of internal glory and prosperity and "the extension of our power and influence among the nations of the earth."[65] At the same time it observed that appointment of Young Americans to Cabinet positions would mean an unsettlement of the financial world, the electrical vibrations of which would be felt even on the London exchange.[66]

The election of Pierce was regarded with concern by those Europeans who feared the growing influence of the United States and the prominence which that influence was lending to republican and democratic ideas. The Prussian minister-resident in Washington, Baron von Gerolt, informed his government that the peace policy of Fillmore had ended, and that a new era designed to show the influence of the United States in Europe as well as the New World was about to begin.[67] The Austrian minister of foreign affairs, Count Buol-Schauenstein, believed that the election would increase popular license in America, "so incompatible with the good faith of foreign relations." Apprehensive of the American movements against Cuba, he feared "a generally aggressive and annexing policy."[68] Hülsemann, the Austrian chargé in Washington, expected that while the new government would be sympathetic with the revolutionary party in Europe, it would be deterred for the mo-

[64] *Democratic Review* (June, 1852), XXX, 491.
[65] New York *Herald*, November 4, 1852.
[66] New York *Herald*, November 18, 1852.
[67] Gerolt to the King of Prussia, No. 23, December 13, 1852, "United States of America" (Geheimes Staats-Archiv, Berlin).
[68] Foote to Everett, December 15, 1852. Correspondence with the State Department (United States Legation, Vienna), IV.

ment from offering any assistance. This was ascribed to the fact that the relations of the United States with Spain were bound to be precarious because of a determination to secure Cuba, and further, that difficulties with Great Britain and Mexico were not unlikely to develop. A victorious revolution abroad, no matter how momentary, would, nevertheless, in Hülsemann's opinion, change the probable pacific policy of the government.[69] Yet Hülsemann clearly realized from the Kossuth excitement that the influence of the South would oppose measures which threatened their commercial and financial interests, as intervention in European affairs was bound to do.[70] Yet the uncertainty in regard to the turn which the expansionist and interventionist sentiment in the United States might take caused Austria to modify her attitude toward this country.[71]

In December, 1852, the *Siècle,* published in Paris as the organ of the Republican party in Europe, represented the newly elected government as favorable to intervention in Europe. The English press, designating the *Siècle* as the organ of the American legation in Paris, regarded this announcement with concern.[72] The conservative press in France was likewise nervous. The *Journal des Débats* believed the election of Pierce was a danger sign.[73] The *Revue des Deux Mondes* lamented that the death of Clay and Webster left the door open to "la Jeune Amérique," and "a violent, perhaps bloody

[69] Hülsemann to Buol-Schauenstein, No. 8, April 10, 1853.

[70] Hülsemann to Buol-Schauenstein, No. 42, November 21, 1852 (Vienna).

[71] The Austrian government sharply reversed its decision that, as a result of Secretary of State Webster's address at the congressional banquet for Kossuth, official relations could not be maintained with Webster (Schwarzenberg to Hülsemann, February 4, 1852). The instructions to Hülsemann to make some sort of a compromise did not reach him until after he left Washington. The conciliatory attitude of the Austrian government was caused chiefly by the realization that "the political and economic importance of the United States are increasing each day, an importance which assures them an influence on the destiny of Europe" (Buol-Schauenstein to Hülsemann, May 11, 1852). See also M. E. Curti, *Austria and the United States,* Smith College Studies in History (April, 1926).

[72] J. Addison Thomas to Marcy, December 26, 1852 (Paris). Marcy Papers (Library of Congress), *XLVI.*

[73] November 11, 1852.

solution" of outstanding issues.[74] Young America was regarded as the most numerous and influential wing of the Democratic party, and its "voracious, insatiable" ambition for power and expansion was evidence that it possessed "les yeux plus gros que le ventre."[75] Émile Montégut observed that since Americans thought of themselves as "patrons of future peoples and the model of universal government," it was not surprising that they had insulted Austria and Russia, and menaced Spain. These were regarded as the advance signs of more grave attacks. The discourse of Cass on the French occupation of Samana was regarded as expressing the jealous anxiety of the United States, and, indeed, Pierce's election might be regarded as a triumph of aggressive passions.[76] Other French writers were also attacking the expansive tendencies in the United States. One, A. de Moges, believed that the system of American expansion ought to become thenceforward the chief preoccupation of the European cabinets.[77] It remained to be seen what influence Young America would actually have on the new administration.

The bitter fight between the Old Fogies and the representatives of Young America for spoils began almost immediately. George Sanders used every possible weapon to prevent the President-elect from offering to Marcy the chief office in the Cabinet.[78] Almost every day and night during the early months of 1853 he was to be seen at the Astor House, with various Douglas men, seizing each opportunity to talk with influential citizens and travelers. A political enemy of Sanders, Thomas N. Carr, had reason to believe that in all these efforts he was financially supported by George Law.[79] Despite everything, including interviews with Pierce,[80] Sanders failed.

[74] (November, 1852), XVI, 792–793.

[75] Ibid.

[76] Ibid. (January, 1853), 606.

[77] A. de Moges, Influence Prochaine des États-Unis sur la Politique de l'Europe (Paris, 1855); M. H. du Pasquier de Dommartin, Les États-Unis et le Mexique l'Intérêt Européen dans l'Amérique du Nord (Paris, 1852).

[78] J. Addison Thomas to Marcy, January 18, 1853 (New York). Marcy Papers (Library of Congress), XXVIII.

[79] Thomas N. Carr to Marcy, February 24, 1853 (New York). Marcy Papers (Library of Congress), XXVIII.

[80] Pierce to Sanders, January 18, 1853. Sanders Papers (Library of Congress).

Marcy was announced as the new Secretary of State.[81] But the leader of Young America was not discouraged. Sanders publicly declared his determination to obtain an office in spite of Marcy's opposition. A letter to this effect was read at Tammany Hall.[82] George Law, it seems, had committed Pierce to Sanders's appointment. It was also believed that Douglas was among the some hundred friends who were aiding Sanders.[83] And so in the face of opposition of Marcy,[84] Sanders was appointed in June (1853) consul at London.[85]

Hülsemann regarded this appointment as an indication that the government intended to maintain intimate relations with the revolutionary refugees in that capital.[86] The Austrian chargé assumed that Marcy had yielded in his opposition to Sanders because of the latter's influence with Pierce.

Sanders arrived in London in November. Although he was on good terms with Buchanan, the American minister,[87] it was Sickles, the secretary of legation, who proved the more valuable friend. This relationship enabled Sanders to make use of the legation seal and dispatch bag for sending personal communications and probably those of his exiled friends, the leaders of the revolutions of 1848. Buchanan was apparently ignorant of the use Sanders was making of the dispatch bags.[88]

The exiles virtually made their headquarters at Sanders's London

[81] This was regarded as a "death blow" to "progress" by that ardent champion of Young America, William Corry. Corry to Holt, May 2, 1853 (Washington). Joseph Holt Papers (Library of Congress).

[82] Carr to Marcy, April 4, 1853 (New York). Marcy Papers (Library of Congress), XXXIII.

[83] Ibid.

[84] Marcy to Buchanan, December 22, 1855. Private Letters of W. L. Marcy (Library of Congress). See also the Lantern (April, May, 1853), II, passim.

[85] The wrath of Marcy's friends ran high with the news of this appointment. By one correspondent Sanders was described as "too lazy to shave and clean himself and out and out a blackguard." W. W. Benson to Marcy, June 25, 1853. Marcy Papers (Library of Congress), XXXIV.

[86] Hülsemann to Buol-Schauenstein, No. 19, August 11, 1853.

[87] J. Addison Thomas to Marcy, November 29, 1853 (London). Marcy Papers (Library of Congress), XLV.

[88] Buchanan to Marcy, December 22, 1854. Marcy Papers (Library of Congress).

house. It was there that Kossuth met Garibaldi for the first time. It was there that Buchanan graced a dinner party whose guests included Kossuth, Mazzini, Ledru-Rollin, Garibaldi, Orsini, Arnold Ruge, and Herzen. "Sitting next to Mrs. Sanders at table," wrote Buchanan, "I asked her if she was not afraid the combustible materials about here would explode and blow us all up."[89] Buchanan was much impressed by the assembly. In reporting the affair to the Secretary of State, he observed that he had been very cautious in his remarks. "But," he added, "they were all evidently much pleased that I was neither ashamed nor afraid to meet them. However indiscreet it might be for me, as American minister, to invite any of them to my house, I should feel myself degraded as an American citizen to have refused the invitation of a friend, simply because men who have suffered in the cause of liberty were to be present."[90]

Sanders was listening to the plans of the exiles and doing what he might to further them. Ledru-Rollin entertained the idea of using the United States as a lever to force the revolutionary movement in Europe. At the time of the *Black Warrior* and the Ostend Manifesto he wrote to Sanders, suggesting that the United States pledge its support to the Spanish republicans, braving even the risk of war with the European governments. The reward was to be the expectation that Cuba, out of gratitude and interest, would apply to the United States for annexation.[91]

With Kossuth the relations of the American consul were more intimate. On July 29, 1852, Kossuth had written from London asking Sanders whether anything was to be expected from the in-

[89] Buchanan to Marcy, February 24, 1854. Marcy Papers (Library of Congress), *XLVIII*.

[90] *Ibid.*

[91] Ledru-Rollin to George N. Sanders, August 1, 1854 (London). *Political Papers of George N. Sanders;* see also A. R. Calmin, *Ledru-Rollin et les Proscrits Français en Angleterre* (Paris, 1921). Sanders's coadjutor, Corry, states that "it is quite probable that it was the urgency of Mr. Sanders that pushed Mr. Buchanan and encouraged Mr. Soulé, at Ostend, to manifest the determination to appropriate Cuba at all hazards, and with no respect for national law as hitherto accepted." *Biographical Encyclopedia of Kentucky*, p. 539. The scattering of Sanders's papers would make it difficult to test this statement.

coming Democratic administration.[92] "The European movement,"
urged Kossuth, "is not only impending, but can by no means be de-
layed long any more. Not only is the organization entirely com-
pleted, but in consequence of this achievement the blow must be
stricken." Kossuth insisted that after the great victory of the
Democratic views signalized by Pierce's election, aid to the cause of
European revolution became a matter of political dignity.[93] "To
speak plainly, the nomination to Constantinople should tell all
Europe explicitly, that it is meant to be energetically anti-Russian
and anti-Austrian because American and Democratic."[94] Kossuth
added that almost anything might be done at Constantinople by
money. This suggestion clarifies the policy Kossuth was at this
time pursuing in Washington. During March and April, 1853,
Pulszky, his former secretary, was urging the administration to
make the uprising in Milan the occasion for announcing its policy.[95]
Pulszky wished the administration to declare that it would support
Turkey in case it was attacked by Russia and aided by Austria.
Such an event was expected, and was to be the signal for an Hungarian uprising. The prestige of the United States would be greatly
enhanced by purchasing as naval bases Kleck and Sutorina. The
influence of Kossuth's chargé at Constantinople was offered to
achieve this end; it was expected in return that the moral influence
of the presence of the United States in this region would aid the
revolutionary outbreak in Hungary. Pulszky seems to have had long
conversations with Cushing, the attorney general, well known for
his sympathy with Young America, and with Soulé, Marcy, and
President Pierce. Hülsemann scarcely expected that the United
States would be led into such an extravagant project.[96] Though
these schemes had in reality little chance of success, there was

---

[92] Kossuth to Sanders, July 29, 1852 (London). *Political Papers of George N.
Sanders.*
[93] *Ibid.*, December 24, 1852.
[94] *Ibid.*; Corry was being pushed for this post. Corry to Holt, May 2, 1853.
Holt Papers (Library of Congress).
[95] Strangely, these activities did not get into the press. Hülsemann to Buol-
Schauenstein, No. 6, March 27, 1853.
[96] Hülsemann to Buol-Schauenstein, No. 6, March 27, 1853.

reason for the Austrian government, none the less, to feel consider-able anxiety.[97]

The spring and summer passed without definite results, but Kossuth's optimism was stimulated by the arrival of Sanders in London in November, 1853. In a letter dated London, November 15, 1853, and published in the New York *Herald*, Sanders an-nounced to America that Kossuth's agent had been openly received in Constantinople. "The Porte made no secret of the fact," con-tinued Sanders, "that unless Austria withdraws her armies from her frontiers, or England and France shall accede to his demand for his guaranty of the neutrality of Austria, that Kossuth will be invited to Constantinople and placed at the head of a strong division to march on Hungary."[98]

But this was obviously mere talk. Two days later Kossuth re-quested Sanders to write a letter to the United States minister in Constantinople recommending to his good offices the Hungarian chargé, and further to use his influence to persuade the Porte not to delay longer in forcing Austria "peremptorily to assume a clear position."[99] Kossuth continued to urge that the United States min-ister in Constantinople should turn the scale in the diplomatic battle being waged between England and France for preponder-ance.[100] In spite of all these efforts, the representatives of the

[97] At this very time, A. Dudley Mann, well known for his friendliness to European revolution, was appointed and confirmed in the newly created office of assistant secretary of state (Hülsemann to Buol-Schauenstein, No. 6, March 27, 1853). This was generally regarded as a concession to Young America, and as such was disagreeable to Hülsemann and his colleagues (Hülsemann to Buol-Schauenstein, *ibid.*). The presence of Cushing in the Cabinet was in itself reason to fear the influence of Young America (Hülsemann to Buol-Schauenstein, February 21, 1853). On the evening of April 10 it appeared that the Cabinet was to be radically reorganized, Cushing to become Secretary of State, Stockton Secretary of the Navy, in which event "it is a complete victory for Young Amer-ica" (Hülsemann to Buol-Schauenstein, April 11, 1853). While the rumor proved to be unfounded, it was clear to the Austrian chargé that there was cause to be nervous as long as Cushing, the representative of Young America, enjoyed the confidence of the President (Hülsemann to Buol-Schauenstein, No. 6, March 27, 1853).

[98] Hülsemann to Buol-Schauenstein, No. 37, December 5, 1853, enclosure.

[99] Kossuth to Sanders, November 17, 1853. Gundlach Collection (St. Louis).

[100] Kossuth to Sanders, February 26, 1854. *Political Papers of George N. Sanders.*

United States remained passive. Kossuth had complained that they were willing to allow the "Black Sea to become a Russian lake or leave it to England's protection."[101]

At the same time that Kossuth and Sanders were pursuing the uncertain paths of diplomacy, they were endeavoring to equip a vessel to transport the Hungarian leader, with such followers as might be assembled, to Constantinople. Sanders not only gave advice, but seems to have acted as a sort of purchasing agent.[102] For lack of financial backing the negotiations came to nothing. "God knows," Kossuth wrote Sanders on December 13, 1853, "how anxiously I have awaited a letter from America. . . . I am sick with excitement and disappointment."[103]

But there were other means of assisting the cause of European freedom. August 21, 1854, Sanders's letter to the President of the Swiss Confederation appeared in the London *Times*.[104] It protested against certain resolutions abridging the rights of asylum in that country. Sanders ventured to hope that the Swiss Confederation would not be influenced by Austrian diplomacy. Full of feeling for republicanism, the letter urged that Switzerland, "like our own America, is charged with certain solemn responsibilities." A few days later, August 24, the *Times* criticized Sanders's position in assuming that Switzerland was the sole abode of "true political faith," and that the duty of its people, therefore, was the conversion of Europe.[105]

August Belmont, American minister at The Hague, wrote to Sanders that "the virulent manner with which the demolition has been attacked by the whole conservative press of England and the continent, is the most evident proof of its importance.[106] The republican spirit in Europe is subdued but not crushed, and mani-

---

[101] Kossuth to Sanders, December 13, 1853. Gundlach Collection (St. Louis).
[102] *Ibid.*, November 17, 1853.
[103] *Ibid.*, December 13, 1853. Kossuth believed that if he could have entered the Bosphorus with a couple of vessels on the occasion of the catastrophe at Sinope, his reception would have been both enthusiastic and significant.
[104] London *Times*, August 21, 1854.
[105] London *Times*, August 24, 1854.
[106] Belmont to Sanders, no date. Sanders Papers (Library of Congress).

festoes like yours can not fail to exercise the most beneficial influence on its dormant powers." Belmont asked for copies of the letter to be distributed in Germany and France.

Sanders had made many enemies before he assumed his position in London, and his open activities in behalf of the revolutionary cause did not diminish them. Hülsemann understood in January, 1854, that Sanders's letter to the New York *Herald* had so displeased the President that he hesitated to transmit the nomination to the Senate.[107] In February, 1854, Sanders's nomination as consul in London was refused confirmation in the Senate by a vote of 29 against 10.[108]

Sanders was outraged at the rejection. Blaming Douglas for deserting him, he even intimated that the Little Giant was one of the conspirators against his character. Douglas was surprised at the direction his wrath had taken. "I am not in the habit of suspecting my friends," Douglas wrote, "much less of condemning them. . . . When, in the prosecution of your cherished revenge, you shall ascertain the true state of the facts, and shall know who stood by you, and defended you to the last, you will feel more mortification and chagrin at having written your unkind letter to me than I did in reading it."[109]

The exiles in London were thoroughly disappointed at the recall of Sanders. On March 1, 1854, Kossuth, Ledru-Rollin, and Mazzini addressed a letter to him expressing "deep regret and mortification

[107] Hülsemann to Buol-Schauenstein, No. 3, D, January 15, 1854. Sanders continued this virulent letter writing, publishing in several languages, according to Corry, an extraordinary assassination letter, which urged the murder of Louis Napoleon, "By any means, and in any way it could be done." *Biographical Encyclopedia of Kentucky*, p. 539.

[108] Hülsemann to Buol-Schauenstein, No. 9, B, March 9, 1854. Sanders's friends believed that Marcy's influence had secured the rejection. Marcy wrote to Buchanan that he had treated Sanders forbearingly, and had done nothing to influence the action of any senator adversely toward him. Marcy to Buchanan, December 22, 1855, Private Letters of W. L. Marcy (Library of Congress). Even Sanders's enemies were surprised, despite Marcy's "conjecture and advice" on the subject, at the large vote against him. N. G. Upham to Marcy, March 3, 1854, Marcy Papers (Library of Congress), XLVIII. Apparently Young America was not such a power in Congress as had been supposed.

[109] Douglas to Sanders, March 27, 1854. *Political Papers of George N. Sanders*.

at this untoward occurrence." The rejection of his nomination by the Senate was "a hard and mischievous blow at the prospects" of democracy.[110] Kossuth became furious when he thought of the way in which Sanders was treated by his government, and "sick at heart at considering what the cause of European democracy" lost by losing him.[111] Louis Blanc took occasion to express his appreciation for the articles which had appeared in the *Democratic Review*.[112] "My admiration rises to affection for you," wrote Victor Hugo. "When you write it is your soul that writes, a soul elevated and free."[113] Campanella, the secretary of Mazzini, thanked Sanders for the favors he had received,[114] and Garibaldi added to "a word of affection and gratitude" the comment that whatever it might be his fortune to accomplish for his country would be inaugurated "under the auspices of generous men (sympathizing in soul with my unhappy land) of whom you are the model."[115]

Sanders's consular colleague in Liverpool, Nathaniel Hawthorne, "hoped to Heaven" that Pierce would do the right thing in Sanders's case, and felt certain that he would "if he follows his nature."[116] Soulé wrote from Madrid that "there will not be a true Democrat throughout the land who will not deplore and bitterly condemn that you were not returned to a post which you filled with so much distinction."[117]

Although Sanders's efforts in London were badly rewarded,

[110] Kossuth, Mazzini, Ledru-Rollin to Sanders, March 1, 1854, *ibid.*
[111] Kossuth to Sanders, September 1, 1854, *ibid.* Kossuth addressed a letter to the Germans of America on the Senate's action. Hülsemann to Buol-Schauenstein, No. 17, March 20, 1854. *National Intelligencer,* March 27, 1854.
[112] Louis Blanc to Sanders, June 14, 1854. *Political Papers of George N. Sanders.*
[113] Victor Hugo to Sanders, October 31, 1854, *ibid.*
[114] Campanella to Sanders, May 17, 1854, *ibid.*
[115] Garibaldi to Sanders, April 11, 1854, *ibid.*
[116] Hawthorne to Sanders, June 2, 1854, *ibid.* Corry says that the appointment was later confirmed as a result of the intercession of William H. Seward, Sanders's political enemy. *Biographical Encyclopedia of Kentucky,* p. 539. The writer has found no record of such action in the *Senate Journal* or in the *Executive Documents.*
[117] Soulé to Sanders, August 21, 1854 (Madrid). *Political Papers of George N. Sanders.*

slightly better success attended those of some other representatives of Young America. August Belmont, agent of the Rothschilds in New York, and sometime consul general for Austria, was thoroughly sympathetic with the program of American aid for European republicanism. Belmont owed his appointment as minister to The Hague very largely to Sanders's influence with Pierce.[118] From The Hague, Belmont wrote Sanders that the Crimean War might very well make possible new and successful revolutions. "The day is not far distant, when self-preservation will dictate to the United States the necessity of throwing her moral and physical force into the scale of European republicanism. To prepare for such a day is the first sacred duty of our Government and Congress, and this can only be done effectively by reorganizing and increasing the navy.[119] The sooner we prepare against the contingencies which our rapid growth and the jealousy of the European powers will bring about, the better it will be for us."[120] But apart from forwarding Sanders's letter to the President of the Swiss Confederation, Belmont's activities in behalf of Young America were confined to the dispatch of high-sounding demands to the Dutch government for the release of one Walter Gibson who had been imprisoned in Batavia on the charge of exciting native chiefs to overthrow Dutch royal authority.[121]

To some extent Edwin de Leon, who as early as 1845 had defined the aims of Young America, executed some of its tenets in his official capacity of diplomatic agent in Egypt. His dealings with Mehemet Ali were high-handed,[122] while his protection of Ameri-

[118] Belmont to Sanders, March 21, 1853 (New York). Sanders Papers (Library of Congress). Buchanan also recommended Belmont as a desirable minister if the administration desired to obtain Cuba in a peaceful way. Buchanan to Marcy, March 8, 1853. Marcy Papers (Library of Congress), XXIX.

[119] A strong navy was a favorite idea with Young America. See "Our Mission—Diplomacy and Navy," *Democratic Review* (July 1852), XXXI, 33–43.

[120] Belmont to Sanders, August, 1854. Sanders Papers (Library of Congress).

[121] See *Letters, Speeches and Addresses of August Belmont* (New York, 1890), *passim;* Marcy to Belmont, August 8, 1853. Marcy Papers (Library of Congress), XLI.

[122] Edwin de Leon, *Thirty Years of My Life on Three Continents* (London, 1890), pp. 150, 193 *et seq.* De Leon corresponded with Sanders in London.

can missionaries in Jaffa must have been applauded by Young America at home.

Although the Secretary of State, Marcy, was not a friend of Sanders, he was certainly somewhat influenced by the group to which Sanders belonged. His circular to the effect that no foreigners be employed in diplomatic chancelleries, and advising diplomatic agents not to wear uniforms, responded to a demand of Young America.[123] Marcy wrote to Buchanan that his course in dispensing with diplomatic uniform had gained him great popularity,[124] but the American representatives in Turin, Paris, and Vienna came out less gloriously,[125] and had either to compromise with or surrender to European and royal custom.

When Douglas failed of nomination in 1852, Young America had been discouraged but not daunted. Now, however, with the return of Sanders from his consular post, and the failure of the group to exert any very important influence on the government, there was no longer any reason for making pretenses, and Young America as a movement died out. But Young America, as a slogan, meant something long after the movement, as such, was dead—its influence was registered in the national self-consciousness.

We have seen that Young America had glorious ideals for the future of the country, and a very ambitious program for realizing them. Yet the ideals were as vague as they were grand. Ways and means of applying the program, of extending aid to the republican movements in Europe, were not definitely worked out, nor, apparently, were the serious practical problems that intervention would involve ever squarely faced. It would not be expected, then, that such a movement would meet with any great degree of practical success, partly because of its inherent weakness and partly because of sectional opposition and that of established economic interests.

Thus the movement itself was a failure. Yet the fact that it

[123] Hülsemann to Buol-Schauenstein, No. 14, B, June 13, 1853.

[124] Marcy to Buchanan, March 12, 1854. Private Letters of Marcy (Library of Congress).

[125] John Y. Mason to Marcy, January 26, 1854 (Paris), Marcy Papers (Library of Congress), XLVII; Wm. Jackson to Marcy, January 30, 1854 (Vienna), ibid.

existed and flourished so strongly for a while is very significant. On the one hand it shows that Young America's grand ideals really expressed the feelings of many Americans. Idealists like Emerson and Whitman entertained the same essential ideals, though they expressed them less crudely. It was probably more true of the United States than of the European countries that its people tended, at that time, to have an exaggerated youthful faith in the glory of their institutions. Some wished to gain still further glory through territorial expansion and foreign trade. Others were especially interested in encouraging democracy abroad. How many of these latter were animated by commercial motives is a question. But such people, idealists and materialists alike, must have found their chief aspirations expressed in the program of Young America. On the other hand, the fact that these already existing feelings found expression and some degree of organization and coherence in Young America could not but have helped to crystallize and still further develop them. Thus, this movement, though it failed of practical results, was significant, first as a political gesture so vigorous as to arouse alarm in Europe, and, second, as a means of expressing and developing a certain type of national self-consciousness.

10

America at the
World Fairs, 1851–1893
(1950)

THE story of American participation in the international exhibitions of agriculture and industry has never been told.[1] It is a story rich in human interest. The increasing American participation in world fairs reflected the expansion of American patriotism and enterprise in the last half of the nineteenth century. At these "tournaments of industry" our exhibits provided a measuring rod for the relative status of American and European technology. They also provided a mirror for the changing attitudes of the rest of the world toward American civilization.

American participation in the foreign exhibits was not taken for granted until the last two decades of the nineteenth century. In the beginning participation was timid and private. The question of

[1] There are references to the Crystal Palace exhibition in John Kouwenhoven's *Made in America* (New York, 1948), pp. 18 ff.; Halvdan Koht's *The American Spirit in Europe* (Philadelphia, 1949), pp. 92 ff.; and Roger Burlingame's *Backgrounds of Power* (New York, 1949), pp. 157 ff. For the Exhibition of the Industry of All Nations, held in London in 1862, see Richard O. Cummings, "American Interest in World Agriculture, 1861–1865," *Agricultural History* (April, 1949), XXIII, 157 ff. The best general account of the international exhibitions is that of Guy Stanton Ford in the *Encyclopaedia of Social Sciences* (New York, 1930–1935, 15 vols.), VI, 23–27.

public support for exhibitors was threshed out in the press and in Congress, opposition being broken down only by a barrage of arguments and pressures, and, as time went on, by the experiences of actual participation.

Among the motives and arguments for American participation in overseas exhibitions was the desire to publicize the nation's resources, industries, and social and economic institutions. Sensitive to European prejudices and attitudes of superiority, Americans, at first haltingly, took with increasing seriousness the opportunity to proclaim at the world fairs the national achievements and potentialities. This note was struck during the discussions of the advisability of being represented at the great exhibition of 1851 in London—the parent of all succeeding international exhibitions. In answer to the widely held view in America that the great show at the Crystal Palace was a mere "mammoth speculation" promoted by John Bull for his own ends, it was maintained that the exhibition of specimens of American industry at London would give Europe "a juster appreciation and a more perfect knowledge of what this Republic is, than could be attained in any other way." Recalling the impression made on the world by the recent victory over Mexico, a writer in one journal remarked that participation in the exhibition would "show to the nations of Europe that our mechanical and inventive resources are equal to what we possess in a military point of view."[2]

In arguing for official support of American participation in the Paris exhibition of 1867, Americans developed still further this point of view. N. M. Beckwith, an American long resident in Paris, called to the attention of John Bigelow, minister to France, the "deficiency of exact information in Europe in regard to America previous to the rebellion, in a political, literary, and moral sense, in a physical, geographical, statistical, financial, industrial, scientific,

---

[2] *Journal of the Great Exhibition of 1851* (February 1, 1851), I, 141. The name of the American newspaper is not given. For American reactions to the proposed Crystal Palace exhibition, see New York *Herald*, January 8, 1851; and New York *Daily Tribune*, January 14, 1851. See also D. Eldon Hall, *A History of the Great Exhibition of Industry of All Nations* (Redfield, N.J., 1852), p. 40.

and productive sense, and in every sense." Though victory in arms had made the United States better known than "all the events of their previous history," Beckwith argued that an exhibition of the products of America in the center of Europe would produce "an impression of surprise analogous to that produced by the disclosures of the war." This impression, he continued, would be most marked among the intelligent, skilled portion of the productive classes, whose labor and knowledge were needed in the United States. American participation, if well planned and truly national, was bound in the end to return to the Treasury, by increased immigration and augmented revenues, more than its cost.[3] The Paris correspondent of the New York *Evening Post* urged that a good exhibit was the best possible advertising medium: it would prove that the United States could be independent of all nations.[4] In London the *Anglo-American Times* echoed all these views. It also urged that a worthy display of American power and wealth would enhance the value of the American bonds presently to be negotiated to meet the national indebtedness and dispel the distrust of European capitalists on whom the United States still depended for loans for the development of resources.[5]

Perhaps moved by such considerations Secretary of State Seward submitted a report to the President in which, on economic grounds, he urged American participation.[6] Since Congress was not in session, the State Department took steps to ensure that participation. Thus in the spring of 1866 when Congress took up the matter, it was in a sense faced by a *fait accompli*. In the heated debates in Congress General Nathaniel Banks of Massachusetts, in supporting the resolution for appropriations and official participation, ar-

[3] N. M. Beckwith to John Bigelow, November 23, 1865, in "Universal Exposition at Paris," *House Executive Document No. 12*, 39 Congress, 1 session, p. 57.

[4] *Ibid.*, pp. 53-54; New York *Evening Post*, December 11, 1865; *The French Universal Exhibition of 1867; Interesting Letters from the United States Commissioner Beckwith and Other Papers* (Washington, 1866), pp. 6-7.

[5] *Anglo-American Times*, July 28, August 25, October 13, 1866; February 9, March 16, 1867.

[6] *House Exec. Doc. No. 12*, 39 Cong., 1 sess., p. 2.

gued that "it is in our power to represent the social and political character of the country in such a way as to attract the attention of other nations . . . and thus place before the world an enlarged view of the condition and the prospect of American civilization." Through its exhibit of the matériel and organization of the armed forces, the government could impress upon the peoples of Europe and Asia the fact that American friendship was worth courting. "It is a duty," Banks concluded, "we owe to other nations, as well as to ourselves, to show them what we are."[7] Henry Raymond of New York looked on the exhibition as a contest between the products of labor under democratic liberty and those under monarchical despotism.[8] These arguments, together with the support of chambers of commerce and the party organization, overrode the opposition, which argued that an appropriation was bound to benefit special interests rather than the people as a whole, that the ingenuity of American enterprise could secure adequate American representation at Paris, and that the United States, "scorned, insulted, and spit upon by every nation in Europe except one during the long and bloody war through which we had just passed," should not kowtow to the despot Napoleon, no friend of ours as his support of Maximilian in Mexico showed.[9]

The arguments for generous support of American participation in the Vienna exhibition of 1873 resembled those heard in 1867.[10] Senator Oliver Morton of Indiana contended that our displays at London and Paris had been so meager as to give Europe improper notions regarding our resources and manufactures. If we sent a first-rate display, we should be engaging in "the best advertisement of the resources, wealth, and the attractions of the United States that can be made."[11] Others argued that participation would enable

[7] *Congressional Globe*, 39 Cong., 1 sess., pp. 1371 ff. (March 13, 1866).
[8] *Ibid.*, pp. 1397–1398 (March 14, 1866).
[9] *Ibid.*, pp. 3156 ff.
[10] The volume of newspaper clippings on the proposed exhibition and American participation reveal widespread enthusiasm for congressional support. "Vienna Exhibition of 1873," Department of State archives, National Archives.
[11] *Congressional Globe*, 42 Cong., 3 sess., p. 623 (January 16, 1873).

the country to make "a perfect and full representation" in central and eastern Europe not only of our mechanical and natural resources but of "our system of government." The exhibit we might send to the rulers of other lands would afford "new proofs of the strength of our Republic, and to their peoples fresh aspirations for comforts and freedom."[12]

In view of circumstances associated with the American participation in the Vienna exhibition and the prevailing hard times, it was necessary to muster heavy arguments and support to break down the opposition to appropriations for participation in the Paris exhibition of 1878—an opposition more formidable than that on any earlier occasion. Abram Hewitt of New York and Charles Williams of Wisconsin maintained that America had benefited measurably from past exhibitions: our exports had been greatly increased.[13] A like emphasis marked the argument of William Crapo of Massachusetts: "Our capacity for production exceeds our consumption. Relief for this industry must come, not through tariffs, but it must come through exportation."[14] Significantly, the votes in Congress on appropriations for subsidies show that support for official participation came chiefly from the industrial northeastern and middle states, and from the commercial centers of the South and West.

Similar arguments accompanied the efforts to ensure generous government support for participation in the exhibitions at Sydney and Melbourne[15] and in the international fisheries exhibitions at Berlin and London.[16] When it was clear that the Columbian Historical Exhibition at Madrid in 1892–1893 was evoking little interest in the United States, the American legation finally persuaded

[12] *Ibid.*, pp. 252–253 (December 17, 1872), Appendix, p. 3 (December 19, 1872).

[13] *Congressional Record*, 45 Cong., 1 sess., VI, 528, 536 ff. (November 19, 1877).

[14] *Ibid.*, p. 542 (November 19, 1877).

[15] O. M. Spencer to Secretary of State F. W. Seward, Melbourne, March 25, 1879, Department of State archives.

[16] Andrew D. White to Secretary of State William M. Evarts, January 5, 28, February 18, 1880, Department of State archives; *Congressional Record*, 47 Cong., 1 sess., XIII, 5116 ff. (June 19, 1882); *House Report No. 1413*, 47 Cong., 1 sess., pp. 203 ff.

the government to take part, not only to ensure Spanish participation at the Chicago World's Fair but as an inducement to Spain to lift the embargo on American pork.[17]

In addition to the arguments that American participation in the international exhibitions was good advertising to attract European skilled immigrants and capital, to increase American exports, and to publicize American institutions and enhance American prestige, champions of American participation brought forth in the debates other considerations. These included the argument that the United States should take part in the Paris exhibitions as a token of appreciation of French aid in establishing American independence; and the further argument, especially evident in the discussions of 1877 and 1888, that the United States was in duty bound to support a sister republic surrounded by monarchies and endeavoring to prove the validity of republican institutions.[18] Representative McCreary of Kentucky struck a related but distinct note when he declared that we must take part in the Paris exhibition inasmuch as "God in His wisdom established this Republic in order that it might stand out before the world as a model by which other lovers of liberty might fashion their governments—as an illustration of what freemen may accomplish in a 'government of the people, by the people, and for the people.' "[19]

Finally, in all the discussions regarding American participation, the argument was made that the United States could learn valuable lessons from the industrial and artistic displays of the Old World. Thus Secretary of State Seward included among his arguments for official support of American exhibitors at the Paris show of 1867 the advantages American agriculture and industry would gain from the diffusion of useful knowledge.[20] This argument generally prevailed over the counterproposition that by sending our products

[17] General E. Burd Grubb to Secretary of State Blaine, Madrid, May 18, 1892, Department of State archives.

[18] *Congressional Record*, 45 Cong., 1 sess., VI, 513 (November 10, 1877), *House Report No. 135*, House Resolution 83, 50 Cong., 1 sess., p. 2.

[19] *Congressional Record*, 50 Cong., 1 sess., XIX, 1651 (March 1, 1888).

[20] *House Exec. Doc. No. 12*, 39 Cong., 1 sess., p. 2. Seward also cited the moral influence of American participation just after the Civil War.

abroad we would enable European competitors to steal our secrets and ruthlessly grab our markets.

Thanks to all these arguments, and to other considerations, the American government provided vessels for transporting exhibits to the Crystal Palace exhibition of 1851 and to the Vienna exhibition of 1873. Additional appropriations varying from $2000 to $200,000 were made, beginning with the London exhibition of 1862. These grants provided for the payment of official American commissioners, for transporting and unpacking exhibits, for decorating and in some cases for constructing quarters for the American exhibits, and for other expenses incidental to participation.[21]

When the efforts of Abbott Lawrence, minister to England, failed to secure a congressional appropriation to aid exhibitors at the Crystal Palace in 1851, many agriculturalists and industrialists, left to their own initiative and resources, hesitated to risk time and money in sending exhibits to the experiment across the seas.[22] The contrast between the official sponsorship of all other foreign exhibitors at London and the private nature of American participation was brought home when it was apparent that of all the compartments in the palace the American rooms alone were bare and undecorated. Worse, no one had money for unloading the cargo of the *Lawrence*, which Congress had provided, and for transporting the exhibits to the Crystal Palace. American chagrin was as deep as the tauntings in the British press were annoying. To the rescue came George Peabody, American banker resident in London. Digging down into his pockets Peabody brought forth $15,000 to decorate the American compartment and to transport and arrange the exhibits.[23]

Nor were these embarrassments the only ones responsible for the

---

[21] The exact amount of the appropriations and the various stipulations regarding their expenditure can be traced in *United States Statutes at Large*, XII, 328; XIV, 362-363; XVII, 637-638; XX, 245-246; XXII, 387-389; XXV, 620-622.

[22] Abbott Lawrence to Secretary of State Clayton (London), April 5, 1850, Department of State archives; Washington *National Intelligencer*, January 5, 1851; *Journal of the Great Exhibition of 1851*, p. 46 (November 23, 1850).

[23] Abbott Lawrence to Secretary of State Webster (London), November 6, 1851, Department of State archives.

initially unfavorable impression created by the American exhibits. In their grandiose expectations the Americans had asked for and got far more space than their exhibits warranted. The New Jersey commissioners believed that after the opening, when knowledge of the great displays reached the United States, many more contributors would have forwarded their articles had not "taunts, aspersions, and petty ridicule" in the English papers at the poverty of the American displays aroused national indignation and deepened the original impression that the United States would not get fair play.[24] In a more sober vein the London *Morning Chronicle* announced that the American exhibit was neither what had been expected of the United States nor an adequate representation of her capabilities.[25] *Chambers' Edinburgh Journal* concluded that on the whole the United States had come out feebly in the arts. It conceded, to be sure, that Hiram Powers' "Greek Slave," which adorned the American compartment, was "marvellously fine," but it added the cutting remark that this one redeeming feature had after all been contributed by its London owner.[26] In commenting on the vacant spaces in the American division the *Eclectic Review* observed that this American "vaulting ambition" which had "overleaped itself" was not untypical of the adolescent republic across the Atlantic.[27]

The tide of opinion suddenly changed after the practical demonstration of agricultural implements at Tiptree Hall. To the surprise of almost everyone the American agricultural machinery, especially the reapers of Obed Hussey and Cyrus McCormick and the draft plow of Prouty and Mears, far exceeded in speed, efficiency, and endurance any and all competitors. European savants had passed by the reapers and plows as unworthy of science, and burly Englishmen had ridiculed them as huge, unwieldy, and unsightly. But the celerity and exactness of the action in the trials surprised the spec-

[24] *Report of the New Jersey Commissioners to the World's Fair* (Trenton, 1852), p. 17.
[25] London *Morning Chronicle*, May 17, 1851, in *Littell's Living Age* (July, 1851), XXX, 34.
[26] *Chambers' Edinburgh Journal* (May 31, 1851), XV, 339.
[27] *Eclectic Review* (June, 1851), XCIII, 746.

tators, convinced the incredulous, and satisfied British farmers that here was something not dreamed of in their fondest reveries.[28] The favorable impression of American technology was heightened when the crack British lock-picker failed to open the American Hobbs' locks, whereas British locks, long deemed impregnable, yielded to American dexterity.[29] In military circles the Colt revolvers and the Robbins and Lawrence rifles—with "the various parts made to interchange"—were clearly superior to all comparable small arms and created a profound impression. *Punch* taunted the amazed John Bull:

> Your gunsmiths of their skill may crack,
> But that again don't mention;
> I guess that Colt's revolvers whack
> Their very first invention.
> By Yankee Doodle, too, you're beat
> Downright in Agriculture,
> With his machine for reaping wheat,
> Chaw'd up as by a vulture.[30]

Still other American exhibits began to attract attention. The sewing machines of Isaac M. Singer, of Lerow and Blodgett, and of Grover and Baker performed admirably, although as yet the great utility of the new invention failed to be fully appreciated; Hayden's ingenious cotton drawing frame and the saw gin for cleansing cotton; stoves and ventilating apparatus; machinery for spinning, sewing, planing, turning; stone-cutting devices; the Morse telegraph; Goodyear rubber materials; fire engines and furnaces; printing presses; clocks and surgical instruments; the Jersey locomotives; oil lamps, pianos, violins, daguerreotypes, and artificial legs; all these

---

[28] See the enthusiastic testimony of an expert witness, cited from the *Journal of the Royal Agricultural Society*, in *Official Description and Illustrated Catalogue of the Great Exhibition of the Works of Industry of All Nations* (London, 1851, 3 vols.) III, 1437–1438. See, on the agricultural displays, William T. Hutchinson, *Cyrus Hall McCormick* (New York, 1930), I, 382–394. See also *Report of the New Jersey Commissioners to the World's Fair*, p. 17.

[29] *Westminster Review* (July, 1851), LX, 198.

[30] Quoted in Charles T. Rodgers, *American Superiority at the World's Fair* (Philadelphia, 1852), p. 91.

won high praise.[31] The very people, in some cases, who had earlier passed by the American exhibits with hurried and indifferent glances, now stopped to admire the wheat, cotton, flax, timber, and fruit, the hams, the copper, the iron ore, the gold, the textiles, the boots and shoes that had crossed the Atlantic.[32] A writer in the *Westminster Review*, in discussing new styles of clothing, observed that the American cousins were introducing more sensible women's garments, just as they were exporting crackers and rocking chairs, sherry cobblers, mint juleps, gin slings, and Wenham Lake ice.[33] To cap the climax the yacht *America*, in the races off Cowes, came through in a "transcendent victory."[34]

The total number of exhibitors from all nations was 15,000, of whom 10,184 were British and colonial. The United States was represented by 534 exhibitors. In proportion to the number of articles displayed, American exhibitors won more prizes than many of the Continental nations, and, indeed, more relatively than Britain herself. Of the 170 Council medals, awarded for especial originality of design, the Americans won only five—the Borden "meat biscuit," the Dick engine tools and presses, the Bond device for observing astronomical phenomena, the Goodyear India rubber, and the McCormick reaper.[35]

British comments, after the announcement of the awards, were revealing. According to Benjamin Pierce Johnson, an agent of New York State, many British and foreign visitors, on learning that the American government had taken no part in the exhibition, marveled that so much had been accomplished. "The influence of our exhibition . . ." he reported, "has more powerfully demonstrated the peculiar advantages of our free institutions in the development

[31] *Lectures on the Progress of Arts and Science* . . . (New York, 1854), pp. 262, 264, 281–282, 313, 325; London *Times*, September 2, 1851; *New York State Register*, November 11, 1851, quoted in Rodgers, *American Superiority*, pp. 90–91; *Journal of the Great Exhibition*, March 8, 1851, p. 182.

[32] Hall, *History of the Great Exhibition*, p. 43; *Daily News*, quoted in Rodgers, *American Superiority*, p. 62; *Eclectic Review* (November, 1851), XCIV, 633.

[33] *Westminster Review* (July, 1851), LV, 197.

[34] London *Times*, September 2, 1851.

[35] *Report of the New Jersey Commissioners*, p. 15.

of the energies of the people, than could have been done if the government had made a large appropriation."[36] In general, the British, while insisting that American industrial products could not approach those of Europe in glamour and splendor, admitted that they far exceeded European products in utility, in comfort, and in appeal to the great masses. The London *Times*, noting the American eye to the mass market, the emphasis on saving labor and time, on utility and comfort, and on the reduction of cost, declared that "Great Britain has received more useful ideas, and more ingenious inventions, from the United States, through the exhibition, than from all other sources."[37]

The superiorities of American industry were related in some European circles to our democratic way of life. The London *Observer* wrote that the industrial system of the Americans, "unfettered by ancient usage, and by the pomp and magnificence which our social institutions countenance, is essentially democratic in its tendencies. . . . No Government of favoritism raises any manufacture to a preëminence, which secures for it the patronage of the wealthy. Every thing is entrusted to the ingenuity of individuals, who look for their reward to public demand alone." While the *Observer* did not admit that American utility and cheapness had as yet affected the mechanical superiority of England, it believed that the Americans had shown how the mother country might improve and extend its achievements in the peaceful arts.[38]

The Liverpool *Times* concluded that the Americans were "no longer to be ridiculed, much less despised." America, continued the Liverpool paper, is in her own phrase "going ahead" and "will assuredly pass us unless we accelerate our speed." The final British reactions indicated that American participation, despite the shortcomings of the exhibit, greatly exalted the country in the eyes of other lands.[39]

[36] Benjamin Pierce Johnson, *Report of the Agent of the State of New York* (Albany, 1852), p. 13.
[37] *Ibid.*, p. 15.
[38] London *Observer*, quoted in Rodgers, *American Superiority*, pp. 127–28.
[39] Liverpool *Times*, August 27, 1851, quoted *ibid.*, p. 89. See also *An Account of the Proceedings at the Dinner given by Mr. George Peabody . . .* (London, 1851), pp. 30 ff.

The favorable impression created in the end by the Americans at London was not sustained at Paris in 1855. Only fifty-four exhibitors found a place in the American section, although space had been reserved for 1200.[40] "One is cruelly disappointed," wrote a French visitor, "when, arriving at the pavillion indicated as the galleries of the Union, one finds only a few bales of cotton, a few machines and diverse rubber objects. Who would have believed that this great American people, which seems to have atrophied all the artistic part of human nature in order to concentrate on agriculture, industry, and commerce, who would have believed that this great nation . . . would have so fallen down in the great exhibition of 1855!"[41] Admitting that the Americans displayed a few ingenious machines to make paper sacks and to work wood, some famous revolvers, some commendable daguerreotypes, the Illinois reapers, several Goodyear rubber objects, a few interesting books, and some well-manufactured objects, the prevailing French view seems to have been that these exhibits had little to teach the Old World.[42] Goodyear received the coveted cross of the Legion of Honor and other Americans were generously recognized by awards and honorable mentions—in high proportion to the total number of exhibits.[43] Nevertheless the expectations that America's reputation for prosperity and ingenuity had aroused emphasized all the more the disappointment in what had been shown.

American participation in the London exhibition of 1862 was still largely unofficial in character.[44] The exhibits included some works of art—J. F. Cropsey's "Autumn Scenes" and examples of the sculpture of William Wetmore Story and Harriet Hosmer. But the steam plows, the milking machines, the McCormick reapers,

[40] *Communication from the Governor* [*Myron Clark*] *transmitting the Report of Alexander Vattemare on the Universal Exposition of Paris* [New York], Senate No. 108 (Albany, 1856), p. 4.

[41] *Visite à l'Exposition universelle de Paris en 1855. Sous la direction de M. Tresca* (Paris, 1855), p. 5.

[42] *Ibid.*, p. 134.

[43] *Communication from the Governor*, p. 5.

[44] Edward Everett to Secretary of State Seward, September 18, 1861, Miscellaneous Letters, Department of State archives; *Congressional Globe*, 37 Cong., 1 sess., XXXI, 226, 232, 288. See also Cummings, "American Interest in World Agriculture, 1861–1865," *loc. cit.*

the Allen engine, the sewing machines, carriages, and locomotives aroused the greatest admiration.[45] The Americans again received a larger proportion of awards to the articles exhibited than any other country (83 out of 95). The *Practical Mechanics' Magazine* was enthusiastic about the Allen engine and other American technological triumphs. The New York commissioner reported that he "found machines on exhibition from the Continent, to which prizes were awarded for their superiority, copied entirely from American machines which had been purchased in this country, and *exhibited as the invention of another country*."[46] In conclusion the New York commissioner wrote that American participation had been "the means of showing the world the resources of our country, and the importance of our free institutions in developing the talents and capabilities of our citizens, which could not have been done in any other manner."[47] If this was the case there was, in view of the dominant hostility toward the North among the conservative classes of Europe, reason for satisfaction.

At the Hamburg exhibition of 1863 American reapers and other machines won awards, as did American livestock. Participation was entirely unofficial. The only note Congress took in 1865 of the international exhibitions at Bergen and Oporto was to pass a joint resolution asking the President to make known to the people of the United States the facts concerning these enterprises.[48]

American participation in the Paris exhibition of 1867 was the first really impressive proof to Europe of the great strides the country had taken even in the midst of civil war. It is true that many of the plans of the American commissioners, headed by N. M. Beckwith, failed. It was hoped, for example, that Indians in various

[45] For comments on American exhibits, see London *Times,* July 12, 1862; and *Record of the International Exhibition* (Glasgow, 1862), *passim.*

[46] B. P. Johnson, *Report on the International Exhibition of Industry and Art* (Albany, 1863), p. 37; New York State Agricultural Society, *Transactions* (1862), pp. 115–119.

[47] *Ibid.,* p. 8. J. W. Hoyt of Wisconsin distributed among representatives of various nations 2000 copies of his report on the *Resources, Conditions and Progress of Wisconsin* (Madison, 1860); J. W. Hoyt, *Reports on the London and Paris Exhibitions of 1862 and 1867* (Madison, 1869), p. 43.

[48] *United States Statutes at Large,* 38 Cong., XIII, 572.

stages of civilization might be brought to Paris, not only to enlighten scientists but to convince Europe that the government was
not guilty, as prevailing opinion held, of having pursued merely
"a cold and cruel policy."[49] But the Secretary of the Interior did
not think well of the idea, and it came to nothing. The long delay
of Congress in appropriating funds made it impossible to calculate
needed space. The general failure of American exhibitors to furnish
inventories caused endless trouble. The situation was made worse
by the fact that most Americans at Paris knew no French.

On the opening day the American section was less ready than
that of any other nation save Italy. Only after the third week did
the American compartment, with its dead-pink walls, take on some
semblance of order.[50] Some of the American commissioners were
bitter in their condemnation of Beckwith. "We felt," wrote one,
"that we were in a big ship, freighted heavily with our nation's
reputation—a cargo that we were unwilling to have sink where all
nations of the earth had assembled and would be witnesses. We
had lost confidence in our captain."[51] Beckwith was, to be sure, in-
experienced in such matters, but there was less point to the jibe
that his long residence abroad had made him aristocratic and ignorant of his country.

Many regretted the lack of certain American displays and the
inadequacy of others. Beckwith himself lamented the absence of
heavy products, such as the Dunderberg gun, at a time when the
whole world was buying heavy guns and ships and when only two
countries besides the United States could supply these.[52] Abram

[49] N. M. Beckwith to J. C. Derby, January 16, 1866; Derby to Beckwith, December 12, 1866; Derby to Beckwith, January 4, 1867; Beckwith to Derby,
December 27, 1866; Beckwith to Seward, September 19, 1866. "Paris Exhibition
of 1867," Department of State archives.

[50] Derby to Beckwith, October 11, 1866; Beckwith to Seward, April 3, 1866,
ibid.

[51] Report of the Commissioner to attend the Universal Exhibition of 1867 at
Paris, Vermont Senate Document No. 2 (Rutland, 1867), p. 42. See also "Report
of James M. Usher, Principal Agent for Massachusetts at the Universal Exposition, held in Paris, France, in 1867," Massachusetts Legislative Documents, 1868,
Senate No. 333, pp. 10 ff.

[52] Beckwith to Thurlow Weed, July 15, 1867, "Paris Exhibition of 1867,"
Miscellaneous Letters, No. 3, Department of State archives.

Hewitt reported that the exhibit of iron and steel was so meager that foreigners could only conclude that this industry was not entitled to the rank that it undoubtedly occupied in the metallic production of the world.[53] The exhibit of printing and books likewise fell short in terms of what might have been done.[54] Nor did the examples of furniture represent American achievements.[55] A few commentators even went so far as to regard the whole American participation as a failure.[56]

Europeans likewise found much to criticize. American manufactures were regarded as deficient in grace, design, fertile combinations of pleasing colors, elegant forms, and elaborate finish. The consul general of the Swedes and Norwegians reported that despite the prodigious abundance of combustible oils in the United States, America was not represented by outstanding specimens and that those shown indicated that production was inferior to that of certain European countries.[57] A British writer contended that American machinery glittered with polish and varnish which too often concealed inferior workmanship; and he stoutly maintained that British steam plows and threshing machines were superior for this reason to American products.[58] A French observer believed that the American exhibits suggested that in the United States the emphasis in industry was on production rather than on perfection.[59] The Belgian commissioners, in contrasting the mass production of American portable arms with the craftsmanship of the Liége shops, implied that the advantage lay with the latter.[60]

[53] Abram S. Hewitt, "The Production of Iron and Steel," *Paris Universal Exposition, 1867; Reports of the United States Commissioners to the Paris Exposition*, II (Washington, 1870, 6 vols.), I.

[54] "General Survey of the Exhibition," *ibid.*, p. 318.

[55] *Ibid.*, p. 60.

[56] *Harper's Monthly Magazine* (July, 1867), XXXV, 242; Rev. E. S. Atwood in the *Centennial Eagle* (August 15, 1876), I, 122.

[57] M. Jules Le Roux, *L'industrie moderne au Champs de Mars* (Paris, n.d.), p. 17.

[58] *Fraser's Magazine* (October, 1867), LXXVI, 421.

[59] L. Tenre, *Les États Américains, leurs produits, leur commerce, en vue de l'Exposition universelle de Paris* (Paris, 1867), p. 91.

[60] *L'Exposition universelle de Paris en 1867; Documents et rapports de la Belgique* (Brussels, 1868, 4 vols.), II, 352.

Yet there was a brighter side to the picture. The Swedish consul general admired the ambulances and pharmaceutical arrangements in the exhibits of the Sanitary Corps: the Republic had obviously spared nothing in organizing and perfecting military hospitals.[61] American food exhibits, together with statistical tables illustrating production, suggested that the United States could virtually feed the world.[62] A distinguished Frenchman told a member of the New York Agricultural Society that the American gallery of raw materials was proof that, once the United States borrowed from the older countries some part of their experience and intellectual wealth, it would dominate the economic world as it had already captured the imagination and the future of the political world.[63]

The Americans came off better than many expected in industrial consumers' goods and far better than Europeans had predicted in technology. Rugs, carpets, textiles, shoes, and other consumers' goods took various awards and honorable mentions.[64] McCormick won a grand prize and the cross of the Legion of Honor for his reaper; Wood went home with a gold medal and the cross for his mowing machine. Cyrus Field was honored for his Atlantic cable, David Hughes for his printing telegraph. American small arms, machine tools, and engines won great praise. Coveted prizes and awards went to the Grant locomotive, the Sharp machine for making screws, the Sellers' planing machines, and above all the reciprocating Corliss engine—with its rotary valves and governor that controlled the admission of steam into the cylinder, an invention that ranks Corliss with Watt. Machines for elevating water in

[61] Le Roux, *L'industrie moderne*, p. 17.

[62] Friedrich Frieherr von Moreau, *Bericht über den Landwirtschaftlichen Theil der Weltausstellung zu Paris im 1867* (Munich, 1867); *Exposition universelle de 1867 à Paris; Rapports du jury international* (Paris, 1867, 13 vols.), VI, 420; XI, 22, 212, 372; *Report of the Special Committee of the Chamber of Commerce of New York* (New York, 1867), p. 26; William P. Blake, *Report of the Commissioner to the Paris Exposition*, California Legislature, Appendix to the *Journal*, 17 sess., 1867–1868, III, 265–266.

[63] Elliott C. Cowdin, *Paris Universal Exhibition of 1867; An Address delivered before the New York State Agricultural Society* (Albany, 1868), p. 22.

[64] *General Survey of the Paris Universal Exhibition, 1867: Report of the United States Commissioner* (Washington, 1870), I, 9, 248 ff.

parks, for peeling apples, beating carpets, cleaning glasses, washing and ironing linen; automatic flour sieves, safes, brickmaking machines, ramps, pumps, haymaking machines, model baking houses, Erickson's hot-air machines, Herring's safes, and Fairbanks' scales; machines for woodworking and typedressing; all these attracted interest and won admiration.[65]

Commissioner General Beckwith concluded that the overall view, expressed by innumerable Europeans, was that the American display was "more fertile than any other in the original, the inventive, the peculiar, the new."[66] As our machines were already being copied in Europe we might hope, Beckwith remarked, that American industrial products, adapted to mass use, might take on the grace, color, and design that distinguished European output. Kings and nobles, declared another American official at Paris, could not but contrast the gewgaws and splendid ornamental articles of their own nations with the "unadorned but highly useful contributions of America" in consequence of which "new and enlarged ideas" entered the European mind.[67] Dr. Otto Thieme, commissioner from Iowa, expressed a typical American view in reporting that "with limited means we have achieved great results. In the branches of ingenious yet simple inventions and constructions, the application of theory to practice, the saving of time and labor, and of grand, practical conceptions, we are, to-day, the admitted champions of the world."[68]

In spheres other than natural resources and technology the American display was, to be sure, less noteworthy. Yet there was much that called attention to American scientific advance: the impressive planetarium, the microscopes, and other instruments of precision. There was general applause as well as prizes for the sensi-

---

[65] *Ibid., passim;* N. M. Beckwith to Thurlow Weed, July 15, 1867, "Paris Exhibition of 1867," Miscellaneous Letters, No. 3, Department of State archives.

[66] Beckwith to Seward, January 21, 1867, "Paris Exhibition of 1867," Department of State archives.

[67] *Report of the Vermont Commissioner,* p. 47.

[68] *Report of Dr. Otto Thieme, Commissioner of the State of Iowa to the Paris Exposition of 1867* (Des Moines, 1868), p. 29.

tiveness, accuracy, and force of American pianos—Chickerings, Steinways, Mason and Hamlins. Minister Bigelow, who on the threshold of the exhibition had noted that the literature of the United States had exerted hardly more influence on France than that of China,[69] must have been disappointed in the display of American books. But dictionaries, encyclopedias, and tracts for the blind won favor. In the art exhibits the Americans did not seem to Europeans to be either impressive or original; but the technical skill and sensitiveness of the "Sleeping Fawn" of Harriet Hosmer and of the landscapes of Kensett and Church were granted. The spectacular paintings of Albert Bierstadt, Winslow Homer's "Confederate Prisoners at the Front," and Eastman Johnson's "Old Kentucky Home" were virile, honest, and American.

In social relations, a new department at the Paris exhibition of 1867, the American standard of living was reflected in both the model Illinois farm and in the Illinois rural school, which, according to Commissioner Beckwith, attracted more interest than anything else. A grand prize was awarded Chapin's Pacific Mills of Lawrence for the "beneficent effects" on the operatives of the superior plan, organization, and management of the plant.[70] More than half the American exhibitors carried off awards from the international juries.[71]

On the lighter side, many Europeans first experienced in Paris another aspect of American civilization in the popular restaurant where enterprising New World chefs and bartenders vended cocktails, eggnogs, smashes, eye openers, corpse revivers, and moustache twisters, as well as porterhouse steaks, green corn, stewed oysters,

[69] John Bigelow, *Retrospections of an Active Life* (New York, 1909–1913, 5 vols.), III, 269.

[70] *Exposition universelle de Paris en 1867: Documents et rapports de la Belgique*, IV, 599; Eugene Rimmel, *Recollections of the Paris Exhibition of 1867* (Philadelphia, 1868), p. 265; *Reports of the United States Commissioners; General Survey*, pp. 27, 38; *L'Exposition universelle de 1867 à Paris; Rapports du jury international*, XIII, *passim;* "Report of James M. Usher," pp. 33–35. For the impressions created by the display of the commissioner of the General Land Office, see John M. Forney, *Letters from Europe* (Philadelphia, 1867), p. 133.

[71] Beckwith to Seward, July 2, 1867, "Paris Exposition of 1867," Department of State archives; *General Survey of the Paris Universal Exhibition*, pp. 8–9.

terrapin, succotash, and prairie chicken![72] All in all, Americans were justified in feeling that, however short their performance may have been, it had made Europe aware of the United States as it had never been before.

The American part in the Vienna exhibition of 1873 did less credit to the country. It is true that the exhibit of an American school, with its maps, charts, textbooks, and other equipment, helped dispel the prevailingly critical European view of American education.[73] In all, 144 exhibitors won awards, ten receiving the Order of Franz Josef. American machinery was again praised. The official report of the American commissioners maintained that there was practically no machinery in the whole exhibition that was not well known in the United States and that American practices had obviously been widely copied by Europeans.[74] The commissioners attributed American superiority to our patent system and our superior technical education. But when all was said and done, the American exhibits were disappointing. Charles Francis Adams was perhaps exaggerating when he compared them with the Worcester County Fair. But he was making no overstatement in writing that "the American department was the least creditable part of the Exposition" if "the civilization, the wealth, the standing, and above all the pride of the country which contributed it" were taken into account.[75]

This poor showing was in part the result of what Adams, who represented Massachusetts at the exhibition, described as complete mismanagement from the very beginning. The principal commissioner, General Thomas Van Buren, a New Jersey Republican politician, was charged by the American minister to Austria-

[72] George August Sala, *Notes and Sketches of the Paris Exhibition* (London, 1868), pp. 372 ff.

[73] *Reports of the Commissioners of the United States; Report on Education* (Washington, 1876), p. 10.

[74] *Ibid.*

[75] Charles Francis Adams, Commissioner of the State of Massachusetts, *Report on the Vienna Exhibition* (Boston, 1874), p. 15. For comments of the French commissioners on the American exhibits, see *Exposition universelle de Vienne en 1873* (Paris, 1874, 5 vols.), *passim.*

Hungary, John Jay, with selling commissions for as much as $6000; with engaging in corruption in connection with the construction of an American building; and with making a questionable deal with a New York liquor outfit by which quantities of liquor were sent, nominally to be exhibited (without customs duty) but actually to be sold at the American bar![76] The press, both in the United States and Europe, publicized the scandals; and Secretary of State Fish instructed Jay to conduct hearings at the legation, to dismiss the existing commissioners, and to appoint temporary ones until new personnel arrived.[77] While Van Buren insisted that nothing was proved,[78] informed opinion took a different view. Charles Francis Adams wrote that "the condition of affairs in the American department was disgraceful, ludicrous, and mortifying."[79] In London the *Anglo-American Times* laid the blame at the door of the administration, with its bent for expediency, favoritism, and corruption.[80] Bayard Taylor, reporting events for New York newspapers, wrote that the "burning disgrace" of American bribery had made the country the laughingstock of the whole world.[81]

At succeeding overseas exhibitions America came off badly in some and creditably in others. At Adelaide (1887) and at Barcelona (1888) the American exhibits were admittedly inferior.[82] The

[76] "Special Commission to Supervise the Commission to Vienna," Department of State archives, Part II, pp. 58 ff.; Letters to the United States Commissioners, Van Buren to Theodore Roosevelt, April 26, 1873, Department of State archives; New York *Herald*, April 20, 1873.

[77] Secretary of State Fish to Minister John Jay (telegram), Washington, April 21, 1873, Department of State archives, "Special Commission to Supervise the Commission to Vienna," *passim*.

[78] *Analysis of the Evidence and Reports on the Vienna Scandal: Letter from General T. B. Van Buren to the Secretary of State* (Hackensack, N.J., 1874), *passim*. Van Buren was appointed consul to Yokohama, where he was charged with corruption, drunkenness, and inefficiency. See Van Buren's appointment papers, Department of State archives.

[79] Adams, *Report on the Vienna Exhibition*, pp. 5–6.

[80] *Anglo-American Times*, April 11, 1874.

[81] Clippings from New York *Herald* and New York *Tribune*, no date, "Vienna Exhibition," Department of State archives.

[82] James M. Morgan to Assistant Secretary of State Porter (Melbourne), July 1, 1887, Department of State archives; *House Exec. Doc. No. 27*, 50 Cong., 1 sess.; George H. Schenk to Assistant Secretary of State Rives (Barcelona), May 24 and August 24, 1888, Department of State archives.

Americans met with only indifferent success at the Brussels international exhibition of 1888.[83] On the other hand our part in other exhibitions was more or less creditable. Thus in 1878 at Paris 853 of the 1200 American exhibitors received awards, twenty of which were Legion of Honor decorations. This was a larger proportion of awards than any other foreign country received.[84] With 339 exhibits at the Melbourne exhibition of 1888, the Americans received 214 awards, of which 110 were of the first order of merit.[85] In 1889 at Paris, Americans carried away 53 grand prizes, 198 gold medals, 266 silver medals, 233 bronze medals, and 233 honorable mentions. Despite the high praise the American exhibit received from the President and ministers of the French Republic,[86] Chauncey Depew expressed the feelings of many Americans when he observed that he entered the grounds with the Stars and Stripes flying and came out with the flag in his pocket.[87]

The American record may be considered under the leading categories into which our exhibits fell—natural resources, technology, and cultural activities. We shall see that the reactions of other countries to our participation reflected the increasing prestige of American economy and culture.[88]

[83] *House Exec. Doc. No. 165*, 50 Cong., 1 sess.; *Congressional Record*, 50 Cong., 1 sess., XIX, 2795 (April 9, 1888); *United States Statutes at Large*, 50 Cong., XXV, 622; William Slade to Assistant Secretary of State Rives (Brussels), November 14, 1888, Department of State archives.

[84] Richard C. McCormick, "Our Success at Paris in 1878," *North American Review* (July, 1879), CXXXIX, 1–22.

[85] "Melbourne Centennial International Exhibition, 1888," Department of State archives.

[86] *Exposition universelle internationale de 1889 à Paris; Rapport* (Paris, 1891, 10 vols.), III, 323.

[87] Theodore Stanton, "The International Exhibition of 1900," *Century Magazine* (December, 1895), LI, 317.

[88] John Robinson Thitley, a Yorkshireman with American business connections, initiated a series of American exhibitions at Earl's Court, London, in 1887, on the ground that Europe "already looks to the United States as the vanguard in the march of both material and moral progress." See Richard Heindel, *The American Impact on Great Britain* (Philadelphia, 1940), pp. 182–183. There are extracts from comments in the English press on the Earl's Court exhibition in *The American Exhibition* (London, 1886).

The agricultural exhibits of the United States attracted favorable attention at several exhibitions: but at Paris in 1889 they were recognized as inferior to none. The French official report held that American superiority rested not only on a vast territory and soil fertility but also on improved means of communication and on the institutions Americans had created in the interest of agriculture.[89] A leading German economist concluded that in the development of technical "know-how," an important factor in the competition for world markets, the Americans had an edge on Europe, and could be expected in the future to be a formidable rival.[90] Nor was American prestige less enviable in the two specialized fisheries exhibitions at Berlin (1880) and at London (1883). The United States took part in the first only by reason of the urgings of the German government and the pressure of our minister in Berlin, Andrew D. White. "It was generally admitted," wrote White in reporting the results, "that the display of the United States was by far the largest and most comprehensive in the Exhibition, and the congratulations on all sides were a pleasing proof that our success has been received in the best and fairest spirit."[91] In urging an even larger appropriation for the London International Fisheries Exhibition three years later, congressmen argued that our exports in fish and fish products had greatly increased as a result of our success at Berlin and that American scientific prestige in this field had been greatly enhanced.[92] At London as at Berlin, Baird and Goode, the government's scientific experts in fish and fisheries, carried off honors, as did the private American exhibitors. The models, maps, and charts showing fishing grounds; the display of the principal fishes; the

[89] *Exposition universelle internationale de 1889 à Paris, VIII,* 414; *Commissariat General des États Unis d'Amérique à l'Exposition universelle de 1889 à Paris* (Paris, 1890); *Rapports sur la production agricoles* (Paris, 1890), *passim.*

[90] Max Sering, *Die Landwirtschaftliche Konkurrenz Nordamerikas* (Leipzig, 1887), p. 716.

[91] Andrew D. White to Secretary of State William M. Evarts (Berlin), January 5, 12, 28, February 18, June 22, 1880, Department of State archives.

[92] *House Report No. 1413,* 47 Cong., 1 sess., pp. 1–2; *Congressional Record,* 47 Cong., 1 sess., XIII, Appendix, pp. 400–402 (June 19, 1882).

specimens of gear and apparatus; the exhibit of the uses of fish and of water products; and the exhibit indicating the economic status of American fishermen—all took honors and awards.[93]

But the mounting reputation of America in technology was even more striking than it was in agriculture and in fisheries. In greater degree than in previous exhibitions, American consumers' goods at the Paris show of 1878 reflected sensitiveness to design, color, and craftsmanship. This was notably true of silverware, watches, photographs, and textiles. But in machinery the Americans truly excelled. Despite obvious evidence that our competitors had copied many original aspects of our machines, there were no real rivals of the Wheelock engine, which supplied power for all American machines; of the Stow flexible shaft, which the London *Times* singled out as the last word in Yankee ingenuity; of the display of the American Society of Engineers, the wood-working machinery of J. A. Fay and Company, and the Edison phonographs and telephones.[94] The English artisans visiting the American department reported that in the machine-tool section "the amount of novelty was inconceivable."[95] The technique of making interchangeable parts by rule and gauge was now admiringly described as the "American system." And as at earlier exhibitions, American agricultural machinery was admittedly unique.

The number of awards in all classes excited surprise and no little jealousy. Several British journals attributed American success to "Yankee management."[96] But it was also true, as the American minister to France reported, that "the American exhibit and its management have been very highly commended here by all classes,

---

[93] James Russell Lowell to Secretary of State Frelinghuysen (London), May 19, 1883, Department of State archives.

[94] Clovis Lamarre and René de la Blanchère, *Les États Unis et l'Exposition de 1878 à Paris* (Paris, 1878), *passim; Lippincott's Magazine* (December, 1878), XXII, 755–770; *Appleton's Journal* (July, 1878), XX, 66–72; *Atlantic Monthly* (November, 1878), XLII, 585–596; Henry Morford, *Paris and Half of Europe in 1878* (New York, 1879), pp. 15, 67; London *Times*, August 22, 1878.

[95] *Nature* (February 26, 1880), XXII, 398.

[96] *Reports of the United States Commissioners to the Paris Universal Exhibition of 1878* (Washington, 1880, 5 vols.), I, 28, 34–35; McCormick in *North American Rev.*, CXXIX, 1–22.

and by the representatives of all nations."[97] The director of the French section of the exhibition declared, "We are not astonished at all by your brilliant success." It was an inevitable result, he continued, of the spirit of freedom, self-help, labor, and popular education. The French director of foreign sections, sharing the wish of his colleague that France might emulate the United States, paid a high tribute to the Americans: "Your vigor, born of yesterday, will be so strong tomorrow that you will be able to aid the world by the benefits of commercial liberty, as you have won its admiration by the liberality of your institutions."[98] Although Richard McCormick, commissioner general, felt that the American exhibit fell short of what might have been done and that it failed to give Europeans a correct idea of our country, he believed that, judged by the exhibits of other nations and by those we ourselves had sent to earlier exhibitions, "the success of our exhibitors at Paris was positive, substantial, and remarkable."[99]

Despite the distance and the many difficulties involved, the United States was fairly well represented at the Melbourne exhibitions of 1880 and 1888. In 1880 the first order of merit was given to our watches, school furniture, and machine tools, to agricultural implements, to railway and metallurgical exhibits, and other industrial products.[100] Thanks to an appropriation of $50,000 the American court at the Melbourne exhibition of 1888, while not as large as many thought desirable, was nevertheless handsomely decorated and much admired.[101] The Australian press praised the American typewriters, sewing machines, carriages, lamps, musical instruments, and other products. One commissioner expressed the belief

[97] Edward F. Noyes to Assistant Secretary of State Robert H. Hitt (Paris), September 20, 1878, Department of State archives. See also *Reports of the United States Commissioners to the Paris Universal Exhibition of 1878*, I, 34–35.

[98] *Universal Exhibition of Paris, 1878: The Banquet to Richard C. McCormick, given in Paris, Nov. 26, 1878* (Paris, 1878), p. 6.

[99] McCormick, "Our Success at Paris in 1878, *loc. cit.*

[100] Official Record, *Melbourne International Exhibition 1880–1881* (Melbourne, 1882), p. 477. See also *State of Connecticut: Report of the Board of Commissioners of the Melbourne Exposition* (Hartford, 1883), p. 11.

[101] James M. Morgan to Assistant Secretary of State Rives (Melbourne), August 6, 1888, Department of State archives.

that the United States, being itself a new country, understood Australian wants better than any other nation. Australian officials were most flattering in their expressions of admiration not only of the American displays but of the institutions back of them. "The mission of Brother Jonathan," declared one in a speech at Victoria, is not to oppress the weak but rather "to stoop to the unfortunate, and uplift the poor and lowly." Australian leaders intimated their desire to have the closest possible commercial relations with the United States. The American commissioners, believing that Australia was not only an important market but that of all English-speaking peoples it was apt to be America's best friend, concluded that the decision to take part in the exhibitions had been fully justified.[102]

We need only point out, in connection with the Paris exhibition of 1889, that the American technological exhibits, although over-shadowed by our agricultural display, excelled those of many countries. In machine tools and other types of machines, and above all in electrical apparatus, the Americans came out unusually well.[103]

It is clear from a study of the official reports of the various European countries that in the sphere of the fine arts Americans were regarded as definitely deficient. William W. Story, the American sculptor long resident in Italy, severely criticized the United States for its failure to support the arts and attributed our poor showing to this fact.[104] At the Paris exhibition of 1878, even so, the work of La Farge, Vedder, Coleman, Homer, Eastman Johnson, and others

[102] *Reports of the United States Commissioners to the Centennial International Exhibition at Melbourne* (Washington, 1889), pp. 129 ff.; Consul General James P. Lesesne to Assistant Secretary of State Rives, February 19, 1889, Department of State archives. The American exhibit at Barcelona (1888) ranked after those of France, Belgium, Italy, and Turkey and according to Consul George H. Schenk was "greatly inferior to what it should be in quantity and quality." Yet the Americans took twenty gold medals, twenty silver medals, and fifteen bronzes. Schenk to Rives, August 24, 1888, Barcelona Exhibition Scrapbook, New York Public Library.

[103] *Exposition universelle internationale de 1889 à Paris*, p. 323; *Reports of the United States Commissioners to the Universal Exposition of 1889 at Paris* (Washington, 1890–1891, 5 vols.), I, 32.

[104] *Reports of the United States Commissioners to the Paris Universal Exposition of 1878*, II, 109–111, 309.

warranted the conclusion that the American exhibit was equal to those of many countries and superior to those of some.[105] Europeans continued, however, to be disappointed that so much American art did not reflect the American soil; but they increasingly admitted, as time went on, that the Americans had achieved skill and competency.[106]

The promising and arresting educational exhibits at Paris in 1867 and at Vienna in 1873 prepared Europeans for what was accomplished at Paris in 1878. Some 200 contributions provided a satisfying picture of American education on every level, public and private. The exhibition, with its illustrations of educational buildings, furniture, fittings, appliances, with the 2500 volumes of educational literature, including reports of city superintendents, state boards of education, regents, and trustees, and the 400 volumes containing specimens of the work of American school and college students, won merited praise in many circles. American superiority in textbooks was generally admitted. The international jury awarded the American educational exhibitors twenty-eight more honors than those of any country save France; and although the educational exhibits comprised only one one-hundreth of the American section, they took nearly one-sixth of the prizes given American participants. Both Paris and London bid for the permanent possession of the American educational display.[107] The catalogue of the American book trade indicated that publishing was well represented; and the work of the American public library was brought to the attention of Europeans.[108] For the first time at any

[105] *Scribner's Monthly* (December, 1878), XVII, 280–281; *Nation* (October 3, 1878), XXVII, 210–211.

[106] *Report of the United States Commissioners to the Paris Universal Exposition of 1878*, I, 35.

[107] See M. Levasseur's review of the American educational exhibit in *La Revue pedagogique* (August, 1878); *Exhibition of Education, Paris Universal Exhibition, 1878* (London, 1878), pp. 8–9; John E. Bradley, *Report of the Legislature of New York on the Educational Exhibit of 1878*, New York Assembly Document No. 71, 1879 (Albany, 1879), pp. 7, 29–30.

[108] *Catalogue of the Collective Exhibit of the American Book Trade* (Paris, 1878), pp. xvi, 26; Lamarre and Blanchère, *Les États Unis et l'Exposition de 1878, passim.*

overseas exhibition it was clear that American cultural achievements could no longer be disregarded.

At the Paris exhibition of 1889 the educational exhibits from the
United States were again excellent. An official from New South
Wales commented favorably on the democratic and practical im-
plications of American education, and spent some time in the
United States observing commercial and technical schools.[109] At
Melbourne, American school exhibits were given the first order of
merit.

The growing prestige of America in scientific matters, evident in
the educational exhibits of technical schools, the Geological Survey, the Naval Observatory, the Bureau of Standards, and other
government agencies, and in our great success at the international
fisheries exhibitions, was threatened by the initial lack of interest
in the Columbian Historical Exhibition at Madrid in 1892 and
1893. In the end the American exhibits were successful testimonies
to a high level of work in archaeology, anthropology, and history.
The Hemmenway exhibit of some 5000 objects of prehistoric New
World anthropology excited much favorable comment. Creditable
exhibits were sent to Madrid by the United States National Museum, the Smithsonian Institution, the University of Pennsylvania,
the Peabody Museum of American Archaeology and Ethnology,
and other institutions. Both the Spanish government and European
experts seemed pleased by the work of Professor G. Brown Goode,
Daniel G. Brinton, and other Americanists.[110]

The two genuinely international exhibitions[111] held on Ameri-

---

[109] Edward Combes, *Report on Technical Education and Manual Training at
the Paris Universal Exposition of 1889* (Sydney, 1891), pp. 53, 103, 105.

[110] *Report of the United States Commission to the Columbian Historical Exposition at Madrid, 1892–1893* (Washington, 1895); Francis McNutt to Secretary of State John Foster (Madrid), November 15, 1892, Department of State
archives.

[111] There were some foreign exhibits at the New York Exhibition of all Industries in 1853. See *Official Catalogue . . .* (New York, 1853); C. R. Goodrich, *Science and Mechanism Illustrated by Examples in the New York Exhibition*
(New York, 1854); *Putnam's Magazine* (August, 1853), II, 843–844; *Harper's
New Monthly Magazine* (November, 1853), VII, 844 ff.; *Bericht der Association
für die Ausstellung der Industrie-Erzeugnisse aller Nationen in New York im
Jahr 1853* (Stuttgart, 1853), *passim*.

can soil—the Centennial of 1876 at Philadelphia and the Columbian Exposition of 1893—can be considered here only in terms of their significance in affecting foreign impressions of American civilization. Strict constructionists and stout nationalists argued on the eve of the Centennial that Europe should not be invited to Philadelphia: it would be an insult to the Republic to have monarchs at the celebration of the nation's birthday.[112] But other arguments prevailed. It was hardly fitting, many maintained, to celebrate the Centennial in splendid isolation in view of the contributions the Old World had made to the New; moreover, if Europe were not invited, it might well suspect we had something embarrassing to conceal.[113] In addition, all the arguments—patriotic, sentimental, and economic—common in the discussions regarding participation in the exhibitions overseas were repeated.[114]

Visitors from abroad were impressed by the show at Philadelphia even when they were critical. The commissioner from Victoria, in assessing the lessons to be learned and applied at home, emphasized the use of electricity in fire alarms and in messenger service; bridges, locomotives, and agricultural machinery as well as metallurgical techniques. He was impressed by American insurance laws and by the practical character of American education.[115] A Belgian civil engineer regarded the Corliss engine, the central feature in the machinery exhibit, as the symbol of American genius and was also much impressed by the agricultural as well as by the industrial production of the United States. At the same time he was critical of what seemed the American emphasis on the idea of "make

[112] See, for example, the speeches of Thomas M. Norwood of Georgia in the Senate on February 10, 1876, *Congressional Record*, 44 Cong., 1 sess., IV, pp. 996 ff.; and the illustrations cited by Senator John P. Stockton in his speech of March 5, 1874, *The Centennial Bill* (Washington, 1874), p. 12.

[113] See, for example, the speeches of Thomas L. Jones of Kentucky in the House on January 20, 1876, of Richard McCormick of Arizona on May 6, 1874, and of John P. Stockton of New Jersey in the Senate on March 5, 1874, *Congressional Record*, 43 Cong., 1 sess., II, pp. 1982–1986, Appendix, p. 499; 44 Cong., 1 sess., Appendix, pp. 2–4.

[114] For example, A. A. Livermore, *The Centennial International Exhibition of 1876* (Meadville, Pa., 1875), and *Anglo-American Times*, March 7, 1874.

[115] *International Exhibition at Philadelphia: Report of the Commissioners for Victoria* (Melbourne, 1877), pp. 9, 15, 35, 62, 84, 159, 200.

money, honestly if you can, but make money."[116] An analysis of the French commissioners' reports indicates that they were impressed by the technological power of the United States; by the promising development of chemical industries, in which Germany, of course, obviously led; by the imposing achievements in book printing, in the making of precision instruments, and in civil engineering. America possessed the power of invention in the highest degree, the French commissioners reported, and Europe must take stock.[117] L. Simonin, a French visitor, concluded that America would more and more learn to dispense with Europe while Europe would learn that she could not dispense with the United States.[118] The Swiss were concerned about the competition of American watches,[119] and the British took stock of the mechanically skilled American artisan whose brains superintended every aspect of the industrial process.[120] Professor F. Reuleaux of the Royal Gewerbe-Akademie of Berlin detected in American consumers' goods not only an emphasis on comfort but also an awakened esthetic consciousness.[121] Richard Wagner's specially composed piece designed to glorify and express the triumph of the United States, while regarded as a musical failure, nevertheless symbolized a changing attitude toward America.[122] Perhaps the most significant proof of the new attitude toward the United States was the seriousness with which the American system of education was analyzed for the light

[116] Paul Jean Marlin, *La Belgique et les États Unis* (Brussels, 1876), pp. 57, 102.

[117] *Exposition internationale et universelle de Philadelphie* (Paris, 1878), pp. 61, 145 ff., 407, 439, 486, 512, 576.

[118] L. Simonin, *A French View of the Grand International Exposition of 1876* (Philadelphia, 1877), pp. 19, 68 ff. For a contrasting French view see Gustave de Molinari, *Lettres sur les États-Unis et le Canada* (Paris, 1876), pp. 34-60. Molinari was especially impressed by the emphasis placed on women's contributions to modern life.

[119] Eduard Bally, *Ein Freies Wort über die Weltausstellung in Philadelphia* (Aarau, 1876), pp. 3, 27.

[120] Francis A. Walker, *The World's Fair* (New York, 1878), pp. 67-68.

[121] Joseph Thompson, *The United States as a Nation* (Boston, 1877), p. 243.

[122] Joseph M. Rogers, "Lessons from the International Exhibitions," *Forum* (November, 1901), XXXII, 504.

it might throw on American achievements.[123] Although an occasional American thoughtfully asked whether the Americans were using their vast power wisely and well,[124] the predominant reaction to European evaluations of Philadelphia was one of rejoicing that America had at last come to have the respect if not the admiration of the world.[125]

The progress of American economy and life that the Centennial revealed to foreign visitors was even more startlingly revealed in 1893 at the Chicago Columbian Exposition. The Europeans had belittled the architecture at Philadelphia. But at the Midwestern metropolis they were impressed by the superb setting, the classical structures, and the promise of a new American architecture suggested by Louis Sullivan's Transportation Building. A study of the official reports of foreign commissioners reveals, to be sure, plenty of criticism.[126] But there was also a deep admiration for American technology and a widespread conviction that Europe had much to learn from American factory management, inventiveness, and organization, as well as from mass production, the extensive use of electricity in industry, and the short day and high pay of American workers.[127] The great importance attached to women in industry and the arts was a matter of comment;[128] and the absence of a building devoted to military exhibits suggested the advantages

[123] United States Bureau of Education, *Circulars of Information*, No. 5, 1879 (Washington, 1879), *passim.*

[124] Edward Atkinson in the *Centennial Eagle* (August 29, 1876), I, 9.

[125] *Memorial to the Honorable Senate and House of Representatives . . . presented by the Centennial Board of Finance* (Philadelphia, 1882), p. 15.

[126] James Dredge, *A Record of the Transportation Exhibits at the World's Columbian Exposition of 1893* (London, 1894), pp. xxii ff.

[127] F. Reuleaux, *Mitteilungen über die amerikanische Maschinen-Industrie . . .* (Berlin, 1894), pp. 85–86; *Amtlicher Bericht über die Weltausstellung in Chicago 1893 erstattet von Reichskommissar* (Berlin, 1894, 2 vols.), *passim; Officieler Bericht der K. K. Osterr-Central-Commission für die Weltausstellung in Chicago im Jahre 1893* (Vienna, 1894, 4 vols.) II, I, ff.; *Ministre du commerce, de l'industrie, des postes et des télégraphes: Exposition internationale de Chicago* (Paris, 1894), pp. 131–133.

[128] *Rapports sur l'Exposition internationale de Chicago en 1893*, III, 588 ff.; Dredge, *A Record of the Transportation Exhibits*, p. xxxiii. See the *Illustrated World's Fair*, I, 27 ff., for further foreign comment.

America enjoyed in her freedom from concern for national security.

The congresses of the sciences, the social sciences, the arts, religion, and education further demonstrated the great strides American learning and scholarship had made. American education was coming to be appreciated as it had never been before.[129] We have yet to realize fully the impact of the learned congresses at Chicago on the intellectual and cultural life both of the United States and of the world. In any case, no one could deny the impressiveness of the American achievements, not only in technology but in cultural matters as well.[130]

In the forty years between the Crystal Palace exhibition of 1851 and the Columbian Exposition of 1893 European attitudes toward American civilization had profoundly changed. These changes must, of course, be attributed to many factors—to the Union's success in the Civil War, to increasing exports and growing competition in world markets, to the changing emphases in foreign travel books dealing with the United States, to cite but a few. However, among the factors that demonstrated to the rest of the world the emergence of a new and powerful America were the international exhibitions. These exhibits have a genuine importance that has not hitherto been appreciated. This study clearly shows that American technology, at least in certain fields, won European praise much earlier and more generally than has commonly been supposed. American participation in these grand displays also facilitated the adoption and modification by Europeans and Japanese of American technological innovations. It is not possible here to evaluate the influence of these exhibitions in attracting skilled artisans and unemployed capital to America and in promoting exports,[131] though

[129] *Ibid.* (October 25, 1893), V, 662.

[130] This is supported by evidence in the *Report of the Comittee on Awards of the World's Columbia Commission* (Washington, 1901, 2 vols.), I, 409, 419 ff.

[131] Worthington C. Ford, chief of the Bureau of Statistics in the Treasury Department, compiled data that, in the opinion of Ferdinand W. Peck, chief commissioner of the United States at the Paris exhibition of 1900, proved "conclusively that the international expositions in which the United States has been interested have had an important and direct effect in increasing its exports." *North American Review* (January, 1899), CLXVIII, 27.

doubtless they contributed in some way to these objectives. American participation in the international exhibitions did something to break down American provincialism and helped to develop an American readiness to meet Europe's criticisms of America by showing what America was and what it could produce. In discussions on the advisability of American official participation and of governmental subsidies, all the arguments that involved America's reputation in the world community were canvassed. The final upshot was a victory for those who maintained that it was no longer sufficient for America to meet foreign criticism merely by verbal defenses, that it was no longer enough just to sit back and watch, but that now the time had come actively to advertise American power and greatness to the world.

11

Prospects
for Future Research[1] (1949)

In CONSIDERING the studies to which Professor Kraus has so skillfully called our attention, and in reviewing the work I myself did twenty-odd years ago on "Young America" and on the expansion overseas of American pacifism, I am convinced that future investigations will profit, first of all, from sharper definitions.

We need to define just what we mean by "American" ideas, techniques, and institutions. In modern western culture ideas and institutions are partly international in their background, scope, and development. Thus it is important to find out whether a given element commonly identified with America is unique or even distinctive. We should, of course, take into account the frequency of occurrence and the intensity of the idea, technique, and institution. In trying to define "American" we ought also to welcome the cooperation of foreign scholars, who should be able more perceptively than we to make additional discriminations and to discover certain (to us) invisible nuances. Once we establish what we mean by "American" it will be less hard to tackle the problem of studying the foreign influence or external impact of such ideas, techniques, and institutions.

[1] This paper was read at an American Historical Association session on "American Influences Abroad: An Exploration."

Let us assume that our definition of "American" leaves a sufficient national residue to proceed to the second part of the process
—a very distinct part which often has not been sufficiently differ-
entiated. This is the foreign reception of American exports. In part
this has depended on the views or images of America which prevailed at a given time in the particular regions or centers of a foreign land and among its several social strata. The next step is to
distinguish between reputation, vogue, influence, impact, example,
and imitation. For instance, the vogue in Europe of the American
dime novel is one thing with its readers; its reputation with critics
is another; and its influence in creating or strengthening images of
American life in the writings of Europeans like Carl May is something else again. The same distinctions must be made in studying
the overseas reception and later career of any American book. Consider the matter of American sports, movies, and business methods
abroad; again it is important to distinguish between terms. The
same distinctions are relevant in examining the relations between
the American federal customs unions and the protective tariff on
the one hand and the *Zollverein* and economic nationalisms in
Europe on the other. Modern apartment houses and the architec-
tural forms of Frank Lloyd Wright have not in general been copied
in other countries, but they are sometimes imitated. The same may
be said of Northcliffe's modifications of certain American journal-
istic developments. And it will be important to make careful distinctions when we explore more thoroughly the reception of the
reports of the foreign missions that came to examine our prisons,
jury system, industrial organization, and educational institutions.

It is important in studying within this field to give careful attention to the problem of chronology and periodization. All of us are
aware that the acceptance in newer fields of the chronological conventions obtaining in older ones has sometimes confused and re-
tarded understanding. This general warning becomes specifically
pertinent in view of the profound changes that have taken place in
America—the impact of the America of today is not that of the
America of 1849 or of any other point in time. The same general

source or institution, which itself is always changing, may have
quite different effects at different times. Chronological considerations are also important since American influences have made themselves felt in some parts of the world sooner than in others, in some
spheres of life earlier than in the rest. The acceleration of means
of communication with the passing of time also presents special
chronological problems.

A specific example may be helpful here. Does present knowledge
permit us to say just when the United States first upset or threatened to upset the equilibrium in Europe? In Asia? Are we in a
position to define an early period in which America was generally
regarded as a revolutionary force and a later period in which she
has been viewed (rightly or wrongly) as the great conservative?
If a shift occurred, when did it occur? Was it related to the passing
of free lands, to the altered balance between agrarian and industrial
forces at home, to America's new role as a creditor nation? If there
was such a shift, was it related to our role as an importer and an
exporter of skills, techniques, and bodies of knowledge, to military
and naval prestige and strength, and to the closing of the safety
valve which our traditional acceptance of Europe's discontented
emigrants represented?

Looking at the problem of chronology and periodization from
another angle, when did the United States become a major cultural
center? Was it in the last two decades of the nineteenth century?
Or was it earlier than this in some particular spheres, later in
others? It is important to bear such considerations in mind in any
effort to gauge the prestige of American exportations at any given
time.

Consider the problem from still another aspect. Was there an
early period when American initiative abroad was largely assumed
by private and unofficial agencies? We know something of the
efforts of individuals to refute mistaken views of America and to
disseminate more adequate conceptions of our institutions. But
we need further studies of these pioneer cultural patriots. Despite
the excellent studies of Gohdes and others, we can profitably ex-

plore the role of American periodicals, newspapers, books, and libraries abroad. In the sphere of private activities, we need a full study of the role of the American Irish and other immigrant groups in the struggles for the freedom of their home lands. And we need to fill in the story of private philanthropy abroad. Can we find fruitful ways of studying the impact of American private benevolence in other lands? One missionary in China testified to the difficulty in making the starving peasants understand how the dimes were collected for food, and what the American spirit back of the enterprise was. We have plenty of literature dealing with American missionaries as agents of God, but we need to know still more about their unconscious role as agents of American civilization.

Until we have more case studies we cannot say whether there is a second phase of American influence abroad marked by a combination of private and official initiative, and if so, when this phase begins. There is yet to be worked out the full story of growing official participation in private philanthropy abroad: governmental support given to scientific investigations, to the medical and other activities of our great foundations, to the Near East Relief, the Friends Service Committee, and the like. We need to know more about the official support given to American business enterprises overseas. We need to study the effects of American official or quasi-official supervision of foreign loans to Mussolini, Pilsudski, and the dictators of Latin America.

We are now in a phase when official initiative and official direction of American activities overseas are playing proportionately larger roles. When did this phase begin? Let us study the overseas activities of such agencies as the Bureau of Agricultural Economics, the Children's Bureau, the Library of Congress, the Voice of America, and the growing number of technical missions. Let us supplement the available stories of the overseas activities of the Creel committee, OSS, and OWI, with investigations of the impacts these official agencies actually had. Above all, let us explore more deeply the shows of naval force, the armed interventions, and the

impacts of military government. What influence have governmental initiatives such as these had, under what circumstances,
and over what spans of time?

Then there is the consideration of the situations in the several
areas to which the export of ideas, techniques, and institutions was
directed. We need to know a great deal about the prevailing ideas
or "images"[2] of America at a particular time—how these developed,
and how they were disseminated. We need to examine the functional role of the American images in the internal tensions and
struggles of the foreign country under examination. We have
considerable knowledge of the role of pro-American and anti-Amer-
ican propaganda in the nineteenth-century conflicts of liberal and
conservative Scandinavians. But we do not yet know enough about
the role of emigration to America in quickening concessions to the
less privileged to keep needed workers at home and to maintain
the influence of the established church. We need similar investigations in other European countries.

Since the initiative to import American ideas and aid sometimes
came from abroad, we need to know who called in American technicians and requested American loans, what groups opposed, and
how their relationships were affected thereby. How did the slogan
"Yankee Peril" influence the internal struggles of our southern
neighbors and, indeed, European and Asiatic lands? We might
well explore the report of Louis Adamic regarding the function of
American symbols and influences in the home-grown challenge to
the Yugoslav dictatorship in the 1920's and 1930's. We might also
profitably study the nature and influence of Fascist, Nazi, and
Communist stereotypes of American institutions and civilization.
These are only examples.

In the study of the situation in foreign countries, linguistic
equipment is paramount, as is knowledge of the history, economy,
and culture of the country under consideration. Thus we need as

---

[2] For my definition of the term "image" see "The Immigrant and the American Image in Europe, 1860–1914," *Mississippi Valley Historical Review* (September, 1950), *XXXVII*, 203–204.

next steps both the coöperation of American historians of other lands and of foreign historians. We also need the coöperation of sociologists, economists, cultural anthropologists, and students of comparative literature, arts, and folklore.

It is unfortunate that the effort to study the impact of the GI's on Britain, at the time they flooded that country, was not carried further by the interview method, which showed considerable promise. It is also unfortunate that carefully planned and well-supported investigations utilizing the interview, case history, and sampling techniques were not used to study from the start the American military occupations of Germany, Austria, Korea, and Japan. There may still be time to do something here. It is also important to launch at once careful current studies of the immediate impact of ECA on Europe. The competency of the historian to handle the interview technique is a matter of record: we need only look at the skillful use Dr. Heindel made of it in his significant pioneer study of American impacts on Britain prior to World War I. But I cannot overemphasize, in speaking to fellow historians, the necessity in this field of using nondocumentary approaches, for the official records of military impacts leave much to be desired. And so, too, we must turn to research instruments we have made little use of if we are, in coöperation with social scientists in related fields, to investigate the role of American music, comic strips, radio programs, and movies in foreign lands.

Any study of existing monographs in this field indicates, I think, the need of comparative investigations. We should study not only the impact of the United States, but of other countries also, on China, Japan, Latin America, and Africa. Only by so doing may we avoid attributing to the United States influences in which Britain and other countries shared. We must also more carefully distinguish between American influence, or alleged influence, and independent parallel developments in a given country. Thus we must be careful about assuming an American influence on movements elsewhere for manhood suffrage, woman suffrage, for separation of church and state, and for technical education. Closely related is the need for distinguishing between verbal attributions of American influence, by both Americans and foreigners, and actual influence. This has not always been done.

In sharpening our tools we also need to determine the point at which an exported idea, technique, or institution ceases to be "American." When, for example, did the homestead law that Argentina seems to have imitated in 1884 cease to be an American imitation and become Argentine? Just when did industrial management cease to be an American import and become British, French, German, Polish, Russian? We may ask the same question about exported fashions in food, drink, and wearing apparel, in music, dancing, and forms of speech.

It might advance work in this field if we investigated relatively successful and unsuccessful efforts to export or import certain "American" ideas, techniques, and institutions. However adapted and modified, there are examples of successful exports of elements of our technology, library management, juvenile courts, our temperance crusade, our evangelical revivals, our progressive education, our jazz, and our Rotary Clubs. Why, and under what conditions, have these been more or less successfully exported?

On the other hand, what examples come to mind of unsuccessful or relatively unsuccessful exports? Would we include federalism, which Mexico, Colombia, and Argentina experimented with only to abandon much that could properly be deemed North American? Would we include the efforts of the Germans of 1848 and of 1919 to adopt certain American constitutional principles, or the efforts of Protestant missionaries to promote the separation of church and state in both Catholic and Islamic countries? Were attempts made to export the idea of the unofficial, voluntary association, or the idea of self-help, or the pattern of racial segregation? If so, with what success? Experts concerned with the introduction of American industrial techniques into Poland and scientific agriculture into Venezuela have testified that part of the resistance encountered arose from the nonexistence of certain underlying habits of thought and action which were closely associated with these techniques in this country.

Turning to another next step, it is obvious that a division of scholarly labor is imperative. Bibliographers might prepare lists of existing studies, American and foreign, published and unpublished. We need to encourage foreign scholars interested in American studies to investigate specific problems for which pertinent materials lie at hand. We could develop a list of topics for which qualified Americans could seek Fulbright aid. We could profitably coöperate more fully with UNESCO in some of its intercultural projects. We certainly might promote careful field studies of the impacts of the Point Four program in the areas where it has operated. Another division of labor is suggested by the foreign-area programs in American universities. Institutions having such programs might well focus their attention on American influences in the areas the universities have chosen to study.

Finally, the importance of collecting materials can hardly be overemphasized. We must have access to the files of foreign newspapers, foreign textbooks, and encyclopedias in which American topics are treated. We require copies of the immense number of books by visitors to the United States. We need to collect letters written by foreign students—Americans in Europe and those from all lands who have come here. We can explore collections of manuscripts of American scholars who, like Charles Sumner, maintained close contacts with learned men abroad. Statistics on the use of American books in libraries overseas might be revealing. We should collect more immigrant letters, especially from Italy and eastern Europe. The role of returned emigrants, as revealed by documents and by field studies, awaits exploration. We need to have the letters of foreign businessmen in this country and of the American agents of foreign investors in our enterprises. There must be pertinent material in the depositories of American firms that carried on business abroad.

We need certainly the reports of foreign commissions that came to study our industry, labor, technical institutions, and our TVA.[3] We shall find a wealth of material dealing with the impact of American technology in the reports of the commissioners to the international exhibitions and of American engineers engaged in foreign projects. Not yet has there been an adequate exploitation of the reports and personal letters of American missionaries in foreign service. And despite the experiences of some scholars in this field, I have found useful the reports of consuls and ministers accredited to foreign countries.[4] We shall also presumably have available some day the reports of our cultural relations officers. These are only a few of the pertinent sources.[5]

We must be on guard against claiming too much for this intricate and, if wrongly handled, dangerous field of investigation. We can certainly claim too much, especially if we limit ourselves to the customary historical study of documentary records alone. But it is possible that something may be learned which may prove useful in developing more adequate programs of intercultural relations and in guiding those concerned with military occupations. It is, of course, hardly necessary to add that, despite the possible usefulness of our studies, we must labor as scholars rather than nationalists. It is certain, as I have suggested, that the field offers an admirable opportunity for the interdisciplinary and international approach to scholarship.

[3] Foreign missions needing further study include those of Siljestrom, Chevalier, Tellkampf, Wyse, Sarmiento, Fraser, Mosley, and the Chinese, Japanese, and Indian emissaries.

[4] For example, Franklin, John Adams, David Warden, George Haven Putnam, Robert Walsh, Samuel Goodrich, Eugene A. Vail, and Nathaniel Miles.

[5] It would be interesting to know more, for instance, about the censorship in post-Napoleonic Spain and France of American writings on the score of their "subversiveness," and of American influences in the struggles between conservatives and liberals in nineteenth-century France and Germany.

INDEXES

Name Index

287

Subject Index